SOCIAL INTERACTION IN CHINESE SOCIETY

SOCIAL INTERACTION IN CHINESE SOCIETY

Edited by

Sidney L. Greenblatt
Richard W. Wilson
Amy Auerbacher Wilson

PRAEGER

PRAEGER SPECIAL STUDIES • PRAEGER SCIENTIFIC

Library of Congress Cataloging in Publication Data
Main entry under title:

Social interaction in Chinese society.

Includes index.
1. China—Social conditions—Addresses, essays,
lectures. 2. Social interaction—china—Addresses,
essays, lectures. I. Greenblatt, Sidney L.
II. Wilson, Richard W., 1933-   . III. Wilson, Amy
Auerbacher, 1934-
HN733.5.S63   1982   306′.0951   82-15019
ISBN 0-03-058021-8

Published in 1982 by Praeger Publishers
CBS Educational and Professional Publishing
a Division of CBS Inc.

© 1982 Praeger Publishers

CONTENTS

LIST OF TABLES

LIST OF FIGURES

SOCIAL INTERACTION IN CHINESE SOCIETY

1 THE SOCIOLOGICAL STUDY OF SOCIAL INTERACTION AND INTERACTION PATTERNS IN CHINESE SOCIETY

Sidney L. Greenblatt

I. THE CRISIS IN SOCIAL PSYCHOLOGY

Jon Saari, author of Chapter Two, concludes his contribution with an aphorism: "He who has made the world look different has already changed it." This statement caps a foray into the world of Chinese childhood during the traumatic, transitional period that began at the turn of the century. It is a statement that encapsulates the author's response to the critical question he poses for himself and his readers at the outset: What are the limits of group control over the individual?

Jon Saari's aphorism, and the question to which it refers, bring to mind another aphorism penned by sociologist William I. Thomas as he entered upon a similar quest through the realm of American childhood over half a century ago: "If men define situations as real, they are real in their consequences."[1] Both aphorisms touch upon matters that are at the heart of contention between schools of thought in social psychology. The shared assumptions that lie behind them suggest where disciplinary and China studies interests might most fruitfully intersect in pursuit of a common course of inquiry into processes of social interaction.

On the matter of contention between schools of thought in social psychology, a rift between sociological social psychologists and psychological social psychologists, latent in the field since the 1930's, has grown to crisis proportions.[2] Sociological social psychologists take to task their "hard" minded colleagues on the other side of the disciplinary fence for their alleged failure to grasp interaction processes as they are actually acted out, free from either experimental artifice or the abstraction from context that survey methods produce.[3] Psychological social psychologists, for their part, retort with critiques of the unverifiable, nonreproducible, and ungeneralizeable "soft" sociological participant-observer studies that seek to capture interaction processes *in situ* and *in vivo* at the expense of a true science of social behavior.[4] What has turned each side's litany of abuses into a genuine crisis has been a series of notable failures in the experimental method headlined by Stanley Milgram's experiments on authority.[5] Milgram's failure to control for "experimenter effects" and the extension of that critique to other experimental research work have raised the prospect that the experimental method is not only an imperfect, but an inappropriate, tool for comprehending the complexities of social interaction. From the point of view of those who criticize the application of the model of the physical sciences to the study of social interaction, faithfulness to the canons of science reduces the subject matter of social interaction to insignificance. From the point of view of the defenders of the experimental approach, departure from the canons of science brings on the symptoms of those same maladies the sociological faction has been accused of perpetrating.[6] Some commentators have argued that the crisis has stranded social psychology in mid-stream. Rather than act to prevent the discipline from sinking, each side has been busily engaged in uncovering holes in the other's theoretical and methodological superstructure.

This vision of the crisis in social psychology overstates the degree of unity in the ranks of either psychological or sociological social psychologists. Sociological social psychologists are divided along lines not dissimilar to those that separate them from colleagues in psychology.

Sociological social psychology is the subject matter of a wide array of schools of thought. Their relationships with one another are most accurately described as in a state of intermittent flux. Schools of thought form and reform their ranks as new problems are discovered, old problems are resolved, and theoretical and methodological legacies are reinterpreted. Rediscovery, resolution, and reinterpretation occur not only when new findings fail to find a suitable framework in old paradigms, but also when critiques by adversaries mount to sufficient pitch to drive those who are their targets to revise their position.[7] Assigning a fixed place to a school of thought or to factions within a school of thought is thus misleading and hazardous— misleading because it fails to capture the fluctuations that actually occur; hazardous because it adds fuel to fires already ignited in the course of earlier rounds of conflict.[8] There are, however, persistent fissures that tend to cut across changing battle lines between and within schools of thought. One of those fissures separates voluntarists from determinists.[9] The question that motivates both of these groups to assume positions on one or the other side of the fissure, or to straddle it, is the one Jon Saari addresses in his essay: What are the limits of group control over the individual?

Among voluntarists, I am including those whose theorizing about so-cial interaction leads them to posit that actors, as individuals, define, inter-pret, negotiate, and construct their social environment. Society, from this vantage point, is built up from an endless array of sometimes divergent, sometimes convergent lines of interaction. Determinists see human actors as products of their social environment, constrained by prescriptions and ex-pectations embodied in the roles they are socialized to assume. Social order emerges from interdependent linkages forged, unconsciously, between units of social structure. Voluntarists and determinists occupy positions at either end of a continuum (or on either side of a fissure to keep the metaphor with which we began). Symbolic interactionists of the Chicago, or Blumer, school fall closest to the voluntarist position; adherents to the Iowa, or Kuhn, school closest to the determinist position.[10] Philosophical phenomenologists whose work draws from the legacy of Austrian social thinker Alfred Schutz and American sociologist Peter Berger straddle the line between voluntarists and determinists.[11] Followers of the exchange school draw closer to the de-terminist position, and ethnomethodologists, like their phenomenologist cousins, tend to straddle the line.[12]

Since voluntarists and determinists are defined in terms of the degree to which they approach idealized positions on a continuum, their answers to the question of group control over the individual are not simplistic. Though vo-luntarists tend to launch discussions of interaction with a conception of the self that stresses the actor's capacity to inject novelty into the social order, they are cognizant of the reflexive mechanisms by which the actor absorbs and internalizes the attitudes of others toward him or herself. They are also cognizant of the lopsided nature of the socialization process in which parents impose their idealizations of the world upon children, and they are cognizant of the degree to which social control, a function of social structural arrange-ments, closes off opportunities for self-conscious self-discovery and self-assertion. Determinists, for their part, acknowledge the limits of conformity principally by reference to society's structural complexity, to the existence of conflicting norms and values, to imperfections in the processes of social con-trol and socialization that open up opportunities for innovative behavior and hence complicate social interaction.

Fundamental differences between voluntarists and determinists remain despite these affinities. They lie at the starting point of theory construction-—the conception of human nature from which propositions about social in-teraction begin. They also lie in the scope for self-conscious reflection and assessment of alternative lines of action human actors are accorded, the per-meability assigned to group and institutional bonds, the reality attributed to social structure, and the means by which any and all of these issues ought to be resolved. The differences are thus theoretical and methodological.

The Chicago school of symbolic interactionism, drawing upon the leg-acy of George Herbert Mead, takes its point of departure from a confrontation with that most fearsome facet of human existence—the mind—the "black box," the contents of which can only be known through hindsight. The reflexive capacity of human beings—the ability to see oneself as an object, to consider the meanings that all things in one's environment have for oneself, to interpret signals from and modify responses to one's environment—distinguishes the human species from all others in the animal kingdom.[13] This starting point permitted Mead to dismiss a stimulus-response theory of human behavior and to posit a unique and controversial definition of the self. The self in Mead's vision has a dual structure comprised of the "me," which is others' attitudes towards oneself internalized, and the "I," an impulsive, creative aspect of the self.[14] This conception, elaborated in the work of Herbert Blumer and his Chicago school successors, leads to the claim that complex forms of social interaction are built up, in diverse situational settings, from the interplay between self and other along sometimes divergent, sometimes convergent lines of interpretation and action. The processes of role-taking and "definition of the situation," made possible by the capacity for reflexivity built into the mind and into language, begin in early childhood and extend throughout the lifecycle. Social order is thus seen as process-like, and social action is given a distinctly voluntaristic and problematic cast.[15]

The voluntaristic orientation of the Chicago school of symbolic interactionism creates a certain kinship with sociologists who adhere to European *verstende* sociology, existentialism, and their offshoots: phenomenological sociology, ethnomethodology, cognitive sociology, and the sociology of the absurd.[16] The positions that they share are that social order is a constructed, negotiated emergent of interaction and that the study of social interaction requires methodologies distinct from those based on the physical sciences. More specifically, they rely on life materials—biographies, autobiographies, novels, transcripts, interviews, participant-observation, and quasi-experiments—in order to grasp interactional processes as they occur.

The research products of these approaches are typically micro-social analyses that are justified first, on the grounds that close-order observation at the micro-level yields data crucial to an understanding of more complex social patterns and second, on the grounds that the meanings actors attribute to their own actions, to the actions of others, or to the situations in which they are involved, are inseparable from the interactional context in which those meanings emerge. This stance is critical of surveys, variable analysis, and controlled experiments, for such techniques are held to interrupt ongoing processes of interaction, strip them of context, or impose an order of interpretation at considerable remove from the empirical event the analyst seeks to grasp.[17] It is a stance that is also critical of rival schools' alleged pursuit of the "fallacy of misplaced concreteness," i.e., the tendency to endow statuses, roles, organizations, and institutions with fixed attributes and the capacity to act as only the actors who occupy and populate them can.

Determinists respond to these suppositions and approaches variously. For exchange theorists who find intellectual roots in the works of George C. Homans and B. F. Skinner, the voluntarist flirtation with the "black box" threatens the viability of a strictly scientific approach to the study of social interaction.[18] Even where George Herbert Mead's depiction of the mind and reflexivity find acceptance, the gap between the Chicago school of symbolic interactionism and the Iowa school, as well as between the Chicago school and its otherwise erstwhile allies in the phenomenological and ethnomethodological schools, is more visible when the issue turns on the definition of the self, the scope allowed for self-conscious reflection, the assessment of alternative lines of action, and the permeability of group and institutional bonds.

To Manford Kuhn, founding father of the Iowa school of symbolic interactionism, George Herbert Mead's vision of the "I" as a critical aspect of the self forms an ambiguous, residually defined conceptual basis for an understanding of the relationship between individual and group.[19] Kuhn holds that Mead defined "I" as the residual "not me;" a poor foundation for empirical research on the self. By resting his own definition of the self on Mead's "me," Kuhn established the grounds for his "Twenty Statements Self-Attitudes Test."[20] Through its influence on role theory, the Iowa school brought symbolic interactionism a step closer to positions held by structural-functionalists and exchange theorists in sociology and mainline psychological social psychologists. The differences between the Chicago and Iowa schools over the definition of the self have further implications for the study of social interaction. To illustrate the meaning of reflexivity, George Herbert Mead describes what he calls "Inner Thought." "Inner Thought" refers to the actor's ability to rehearse alternative lines of action, imagine the responses of others, and modify alternative reactions to the responses imagined before they actually occur or in the very course of their occurrence.[21] Herbert Blumer and his successors in the Chicago school take seriously the implications of "Inner Thought" and posit a degree of self-consciousness in interactive behavior that other schools deny. Structural-functionalists and exchange theorists rest their cases for the stability of interaction patterns on the supposition that most behavior is unreflective custom and habit, reinforced by socialization and social control. In assuming this position, they are allied with phenomenologists and ethnomethodologists who are otherwise antipathetic to either structural-functionalism or exchange perspectives.

In the language of Alfred Schutz, Peter Berger, and Thomas Luckmann, actors enter the world of everyday life as a "finite province of meaning"—a common-sense world of taken-for-grantedness, of self-evident routines laid down as if they were objective and unproblematic.[22] The attitude of the actor, the "natural attitude," is that the reality of everyday life is given, factual, and unassailable. By virtue of the "reciprocity of perspectives," actors in the common-sense realm assume that their "stock of knowledge" about the world, their "recipes" for action, their "typifications" of others and of situations are more or less congruent with one another. If in the course of interaction such assumptions are challenged, as they often are, the fabric of the natural attitude may be threatened and taken-for-grantedness momentarily suspended.[23] The logic of common-sense reasoning, however, calls for reinterpretation and negotiation of interactive disjunctures through devices that restore the texture of everyday life.[24] In many interactive relationships common-sense assumptions are never tested because the relationship is too remote from the actor's "here and now" to warrant concerted attention, apart from the typifications that are ready at hand.

The sum total of common-sense typifications is what constitutes social structure.[25] Seen in these terms, social structure presents a formidable barrier to crack for those who would bring the common-sense world to self-consciousness and suspend the "natural attitude." For the ethnomethodologist, suspending the "natural attitude" is requisite if one is to grasp the question central to all sociological inquiry: How do actors come to agree that the world about them *is* real? Harold Garfinkel, the father of ethnomethodology, demonstrates the consequences of suspending the "natural attitude" through what have been called his "nasty surprises"—quasi-experiments designed to reveal both the obduracy of common-sense understandings of the social world and the specific steps in the process of interaction by which the sense of social order is negotiated, reified, and sustained.[26]

The differences between ethnomethodological and symbolic interactionist treatments of role-negotiation indicate how far ethnomethodology strays from the voluntarist position. For the Chicago school symbolic interactionist role perscriptions are insufficient to describe either how individuals adapt to roles or how individuals relate to one another as role performers. Through close-order observation and putting themselves into the shoes of the actors who perform roles, symbolic interactionists search for the intricacies of role-negotiation. From the ethnomethodologist's perspective, the symbolic interactionist focuses on the "surface rules" that govern interactive processes but misses the constitutive rules that underlie surface behavior of which the actors themselves are unaware. Aaron Cicourel, taking a page from Noam Chomsky, argues that surface rules are dependent upon interpretive procedures that are tacit, deep structural features of social interaction. Unveiling generative rules that underlie surface behaviors requires an examination of their roots in language acquisition and development.[27]

While these features of ethnomethodology and phenomenology appear more deterministic than voluntaristic, adherents to the two schools of thought have little in common with determinists. First, phenomenologists refuse to define the world of common-sense reasoning, however obdurate, as a reality. It is a "finite province of meaning" and as such is subject to change. Second, ethnomethodologists focus not on the question of what reality is, but how the sense of it is established.[28] Both positions lead to a rejection of the view that social order should be grasped as an immutable fact and that the model of the physical sciences is appropriate to its apprehension. Both schools of thought, then, take a radical methodological departure from a deterministic position. Indeed, one might argue that both schools are voluntaristic, for revealing the underpinnings of social conventions holds out the promise of a radical redefinition of the bases of social interaction.

A natural law is some statement that describes a phenomenon for those governed by paradigms in the physical sciences. For those so governed, the law itself cannot be changed merely because humans want to change it (although humans can, of course, modify the consequences of phenomena within its purview). But normative law, being man-made, can be changed merely by doing so: "If men define situations as real, they are real in their consequences." The critical distinction, for our purposes, is implied by the statement that men can change the law in one case but not in the other: Men both make and describe one kind of law, but only describe the phenomena of the other. Man, himself, imputes his history, whether it be of a nation, an economy, or an interaction and can affect its course in so doing; physical objects cannot. In one case, men are their own subjects, in the other they are not. The investigator in physical science is not confronted with what his objects of investigation make of something, because these objects do not make anything of anything. The scientist's version of an affair is the only one that need be sought. In social science, however, the possibility that the subjects of study will impute one thing at Time 1 and another at Time 2, and change their behavior accordingly, makes it imperative that we observe the process of imputation itself. In the one case, meaning (imputation) is totally a province of the scientist, in the other it belongs to both the scientist and his subjects.[29]

II. SELF, SOCIETY AND CULTURE IN TRANSFORMATION

Peter McHugh's reference in the above citation to W. I. Thomas' statement "If men define situations as real, they are real in their consequences," brings us back to Jon Saari's aphorism: "He who has made the world look different has already changed it."

The similarity of the two aphorisms is more than coincidental. Both authors recognize the capacity of human beings to impose their intentions and projects on the world, attribute meaning to and draw meaning from every aspect of the environment, and to reify the environment they have thus made meaningful. Intentionality and reflexivity, both of which are implied in these aphorisms, are the starting points for a voluntarist conception of social interaction and social order. For both Saari and Thomas, the individual is the focal point of analysis; groups are derivative. As Saari puts it:

> . . . while capable of devouring individuals, the group was neither omnipotent nor dominant by itself; it was a debtor, borrowing its power from individual members. And the individual, in hundreds of unconscious appropriations, habitual acts and conscious decisions, negotiated how much power would be lent to others or reserved for self.

The obduracy of the meaningfulness "lent" by individuals to the group is no less evident by virtue of its derivation. Children entering the world of the group, into the world of valuations taken-for-granted by adults, confronted a "massive first reality" that bound them to group conventions. Group conventions, in turn, were reinforced by the vital co-presence of ancestors, the security experienced by basking in the affections of extended kin networks, the rewards promised for conformity to ideals embodied in paternal role models, and the anxieties created by the threat of the loss of group affection and support expressed in the language of *lian*.

Saari treats the language of *lian* not only as a tool by which to interpret the social world or a "set of coordinates" for measuring one's own behavior and the behavior of others, but as an instrument that "posed the very nature of social existence as a moral order that embraced all the members of a civilized group." Although he does not approach language as a socio-linguist, his interpretation suggests that rules of interactive behavior were grounded partly in the language of *lian*. Coupled with the intensity and extensity of clan and family ties, this feature of the language of *lian* may constitute a uniquely and specifically Chinese cultural component of social interaction and serve as a strategic cue to the Chinese construction of social reality.

The implications of language and social structure for the constitution of the self lie in the split between what Saari calls the "inner self" and the "outer self," or in slightly different terms, between the self as presented to others and the self as it is experienced in the lively give-and-take of "Inner Thought." The split present in every culture, as Saari points out, is more pronounced in the Chinese case because of the massive weight of convention imposed upon interaction in the world beyond Inner Thought. What may be unique to Chinese culture, at least at the turn of the century, is the degree to which the self is privatized and the extent to which its sanctity rests upon the vitality of Inner Thought. The potency of group conventions and its consequences for social interaction are what lead Saari to propose that group control of the individual terminated "near the threshold of individual minds."

However few the routes one might take to break out of the world of Inner Thought to reach beyond accepted convention to new visions and new standards, such routes did exist. Saari explores family and community interactions with the *taochi* child, the *shentong* youth, identification with sages transcending established conventions, and the experience of shame.

> In the experience of shame—of being out of step with society—lay the possibility of identification beyond the morality of the particular social group and its prescribed rules. It permitted the discovery of other standards with which to measure oneself and one's society, and could liberate one into a larger historical and human perspective.

Saari finds echoes of the distinction between the small man and the superior man in Helen Lynd's distinction between "normal" and "restless" persons. It is also echoed in Erving Goffman's *Stigma*, where deviants are forced to reflect self-consciously on the stock of shared assumptions that underlie social conventions.[30] How the restless and the deviant might emulate Lu Xun to reshape the consciousness of whole groups is a question that remains to be explored.

Jon Saari's essay demonstrates an affinity with the phenomenological school of inquiry, an approach rarely called upon in research on Chinese society. His work throws light on the voluntaristic underpinnings of social interaction by exploring the meaning of the self in the Chinese context. By focusing on the perspective of the actor, it undermines reliance on reified notions of ideology and practice for explanations of Chinese society. This is particularly evident in his treatment of tradition as a "world of possibilities embodied first of all in people and only secondarily in books and artifacts." Saari's treatment of motives avoids the tendency in symbolic interactionism, and in China field research, to allow the actor's publicly expressed attitudes to stand for explanations. In response to Leon Stover's assertion that the Chinese are uninterested in motives, Saari stresses the grounded features of attitudes that "protect the private sphere by formally denying its importance."[31] These insights drawn from disciplinary perspectives are of strategic value in research on Chinese society beyond the period Saari studies.

At the same time, Saari's essay provides food for thought among schools of sociological and psychological social psychology by taking the question of the limits of group control over the individual to a cultural setting rarely tapped as a source of theoretical insight. Of particular importance in this regard are Saari's approach to the split between the "inner" and "outer" self and the language of *lian*.

Nishan Najarian's paper takes the voluntarist approach to social interaction into another historical setting, involving encounters between Protestant missionaries and Chinese converts during the period between 1845 and 1900. Where Saari addresses his work to the conditions under which individuals break through group constraints to define new and untried standards for assessing self and others, Najarian turns to the question of how individuals break through the confines of one group's constraints to embrace those of another.

While interactionist studies address the problem of conversion, little attention has been paid to the voluminous literature on missionary activities as a source of data on cross-cultural interaction patterns and the conversion process. John Lofland and Rodney Stark, in a well-known study of a West Coast millinerian cult, adopt a symbolic interactionist approach to the process of conversion. They lay out the conditions requisite to a total embrace of the cult. The critical factors include acutely felt tensions as a precondition to conversion, a predisposition to seek out religious solutions to those tensions, a self-definition as a seeker of religion, the availability of an alternative world view buttressed by intensive affective bonds with the agents of conversion, the neutralization of extra-cult interactive ties, and intensified interaction with agents of the cult to anchor the convert's new affiliation.[32] Peter Berger, employing a phenomenological approach to what he labels the process of "alternation," stresses the critical importance of a "plausibility structure," a social base ready at hand to redefine the potential convert's world of relationships and activities, to support the convert with powerful affective bonds, and to provide the legitimation by which the convert's biography is reconstructed.[33] Both studies postulate the importance of affective and cognitive bonds between the agents of conversion and their targets.

In the context of cross-cultural encounters between Protestant missionaries and potential Chinese converts, those bonds would appear to have been tenuous. As Najarian demonstrates, Protestant missionaries and the Chinese with whom they came into contact viewed one another through the opaque lenses of stereotypes. While Chinese views of the missionary allowed for varying degrees of proximity to "civilized" behavior, the gradations that separated *yang guizi* from *lao fan* measured varying degrees of strangerhood. Missionaries, for their part, viewed the Chinese almost exclusively as targets for conversion—"heathens" whose statuses, as assessed by missionaries, were transformed only as they "progressed" toward a tentative and ambiguous acceptance into the "family of Christ."

Given these conditions, it is not surprising that missionaries had trouble finding a social niche within which to operate. The tendency, later a strategy as Najarian points out, was to seek out and attract audiences of Chinese with fragile ties to primary groups in social locations where the fabric of Chinese society was at its weakest. Once they had established themselves in such locations and absorbed a modicum of Chinese language and culture, missionaries launched incessant attacks on Chinese values and beliefs.

Meaningful interaction toward conversion, for missionaries, rested heavily on the material resources and legal protections that afforded them a degree of dominion over the Chinese. For the Chinese, it rested on the attractiveness of the material advantages and protections that might be won by submission to missionary demands and perspectives. Interaction in the "induced incentive" mode led to a relationship between missionary and convert based almost entirely on a calculus of utility. Both parties to the relationship achieved the results they expected.

> The cognitive negotiation of the relationship by the missionary resulted in his "winning" a convert, and the cognitive negotiation of the relationship by the recruit resulted in his taking advantage of those incentives which enhanced his position in life.

Najarian's second "induced conflict" mode of conversion describes converts as making a radical break with past value commitments and social relationships and relocking into a new set of beliefs and group affiliations. To accomplish radical transformation in their recruits, missionaries tailored their roles to establish a flexible pattern of conduct against which recruits might either play off their responses or with which they might identify as they moved through a series of painful steps that led either toward a return to the Chinese fold or toward a new commitment. At each of these steps, missionaries played out their roles as moral exemplars, unbending patriarchs, therapists, and surrogate parents, cajoling recruits into the renunciation of past commitments and ties, checking the tendencies toward backsliding, and leading recruits across the threshold into the Christian community.

Success in the pursuit of this form of conversion depended on the missionary's command, not only of the target language and culture, but also of the dynamics of interaction as a social process. Missionaries set the timing of each shift in role style, determined interaction strategies, and manipulated the support of the mission community to buttress each successive ploy. Unlike "induced incentive", "induced conflict" required that missionaries bridge the barriers that distanced their relations to recruits and converts. As Najarian makes clear, however, both modes rested on the missionary's domination of the situation and on the Chinese convert's sense of inferiority in the face of that domination.

Najarian's study of conversion employs a rich, eclectic choice of schools of thought, including symbolic interactionism, phenomenological sociology, dramaturgical sociology, and planned change. This choice serves to highlight both the formal properties of interaction aimed at radical change and the nuances of interpersonal encounters. It enriches and enlivens the documentary materials upon which historical research depends, and it is an approach that holds promise for studies of interaction between Westerners and Chinese in contemporary settings. Najarian's depiction of the "artful and adroit accommodations" evident in interactions between missionaries and converts also reiterates the importance of the voluntaristic approach to interaction processes—the open-ended, negotiable character of role-relations across a pronounced cultural divide.

Nishan Najarian's paper touches upon the link between micro-level interaction processes and larger patterns of domination and submission. Richard Kagan and Anna Wasescha's essay on the Taiwanese *Tang-ki* attempts to elaborate the linkages between micro-level interaction and macro-level patterns of domination by examining the role of shamanistic practitioners of non-allopathic medicine in the conflict between Taiwanese and Mainlanders.

Kagan and Wasescha claim that shamans play a dual role in Taiwan as healers in the Taiwanese tradition of holistic medicine and as guardians of Taiwanese culture and its underlying archetypal myths. According to the authors, shamans protect Taiwanese culture against Mainlander disparagement of Taiwanese language and customs, police harrassment, and Kuomintang (pinyin Guomindang, hereafter KMT) governmental suppression of cultic activities. The means used to achieve these ends only occasionally fall into the domain of politics and political ideology as such. For the most part, shamans refrain from making political statements and participating in opposition political movements. The politics of shamanism rests rather on the growth in the numbers of practitioners and followers (despite government sanctions), on the vitality of temple life, magico-religious and medical practices (particularly those that address the dysfunctions of rapid industrialization), and on inter-village networking. These are activities which serve to undermine Nationalist claims that Confucianism, anti-Communism, and modern western economic and scientific rationalism unite the people of Taiwan into a single, integrated body politic.

Drawing upon field observations of *wen* and *wu Tang-ki*, the authors provide a detailed accounting of *Tang-ki* role-performances, the situational settings in which they perform, and their interactions with clients, client groups, and other practitioners of the shamanistic arts. Features of the setting in which *Tang-ki* perform, including the theatrical "props" that support performances, give evidence of the *Tang-ki's* status in the cultic community, of the client community's involvement in the magico-religious world of the shaman, and of the *Tang-ki's* function as a "liaison between the pantheon of gods with their supporting myths and the world of humans with their supporting culture." The shamans' organization of space and time, as the authors point out, contrasts sharply with the linearity and insularity characteristic of the Western-trained and Western-style physicians. The differences between the two bear implications for the meaning of "politics". For the Western-style physician, "politics" constitutes a specific realm of meaning and activity distinct from one's role as a medical professional. Shamans, embracing a cosmic view, recognize no separate spheres of meaning; politics is nebulously and diffusely interwoven with everyday behavior into the fabric of the cosmos.

Through transcripts of *Tang-ki*, responses to client questions, and enumerating client problems addressed by *Tang-ki* in trance states, Kagan and Wasescha provide additional evidence of the *Tang-ki's* role as an intermediary between the gods and human kind. These same data also permit the authors to profile the shaman's syncretic approach to illness. Shamans ignore medical symptomology to define illness as a cultural and social problem arising from psycho-social imbalances in the lives of their clients. Psycho-social imbalance refers not only to the client's attitudes towards, and relationships with, the living, but also to the world of spirits, gods, and ancestors. Health is restored by redressing imbalances through the performance of prescribed rituals, both by the shamans and by their clients. Thus ancient archetypes of cosmic harmony are simultaneously revitalized and diffused through networks of shamans and their followers. The resolution of individual problems serves as the basis for the formation of collectivities bonded by adherence to shared myths and ritual practices. These definitions of illness and health are sufficiently encompassing to incorporate the effects of socio-economic and political policies as sources of "unhealthy" imbalance requiring redress. Kagan and Wasescha demonstrate this point in their description of public exorcism. Using secondary sources, they document instances in which shamanism, from the Qing Dynasty to the present, has served to articulate political factions and opposition movements that in Mainlander eyes legitimate the KMT's effort to label such cults as subversive.

Kagan and Wasescha's close-order observation of *Tang-ki* practices resonates well with the dramaturgical school's approach to interaction.[34] The data derived from it provides a base-point for an examination of how micro-level interaction between shamans and individual clients leads to the formation of larger collectivities with a shared, though in this case amorphous, view of the world. The authors' approach is important because it offers insight into the process by which popular beliefs emerge to confront official ideologies and to challenge the legitimacy of dominant groups. Shamanism presents no coherent political philosophy nor program of action with which to challenge KMT domination. Its challenge appears to derive from its ability, as a syncretic belief system, to incorporate all phenomena within its flexible framework including phenomena relating to policy where the KMT claims preeminence. Shamanism also challenges the dominant minority through its ability to mobilize individuals and collectivities to pursue the moral redress of actions and events judged to be morally "unhealthy." Studies of non-allopathic medical practices and systems of belief are becoming increasingly widespread, but it is rare that those systems are tapped for information relating to political domination and conflict.[35]

III. SOCIAL INTERACTION IN CHINESE INSTITUTIONAL AND ORGANIZATIONAL SETTINGS

Bernard and Rita Gallin in "The Chinese Joint Family in Changing Rural Taiwan" examine the impact of modernization on the structure of families in

Xin Xing village through field research conducted at five separate intervals over a span of twenty years. Changes in family structure, impelled by modernization in the Xin Xing area, provide a key to changing patterns of interaction within a revitalized and modified joint family structure.

As the Gallins point out, the pattern of family organization in Xin Xing villages belies the generalization, prominent in the literature on modernization and development, that the dissolution of the joint family in favor of the nuclear type is an inevitable consequence of the phenomenon of modernization. While joint families appeared to be headed toward dissolution in the 1950's and 1960's, in the early and mid-1970's their fortunes reversed. As Xin Xing registered the effects of a rapid growth in small-scale, labor-intensive, family operated non-farm and service industries, the joint family underwent a "rebirth." Although it shared some features with the traditional joint family, the modified joint family of the late 1970's was restructured to avail itself of the profitability of non-farm businesses and the increased earning power of the younger generation. These changes have had significant ramifications for interaction within the joint family.

The effects of the independence of married sons and daughters-in-law in particular are registered in the narrowed status gap between fathers and sons, and between mothers-in-law and daughters-in-law. In recognition of their contribution to the family treasury, sons play a more important role in family decision-making and have the economic wherewithal to support the independence of their own conjugal households. Daughters-in-law, encouraged by the family to participate in non-farm business activities, are freed from the tight constraints of the traditional mother-in-law—daughter-in-law relationship to invest time, energy and money into their own households and into their relationships with their own natal families. Husband and wife interactions are invested with a greater degree of egalitarianism, mutual respect, and shared recreational activity than traditional joint family patterns accommodated.

The Gallins note that these changes in interaction patterns have served to diminish the authority of the head of household and the mother-in-law. Yet, household elders and the younger generation both work to maintain the joint family because of the socio-economic advantages that both derive from joint family arrangements. Release from the constraints of the traditional joint family, economic independence of the family's constituent units, closer affinal and conjugal relations, all function to remove sources of strain and tension that in the past led to the premature division of property and offset the traditional joint family's advantages of mutual liability and occupational diversity. The modified patterns of interaction that follow in the wake of structural change produce a more effective and stable family system, able to cope with changing economic conditions.

Janet Salaff's essay on marriage relationships in Singapore Chinese families also focuses on the role of interaction patterns in the context of the structure of social institutions and the impact of economic conditions. In this case, however, the setting is urban and the key structural factor is social class. Through in-depth interviews with one hundred Chinese couples with at least one child, drawn as a sample roughly representative of Singapore's socio-economic structure, Salaff analyzes the effect of social class determinants on interaction patterns among the couples in her sample, with an eye to their import for these families' abilities to avail themselves of state programs for development. Interaction is thus seen as a link in a causal chain.

As Salaff notes, the Singapore government's approach to development eschews welfare state policies and income equalization. Breaking the cycle of poverty requires that each family mobilize its own resources and plan ahead in order to take advantage of job retraining, educational and housing programs. Socio-economic position, however, fixes patterns of interaction that, in turn, determine the ability of families to mobilize and plan. Salaff examines families, located differentially in Singapore's class structure, along four interactional dimensions: sharing of tasks at home between husbands and wives (the bi-lateral division of labor), shared or segregated patterns of leisure time activity, the sharing of confidences, and joint planning. With few exceptions, lower and average working-class families are entwined in a nexus that inhibits future planning and reproduces their class standing. Laboring for long hours at jobs that offer little prospect for advancement, lower and average working-class husbands work and spend their leisure time in the company of other men. There is sex-segregated division of labor, mutual secrecy about working conditions on the job or at home, about money and health. Traditional attitudes shared by husbands and wives give primacy to parents-in-law, minimize the possibility of shared communications between men and women, weaken the marital bond, obstruct interaction between spouses, and impede joint planning, either for their own or for their children's futures. Lower and average working-class wives live sex-segregated lives focused almost exclusively on child-care. They are dependent upon networks of female friends and relatives for aid and advice and are restricted, even in these choices, by the demands of parents-in-law. By contrast, upper working-class and middle-class men share household chores with their wives to at least some minimal degree; husbands and wives spend leisure time together, discuss confidential matters, and give primacy to the marital bond, while at the same time preserving a viable relationship with parents and parents-in-law. These patterns facilitate marital couples' joint planning for themselves and their children.

In terms of the effects of interaction, Salaff finds that interaction between spouses has a direct bearing both on the family's place in the social pecking order and on its members' participation in a modernizing economic order. This is a crucial finding because criticism is so often aimed at micro-level interactional analysis for its alleged failure to generate theory applicable at the macro-level.[36] By examining interaction patterns within the context of social structural change and economic conditions, both the Gallins and Salaff facilitate linkages between micro-level interaction and economic development. Despite obvious differences in setting, in the specific features of the economic system they describe, and the units of social structure they analyze, the findings of Salaff and the Gallins overlap in two significant respects. Both depict egalitarian patterns of interaction between young husbands and wives and their sharing of recreational and leisure time as outcomes of structural change (in the case of Xin Xing), structural determinants (in the case of Singapore), and economic conditions. Both studies also hold that these features of spousal interaction play an important part in producing a stable foundation for families' participation in the modernizing economic sector. This end is achieved, however, not by the sundering of bonds between the elder and younger generations in the family unit and the creation of nuclear families, as the Parsonian literature predicts, but by modifications in the intensity of marital couples' interaction with and their obeisance to, the elders with whom they share a common residence.[37] The maintenance of multi-valent interactional bonds characteristic of the joint family in rural Xin Xing or the extended family in urban Singapore is not incompatible with the thrust of modernization and development. What is incompatible with modernization is the skewed pattern of traditional intra-familial interaction that favored the domination of parents or parents-in-law over the conjugal couple and legitimated norms of sex-segregation. Interaction across boundary lines of gender and generation is thus a key factor in the adaptation of social institutions to social and economic change.

Richard Wilson and Anne Wang Pusey in "Achievement Motivation and Small Business Relationship Patterns in Chinese Society" offer a different perspective on the interplay between social structure, social interaction, and economic conditions. Their foci are Chinese "familism," rather than family, in a small business setting, and the implications of "familism" for both organizational success and individual achievement in a rapidly changing socio-economic environment.

The essay comprises two separate but complementary parts. The first part presents Anne Wang Pusey's findings from tests of achievement motivation performed by a selected group of Chinese and American college students. Her analysis of test scores and inter-item correlations leads her to the discovery that the basis for achievement among the Chinese subjects cannot be derived from hypotheses generated by the study of Western subjects. For the Chinese subjects, individual achievement is inseparable from their ties to the group.

> Success for Chinese tends to be a group enterprise rather than a striking out on an individual path of discovery. The group for whom Chinese achieve, however, is the one toward whom they have the greatest sensitivities concerning loss of face. Traditionally this group was the family and

for it individuals would work incredibly long and hard hours. The warmth and security of the family, however, were never perceived as duplicated in the larger environment which had to be approached with caution and reserve.

The implications of this "familism", which underlies group-orientedness and face-consciousness in Chinese achievers, are explored further in the second part of the essay, written by Richard Wilson. Wilson takes on the role of participant-as-observer assaying relationship patterns between workers and staff in a small Chinese restaurant business in New Jersey.[38] These relationship patterns are examined along two structural dimensions (vertical, between leaders and followers; and horizontal, between "insiders" and "outsiders"), four interactional dimensions (greatest obligation/least obligation; loyalty; exploitation/sharing; cooperation/conflict), and two attitudinal dimensions that refer to the social environment in which the business was situated (trust/suspicion; risk-taking/risk-avoiding).

Permeating interaction at every level of the organization was the primacy each member gave to family over any other type of obligation, whether to the organization itself, fellow workers and staff, clients, creditors, or suppliers. To outsiders, the organization presented itself as "one large family group" with a high degree of internal unity and quasi-kinship patterns of speech and deference suggestive of the kind of intimacy that binds kin. Bereft of true kin ties, these quasi-kinship patterns and the harmony they pretended, constituted a thin veneer over what in reality were exploitive conditions of labor, insensitivity of the staff to employee welfare, a high degree of job insecurity, a high expectation of conflict, and an accompanying readiness to search for cues of impending disaster in the form of either abrupt dismissal by the staff or sudden walkouts by the employees. The organization's survival depended upon personal relations, custom, the maximization of immediate profits, not upon contracts, negotiation of disputes, formalized cooperation, trust in the outside world, and long-term investment either in employee welfare and organizational commitment or in promotional programs designed to improve long-term business prospects. Competing family claims lay at the base of the organization's conflictual patterns of interaction, stifling the potential for organizational success and the effectiveness of individuals within the organization motivated to achieve success.

Wilson and Pusey hold that organizational and individual success in business enterprises rested, traditionally, upon single family domination or strong pseudo-familial bonds among organizational members. In its most effective form, "familism" provided the group support necessary to release the energies of achievement motivated individuals. In its least effective form, business enterprise, buttressed by "familism", fell victim to strains similar to those that led to the premature division of property in the traditional family. In their zeal to overcome the limitations of "familism" and to modernize,

Chinese elites have attempted to supplant the primacy of family loyalties with loyalty to the society, an approach that threatens to destroy the very bonds that sustain achievement motivation and individual and organizational success. The authors imply that adaptation to a modernizing economic environment requires not the demise, but the modification of traditional forms of organization and the interactive patterns within them. In this regard, Wilson and Pusey's conclusions parallel those of the Gallins and Janet Salaff.

These three papers on family and "familism" offer three disparate approaches, at three distinct sites, to studying data on interaction. The Gallins provide a diachronic survey of changing family structure and interaction patterns in Xinxing, Taiwan. Jane Salaff employs ecological sampling and intensive interviews to achieve a cross-sectional analysis of interaction patterns among Singapore Chinese families. Richard Wilson and Anne Wang Pusey combine standardized testing and participant observation to carry out a case study of a quasi-familial business organization in New Jersey. Despite the idiosyncratic methodological features of each of these studies, all three place the analysis of social interaction in a framework which takes into account both specific institutional and organizational structural characteristics as well as the larger socio-economic environment. Although they do not state it explicitly, all three appear to embrace a theoretical model of interaction processes that is both deterministic and voluntaristic. On the one hand, actors do not define their social worlds free from the prior social constraints that emanate from their place in the system of social stratification and from economic conditions over which they have little or no control. On the other hand, within given limits, their definitions of the situations in which they find themselves, their negotiation of relations with each other, have effects on their social environments that are not traceable solely to predetermining structural and environmental conditions. Accounting for both the deterministic and voluntaristic aspects of human behavior calls for flexible methodological and syncretic theoretical approaches of the kind that are evident in the essays presented here—approaches that warrant consideration in the study of social interaction in other Chinese social settings. The analytical frameworks applied in these three studies and the data derived from them are particularly amenable to exchange and symbolic interactionist perspectives.[39] A knowledge of how relative utilities help to shape differential rates of interaction between younger and older family members, mothers-in-law and daughters-in-law, agnates and affines, "insiders" and "outsiders," workers and staff, and networks of friends, relatives, and neighbors might well serve to pinpoint the sources of change in interactional patterns and in the meanings actors attribute to and derive from those patterns. The Gallins, Salaff, and Wilson and Pusey provide points of departure for a more explicit formulation of theoretical and methodological research strategies aimed at analyzing the role of social interaction in sustaining and changing large-scale social institutions and societal processes.

IV. SOCIAL INTERACTION AND THE POLITY IN CHINESE SOCIETY

J. Bruce Jacobs' "The Concept of *Guanxi* and Local Politics in a Rural Chinese Cultural Setting" offers an incisive analysis of a ubiquitous feature of social and political relationships in Chinese society. The term *guanxi* describes "a commonality of shared identification" between two or more persons. It is a uniquely Chinese particularistic tie that serves, for the purposes of Jacobs' study, as a base from which political alliances are formed and a means by which the people of Mazu Township, Taiwan, mobilize to attain their political goals. *Guanxi* are not explicable in terms of such Western concepts as "role relationships," nor, as Jacobs makes clear, are they encompassed in the notion of patron-client relationships. *Guanxi* vary in value in terms of "closeness" or "distance" and vary in salience for people located at different levels of the political system and territorial hierarchy, for different political actors, in different political arenas, and over time. Jacobs considers each of these factors and from field research data develops a typology of *guanxi* bases of political alliances in Mazu Township.

While establishing *guanxi* on one or more of the seven principal bases Jacobs identifies is important to political success, merely having *guanxi* does nothing to guarantee their value. The political utility of *guanxi* rests on their "closeness," and "closeness" depends on other intervening factors. Most important among those factors is *ganqing*, a concept that translates poorly into English equivalents. Jacobs calls it the "affective component." It admits of a certain amount of emotional commitment, but also of a degree of utility, and it is distinct from friendship. In Mazu Township, groups can be described as having *ganqing*, and *ganqing* is seen as transitive. It is frequently measured by Mazu citizens in terms of closeness, goodness, distance, or absence, although Jacobs argues that it can actually be measured along an infinite range of gradations. *Ganqing*, particularly in Mazu Township, is an essential element in eliciting group cooperation and maintaining group harmony.

As Jacobs indicates, investing *guanxi* with *ganqing* requires social interaction between parties to the relationship. Various strategies are employed to initiate social interaction, and the consequences of their employment are such as to limit the total number of close *guanxi* an individual can establish and sustain. In this respect, the dynamics of *guanxi* closely resemble the dynamics of role-set relationships. Limitations on the depth of *guanxi* are offset by the establishment of new *guanxi* bases to extend the range of alliances essential to secure one's objectives at minimal cost in time, in particular, and in financial terms. Jacobs demonstrates how "utilizing," i.e., taking advantage of the resources and status of others in return for favors, and "helping," i.e., seeking out and meeting the needs of others, add to the "closeness" of *guanxi*.

The failure to maintain social interaction or the emergence of conflict of interest in the course of the mobilization of *guanxi* can lead to deterioration of *guanxi* ties which may fuel resentments and foster factionalism. Despite the difficulty in its accomplishment, because of the resentment a withdrawal of *ganqing* generates, *guanxi* can be repaired through third party intervention.

Securing political alliances within the township and expanding *guanxi* is facilitated by the number of possible bases that are available. At higher levels, *guanxi* bases are more limited, a problem that is resolved by "pulling" *guanxi*, i.e., searching for linkages that are often quite remote and mobilizing a chain of interactive relationships to establish or deepen one's ties to people of political importance. As in the case of cross-cutting cleavages in other political systems, competition for *guanxi* generates cross-pressures which are resolved either by adopting a stance of neutrality or by favoring one set of *guanxi* over another. As Jacobs notes, the politically less involved tend to assume a neutral stance, and he illustrates the dynamics of interaction under conditions of cross-pressure by drawing upon case study material.

Apart from its importance for understanding Chinese politics in Mazu Township and in other Chinese settings, Jacobs' treatment of *guanxi* and *ganqing* affords Western social scientists an opportunity to grasp the import of culturally distinctive patterns of association and interaction and to evaluate the usefulness of conceptual metaphors for those processes generated by studies of Western institutions and processes and applied to non-Western settings. "Relationships," the term into which *guanxi* is often translated, and "feelings" or "affect," the translation often provided for *ganqing*, fail to convey the complexity of the Chinese conceptions. As a consequence, the grounds of social and political order and conflict are subject to distortion. By embedding the Chinese conceptions in the context of their use, i.e., into scenes of political interaction, Jacobs helps to clarify their meaning and their consequences for the achievement of political goals, the maintenance of community solidarity, and the management of conflict.

The approach most commonly employed to link micro-level patterns of social interaction with macro-level institutions and processes is one that begins at the micro-level and builds toward more complexity.[40] Victor Falkenheim, in "Popular Values and Political Reform: The 'Crisis of Faith' in Contemporary China," focuses on interaction at the macro-level between collectivities, in this case the Chinese leadership and their mass constituency. Drawing principally on documentary sources, Falkenheim assesses the scope, significance, and severity of what the Chinese press has defined as a "crisis of faith and confidence" that is perceived to have emerged in the aftermath of the "decade of disaster." With this information as a base, Falkenheim examines proposals to resolve the "crisis," the sources from which they receive support, the implications of these proposals, and their prospects for success.

No matter how the documentary materials describe its specific features, there is a consensus expressed in them that China's "social atmosphere" has suffered serious deterioration since Liberation. Documentary evidence suggests that widespread alienation and pessimism, cutting across all social and political strata, threaten the bond presumed to have been held between leaders and the masses. The particular manifestations of the "crisis" include the resistance of graduates to unpalatable job assignments; interference with production; immoral behavior; retreat from political study into privatized, "individualistic" activities; participation in dissident movements; indifference towards the law; and doubts about the success or even the legitimacy of the dictatorship of the proletariat and the pursuit of communism. Evidence provided in surveys, letters to the editor, and investigatory reports suggests that the "crisis" affects a minority, but the size of the minority, its composition, and the attitudes its constituents express must give cause for concern.

As Falkenheim points out, attitudes toward the causes and characteristics of the crisis are more important than the data available for its assessment. To some, the phenomenon is restricted to a tiny minority of insufficient importance to warrant great concern. Others agree that it is a minority phenomenon, but one that threatens disaster for the body politic. Still others see it as the product of youth's immaturity, particularly those youth who suffered neglect during the Cultural Revolution and the years preceding the arrest of the Gang of Four. Yet others regard it as a manifestation of a new generation's healthy skepticism and commitment to change.

These varied attitudes have jelled into two distinct, official lines: conservative and reformist. While the supporters of these two lines share a common commitment to economic reform, the conservatives seek to return to Party primacy, orthodoxy and discipline. They also seek to restrict economic liberalization and foreign contact. The reformists seek more sweeping changes: decentralization, the reorganization of mass associations to serve interest articulating functions, the restriction of Party authority, and experimentation with various open-ended approaches to mass representation as a way of eliciting support for modernization and social change. For the reformists, the "crisis" presents an opportunity to break new ground; for the conservatives, the "crisis" represents a dangerous threat to continued Party control.

Falkenheim's essay serves as a reminder that "definition of the situation" applies as well to interaction between large collectivities as it does to interaction between individual actors and small face-to-face groups. Manifestations of privatism, of retreat from commitments to the collective, are replete in the descriptions of China's "crisis of faith". Their presence is reason enough to suspect that the impact of officially sanctioned, ideologically derived statements of national purpose and identity on norms governing interaction at every level of the social system has been undermined by prolonged political conflict. The "crisis," whatever its real dimensions, thus justifies elite efforts either to revitalize ideological symbols of the past or to define new symbols that might be infused into norms governing interaction between citizens, collectivities, society and polity. Conservatives and reformists offer counterpoised "definitions of the situation" from which to reconstruct a sense of national commitment. The relationship between official ideology and popular perception and the impact that both have on patterns of interaction are poorly understood. As Falkenheim suggests, that impact will be affected by shifts in the generational composition of the population and by perceptions held by citizens that are distinct from those embraced by China's ruling elite. China's "crisis of faith" points up the need for studies that focus specifically on the relationship between ideology, popular perception and patterns of interaction.

V. CONCLUSION: POINTS OF DEPARTURE FOR THE STUDY OF SOCIAL INTERACTION IN CHINESE SOCIETY

The topics treated in the papers in this volume deal broadly with social interaction at three distinct structural locations in Chinese societies. The papers by Saari, Najarian, and Kagan and Wasescha focus principally on the definition, transformation, and cultural articulation of the relationships between self and society. The papers by the Gallins, Salaff, and Wilson and Pusey have as their central focus social interaction in specific organizations and institutions that occupy a place intermediate between society and polity. Finally, the papers by Jacobs and Falkenheim examine patterns of interaction within the polity.

Because the authors address interaction in three different Chinese societies (or four different settings, if we include Chinese business in New Jersey) at varying periods of time, it is impossible to generalize about the links between definitions of the self, patterns of interaction in intermediate social organizations and institutions, and patterns of interaction at local and national levels of the polity. This fact alone warrants a plea for studies that aim at integrating these three levels of social and political interaction. There are, however, common threads that cut across the specific foci in each of the papers. Virtually all the contributions to the volume describe social and political interaction patterns in terms of culturally distinctive values and traditional social institutions that persist in different Chinese societies and settings right to the present day despite modifications in form, function, and *modi operandi*. Group-orientation and face-consciousness underlie definitions of the self and the articulation of the self's relationship to the group as Jon Saari portrays these facets of self and society in early twentieth-century, transitional China. Richard Wilson and Anne Wang Pusey reiterate the importance of these same values in the contemporary American Chinese business community, and J. Bruce Jacobs does the same when he treats these values in terms of their import for interaction in the establishment and articulation of *guanxi* bases in Taiwan in the 1970's. Face-consciousness is related to another important factor, namely, national identity (or more appropriately, "national humiliation") as Jon Saari makes clear in his sensitive treatment of Lu Xun's effort to reach beyond established conventions in response to the dilemmas posed by China's transition into the modern era. Though he does not explicitly state it in these terms, Nishan Najarian implies that face-consciousness and cultural identity underlay Chinese responses to Western missionary strategies of conversion. These considerations play no role in Victor Falkenheim's analysis of contemporary China's "crisis of faith," but by extrapolating from the work of Saari, Najarian, and Jacobs it seems plausible that face-consciousness and a sense of national humiliation stemming from the "decade of disaster" combine to play a significant role in what is perceived to be a deterioration in group-orientedness and public spiritedness, particularly among the younger generation in present-day China. These generalizations suggest that the study of social interaction in Chinese society, and by extension in other cultural settings, would profit from closer attention to the specific mechanisms by which values that transcend concrete situations and encounters are infused into social interaction, give meaning to encounters between persons and groups, and shape patterns of relationships at all levels of society. Richard Kagan and Anna Wasescha's treatment of shamanistic cosmology, its infusion into face-to-face encounters between shamans and clients and its import for Taiwanese identity, offers an example of one possible approach to the problem posed by transcendent values.

The persistence of traditional forms of social organization in modified form and their impact on intra-organizational patterns of interaction have been taken up in the summary of the work of Bernard and Rita Gallin, Janet Salaff, and Richard Wilson and Anne Wang Pusey presented earlier in this essay. Here, however, a brief digression into the differences among the papers might be warranted. In varying ways, all three papers take a multivariate approach to social interaction. Values, social structure, interaction processes, and environing economic conditions are examined for the interrelationships they reveal. The differences are most evident, however, in the assignment of causal significance. Wilson and Pusey imply that culturally distinctive values give shape to Chinese organizational structure which, in turn, shapes patterns of interaction. The Gallins suggest that change in environing economic conditions has re-shaped the structure of the joint family with consequent effects on patterns of interaction between family members. Salaff explicitly identifies class as a determinant of patterns of interaction, but interaction, in turn, functions as part of a causal chain affecting participation in state modernization programs. Resolution of these differences requires closer attention to the interrelationship between these multiple variables through a range of case studies of interaction. Additional case study data would go far toward clarifying the specific steps that compose complex causal chains and yield information essential to a determination of the limits of flexibility in traditional institutions and patterns of behavior.

Apart from their shared concern with the persistence of traditional values and institutions, the authors represented here also share a theoretical and methodological openness to their subject matter. Jon Saari and Nishan Najarian adopt explicitly voluntaristic positions in dealing with certain aspects of social interaction. Most of the remaining papers implicitly combine voluntaristic positions in dealing with certain aspects of social interaction. Most of the remaining papers implicitly combine voluntaristic and deterministic positions as they are reflected in the problems they address and the methods they use to address them. The syncretic approaches one encounters in these papers permit one to grasp both the options open to social actors—in defining their place in the social and political order, in negotiating their relationships with one another, and in modifying the arrangements in which they live out their lives—and the constraints that a pre-existent society, culture, and polity impose upon them. The open-endedness illustrated in the contributions to this volume facilitate interaction of another kind: that between China specialists and their colleagues in the parent social science disciplines. On the one hand, open-endedness encourages China specialists to examine the full range of Western-derived concepts and orientations as they might apply to Chinese society. On the other hand, application of the full range of Western social science concepts to the study of Chinese society stands a greater likelihood of attracting the attention of colleagues in the social sciences to the importance of data about Chinese society. Debates in the China field over the applicability of Western social science concepts, particularly sociological concepts, to China generally lack cogency because critics of the disciplines seldom reach beyond a limited number of paradigms available for consideration. At the same time, the ranks of contenders for paradigmatic primacy within the social science disciplines seldom include China specialists, and the orientations over which they contend are seldom informed by data from the study of China—factors that limit the cogency of debates between schools of thought in the parent disciplines. The essays presented here are an attempt to open a dialogue among practitioners of Western social science disciplines—between those within and those outside the China field.

NOTES

1. William I. and Dorothy Swaine Thomas, "Situations Defined as Real are Real in Their Consequences," in *Social Psychology Through Symbolic Interaction*, ed. Gregory P. Stone and Harvey A. Farberman (Waltham, Massachusetts: Ginn-Blaisdell, 1970), pp. 154–55; reprinted from William and Dorothy Swaine Thomas, *The Child in America* (New York: Alfred A. Knopf, Inc., 1928), pp. 571–73; 575. See also, "Situational Analysis: The Behavior Pattern and the Situation," in *W. I. Thomas On Social Organization and Social Personality: Selected Papers*, ed. Morris Janowitz (Chicago: The University of Chicago Press, 1966), pp. 154–67.

2. Robert A. Boutilier, J. Christian Roed, and Ann C. Svendsen, "Crisis in the Two Social Psychologies: A Critical Comparison," *Social Psychology Quarterly*, 43 (1980): 5–17.

3. Herbert Blumer, *Symbolic Interactionism: Perspective and Method* (Englewood Cliffs, New Jersey: Prentice-Hall, Inc., 1969), p. 172.

4. See Jonathan H. Turner, *The Structure of Sociological Theory* (Homewood, Illinois: The Dorsey Press, 1974), pp. 184–87. For responses, see Robert H. Lauer and Warren H. Handel, *Social Psychology: The Theory and Application of Symbolic Interactionism* (Boston: Houghton Mifflin Co., 1977), pp. 318–23.

5. Boutilier, Roed, and Svensen, "Crisis in the Two Social Psychologies," pp. 6–7.

6. Ibid.

7. Kuhn's notion of paradigms as "exemplars" is still relevant here despite the limitations of the concept of paradigm applied to sociology. For an excellent review of the concept and the critique, see Douglas Lee Eckberg and Lester Hill, Jr., "The Paradigm Concept and Sociology: A Critical Review," *American Sociological Review*, 44 (1979): 925–37.

8. A good example, as William J. Goode notes, is the debate over functionalism. See William J. Goode, "Functionalism: the Empty Castle," in *Explorations in Social Theory* (New York: Oxford University Press, 1973), pp. 64–94.

9. There is a plethora of classifications now in use to describe what variously pass as "theoretical orientations", "frameworks," and "schools of thought" in sociology and social psychology. Margaret M. Poloma, in a recent text, distinguishes "naturalistic sociological theory," "interpretive sociology," and "evaluative sociology." Her labels of naturalistic and interpretive theories come closest to the schema adopted here. See Margaret M. Poloma, *Contemporary Sociological Theory* (New York: Macmillan Publishing Co., Inc., 1979), pp. 1–11. For a schematic sample of classifications in use, see Eckberg and Hill, "The Paradigm Concept and Sociology," p. 930.

10. Bernard M. Meltzer and John W. Petras, "The Chicago and Iowa Schools of Symbolic Interactionism," in *Symbolic Interaction: A Reader in Social Psychology*, 2nd ed., ed. Jerome G. Manis and Bernard N. Meltzer (Boston: Allyn and Bacon, Inc., 1972), pp. 43–57; Jonathan H. Turner, *The Structure of Sociological Theory*, rev. ed. (Homewood, Ill.: The Dorsey Press, 1978), pp. 326–46.

11. *Alfred Schutz On Phenomenology and Social Relations: Selected Writings*, ed. Helmut R. Wagner. (Chicago: The University of Chicago Press, 1970); Peter L. Berger and Thomas Luckmann, *The Social Construction of Reality: A Treatise in the Sociology of Knowledge* (New York: Anchor Books, 1967).

12. Representative works in exchange theory include George C. Homans, *The Human Group* (New York: Harcourt, Brace and Company, 1950) and *Social Behavior: Its Elementary Forms* (New York: Harcourt, Brace and World, 1961); Peter M. Blau, *Exchange and Power in Social Life* (New York: John Wiley and Sons, Inc., 1964); Peter Ekeh, *Social Exchange Theory and the Two Sociological Traditions* (Cambridge, Massachusetts: Harvard University Press, 1975). Representative works in ethnomethodology include Harold Garfinkel, *Studies in Ethnomethodology* (Englewood Cliffs, New Jersey: Prentice-Hall, Inc., 1967); *Ethnomethodology: Selected Readings*, ed. Roy Turner (Baltimore, Maryland: Penguin Books, Inc., 1974); Aaron V. Cicourel, *Cognitive Sociology: Language and Meaning in Social Interaction* (Baltimore, Mary-

land: Penguin Books Inc., 1973); *Studies in Social Interaction*, ed. David Sudnow (New York: The Free Press, 1972); Peter McHugh, *Defining the Situation: The Organization of Meaning in Social Interaction* (New York: The Bobbs-Merrill Co., Inc., 1968).

13. *George Herbert Mead on Social Psychology: Selected Papers*, ed. Anselm Strauss (Chicago: The University of Chicago Press, 1956), pp. 37-41.

14. Ibid., pp. 228-41.

15. The extent of agreement among interactionists on this perspective is tapped in Ted R. Vaughn and Larry T. Reynolds, "The Sociology of Symbolic Interactionism," in *The Sociology of Sociology: Analysis and Criticism of the Thought, Research and Ethical Folkways of Sociology and Its Practitioners*, ed. Larry T. Reynolds and Janice N. Reynolds (New York: David McKay Co., Inc., 1970), pp. 324-39.

16. Stanford M. Lyman and Marvin B. Scott, *A Sociology of the Absurd* (New York: Appleton-Century-Crofts, 1970).

17. Herbert Blumer, "Sociological Analysis and the Variable" in *Symbolic Interactionism: Perspective and Method* (Englewood Cliffs, New Jersey: Prentice-Hall, Inc., 1969), p. 134.

18. As Jonathan Turner notes, Homans does admit "black box" assumptions into his theoretical schema but in such a way as to leave the question of values highly ambiguous. See Turner, *The Structure of Sociological Theory*, pp. 244-45.

19. Manford H. Kuhn, "Major Trends in Symbolic Interaction Theory in the Past Twenty-Five Years," in *Symbolic Interaction: A Reader in Social Psychology* 2nd ed., ed. Manis and Meltzer, pp. 59-60.

20. Manford H. Kuhn and Thomas S. McPartland, "An Empirical Investigation of Self-Attitudes," in *Symbolic Interaction: A Reader in Social Psychology* 2nd ed., ed. Manis and Meltzer, pp. 112-24.

21. *George Herbert Mead on Social Psychology*, p. 39.

22. *Alfred Schutz On Phenomenology and Social Relations*, pp. 79-80; Berger and Luckmann, *The Social Construction of Reality*, pp. 23-26.

23. Berger and Luckmann, *The Social Construction of Reality*, pp. 24-25.

24. Ibid., p. 24

25. Ibid., p. 33

26. Garfinkel, *Studies in Ethnomethodology*, pp. 35-75.

27. Cicourel, *Cognitive Sociology*, pp. 48-49.

28. Harold Garfinkel, "The Origins of the Term 'Ethnomethodology'," in *Ethnomethodology*, ed. Turner, pp. 16-18.

29. McHugh, *Defining the Situation*, p. 131.

30. Erving Goffman, *Stigma* (Englewood Cliffs, New Jersey: Prentice-Hall, Inc., 1963).

31. Leon E. Stover, *The Cultural Ecology of Chinese Civilization: Peasants and Elites in the Last of the Agrarian States* (New York: The New American Library, Inc., 1974), p. 244.

32. John Lofland and Rodney Stark, "Becoming a World-Saver: A Theory of Conversion to A Deviant Perspective," in *Social Interaction: Introductory Readings in Sociology*, ed. Howard Robboy, Sidney L. Greenblatt and Candace Clark (New York: St. Martin's Press, 1979), pp. 458-70.

33. Berger and Luckmann, *The Social Construction of Reality*, pp. 157-63.

34. Doyle Paul Johnson, *Sociological Theory: Classical Founders and Contemporary Perspectives* (New York: John Wiley and Sons, 1981), pp. 325-41.

35. An example is Vivian Garrison, "Doctor, *Espirita* or Psychiatrist?: Health-Seeking Behavior in a Puerto Rican Neighborhood of New York City," *Medical Anthropology*, I (1977): 66-180.

36. Sheldon Stryker, *Symbolic Interactionism: A Social Structural Version* (Menlo Park, California: The Benjamin/Cummings Publishing Co., 1980), pp. 150-51; Boutilier, Roed, and Svensen, "Crisis in Two Social Psychologies," p. 8.

37. Marion J. Levy, "Aspects of the Analysis of Family Structure," in *Aspects of the Analysis of Family Structure*, ed. Ansley J. Coale, *et. al.*, (Princeton, New Jersey: Princeton University Press, 1965), pp. 57–63.

38. Raymond L. Gold, "Roles in Sociological Field Observations," *Social Forces*, 36 (1958): 221.

39. Sheldon Stryker finds a particularly useful analytical framework in the eclectic thought of Eugene Weinstein. See Stryker, *Symbolic Interactionism*, pp. 124–29. See also Richard M. Emerson, "Exchange Theory, Part I: A Psychological Basis for Social Exchange," and "Exchange Theory, Part II: Enchange Relations and Network Structures," in *Sociological Theories in Progress*, ed. Joseph Berger, Morris Zelditch, Jr., and Bo Anderson (Boston: Houghton Mifflin Co., 1972), II, pp. 38–87; Turner, *The Structure of Sociological Theory* rev. ed., pp. 278–305.

40. Jack Douglas argues that such an approach is the *sine qua non* of sociological research. See Jack D. Douglas, "Understanding Everyday Life," in *Understanding Everyday Life: Toward the Reconstruction of Sociological Knowledge*, ed. Jack D. Douglas (Chicago: Aldine Publishing Co., 1970), pp. 3–12.

2 BREAKING THE HOLD OF TRADITION: THE SELF-GROUP INTERFACE IN TRANSITIONAL CHINA

Jon L. Saari

In 1905 in Japan twenty-five year old Lu Xun (the penname for Zhou Shuren) saw a news slide on the Russo-Japanese war showing a group of Chinese—strong in body but apathetic in expression—waiting for the Japanese military to execute a bound Chinese accused of being a spy for the Russians. Lu Xun's shame, not only for the Chinese spy who was used and executed by other nationals but also for the pathetic Chinese onlookers who had come to enjoy the spectacle, forced him to reconsider his medical study in Japan and his analysis of the locus of China's problems. "The people of a weak and backward country, however strong and healthy they may be, can only serve to be made examples of, or to witness such futile spectacles; and it is not necessarily deplorable no matter how many of them die of illness. The most important thing, therefore, was to change their spirit. . . ."[1] Literature was to be the way to change the inner spirit of the Chinese people, to awaken them to a sense of their national failings, and to point out how they might become "real human beings," freed from the tyranny of the group and tradition.

The spectacle of the conformist, mindless crowd that so struck Lu Xun in this incident in Japan recurs again and again in his short stories. In the story "Medicine," during an execution scene the people "craned their necks as far as they would go . . . [looking] like so many ducks, held and lifted by some invisible hand." In "Kong Yiji" the theme centers on the "fierce-looking" employer and the "morose lot" of the customers as much as on the pathetic figure of the old scholar-failure. In the "Diary of a Madman" the protagonist is tormented by the strange, fierce expressions in people's eyes, even in those of children, and by their ghastly pale, longtoothed faces that come alive with derisive laughter. Ordinary villagers who had themselves endured shame and wrong had had the experiences to identify with the protagonist: "Some of them have been pilloried by the magistrate, some slapped in the face by the local gentry, some have had their wives taken away by bailiffs, some have had their parents driven to suicide by creditors." Yet these experiences only made them more frightened and fierce, more ready to persecute than empathize.[2]

In his short stories Lu Xun presented individuals caught in this callous, self-righteous group setting. The environment of the traditional group bound them with a thousand threads. Sociologically, whole classes of people, particularly women and youth, were held in a state of servile dependence; psychologically, all participated in binding themselves as they grew up and internalized the cultural style. Change was predicated on breaking the hold of tradition within oneself as well as others. The pathos of the reformer or rebel lay in the almost futile effort to free oneself from four thousand years of history. As the protagonist in "The Diary of a Madman" finally realized, it was not just the others around him in a "man-eating" environment who were implicated in the status quo, but he himself; for he too had ingested the tradition unknowingly as a child. Only the not yet socialized children of the future could be saved, could offer a way out of the predicament.

Becoming an agent of change meant not only a conscious reorienting of the self—a desocialization through awareness—but also an attempted unmaking of the whole inner world of ordinary Chinese villagers. Change could not happen as long as this great majority preferred to destroy an innovator as a "crazy man" rather than to open themselves to doubt about the traditional wisdom and to the possibility of new ideas and forms in politics, ethics, and social life. This failing of ordinary Chinese was addressed by Lu Xun most fully in his satirical piece "The True Story of Ah Q." The nameless Ah Q was held up as a mirror in which all could see their reflections; by implication all Chinese shared his faults.[3] Ah Q is timid, even cowardly, full of resentments but releasing them only when confident of getting away with it. He has a repertoire of ways to achieve subjective victory and wipe out objective defeats and losses. He has keen eyes to find his own advantage in any situation, whether avoiding pain or securing fame and profit, despite the idealistic labels he may attach to his own behavior. And he readily inflates his own self-image and thinks himself above others, although he can also be very self-effacing if necessary—"I am an insect—now will you let me go?" Ah Q is a spineless creature, finely attuned to living within the prejudices of his group, yet trying desperately to enhance his self-image at every opportunity. He is open to manipulation and abuse by his social and political "betters" because of his ignorant imprisonment in the group's ways.

Ah Q's weakness, however, was also a strength, for his capacity for psychological victory lent him a resiliency when he faced defeat and humiliation. Being situation-oriented permitted a variety of behaviors, all in good conscience; this undoubtedly enhanced his survival as it meant avoidance of clashes over principle with stronger parties as well as the absence of debilitating self-doubts and recriminations. The long range costs of these "strengths," however, were continuing to live in a world of dangerous illusion and facing an eventual crisis of moral integrity and self-respect. Among the characters in "The True Story of Ah Q," individual identity and responsibility were reduced to role-playing: condemned criminal, returned student, would-be revolutionary, disgraced mate, competent thief. Furthermore, the roles were played within a drama whose script was now outdated and inappropriate for twentieth-century Chinese society. China needed, in Lu Xun's vision, strong individuals with empathy and honesty who could redefine roles and create a new drama.[4] But where were such individuals to come from? How was an individual to break the hold of tradition and stand up to the power of the group? What were the psychological-sociological-historical determinants of "being held" as well as "breaking free"? We do well to build upon the self-group interface so richly posed in Lu Xun's works. For, while capable of devouring individuals, the group was neither omnipotent nor dominant by itself; it was a debtor, borrowing its power from individual members. And the individual, in hundreds of unconscious appropriations, habitual acts, and conscious decisions, negotiated how much power would be lent to others or reserved for self.

THE SOCIALIZATION PACT

The power of the group, at its deepest level, must lie in the socialization pact that young dependent children come to make with the seemingly given world of the adults around them. Emotions find objects, ideas take form through the dawning of our first conceptions of what the world is and what it requires of us. Growing up is an apprenticeship in "becoming human" (*zuo ren*) by adult cultural standards, as children are initiated, harshly or gently, into the ways of the group. They are drawn along or levered into ever higher stages of social interaction and environmental mastery, initially by the desire to keep the love and meet the demands of the mother or nurturing adult. Hu Shi (1891–1962), whose father died when he was four, has given us a vivid glimpse of these universal elements—the mother's love and demands, the child's dependence and intense emotional participation in the process of learning.

> Every day just before dawn, my mother would call me to wake up, tell me to put my clothing around my shoulders. I never knew how long she herself had been up and sitting there on my bed. When she saw that I was clearly awake, then she would tell me what I had done wrong and said

wrong the day before, and that she wanted me to study diligently. Some days she would tell me each of my father's good points, saying "You should always follow in your father's footsteps. He was the only complete man that I have known in my life. You want to emulate (lit: study) him, not discredit him (lit: cause him to lose face or appear disgraced). When she talked about things that hurt her, she always began to cry. When it was broad daylight she would dress me and urge me off to my early studies. . . . My mother disciplined me very strictly. She was a mother who doubled as a father. But she never scolded me in front of anyone else, nor hit me physically. When I did something wrong, she would only give me a look. When I saw the reproach shining in her eyes I was struck still. If the misdeed was small, she would wait until evening when people had settled down. She would close the door, first reprove me and then punish me, sometimes by kneeling or by pinching and twisting my skin. No matter what kind of heavy punishment she gave me, she never permitted me to cry out loud. Her discipline of her son was not a way of using him as a target for the display of her own emotions.[5]

Slowly the child learns how to live within ever larger and more complicated collectivities and how to monitor its own behavior at the same time. In the process of differentiating the world of objects "outside" and coming to discover the self at the same time, it is the external environment, perceived as systems—at first the mother, then the family, and larger society—that controls and pressures the learning child until it can function autonomously via self-control and self-regulation. The child learns to act autonomously by identifying the operative values in these collectivities and internalizing them as its own guidelines.[6] This early learning has a certain fatedness about it, for given the basic inequality of childhood, the child is acted upon more than it enacts its own script. This imbalance gives the first world of childhood a massive, indubitable reality that is more firmly entrenched in consciousness than the worlds internalized in secondary socializations. "Primary socialization . . . accomplishes what (in hindsight, of course) may be seen as the most important confidence trick that society plays on the individual—to make appear as necessity what is in fact a bundle of contingencies, and thus to make meaningful the accident of birth."[7]

The maturation of children is indeed impossible apart from a human group, but the visions of "meaningful necessity" taught by human groups to children are quite diverse. The very starting point in China in defining the self-other relationship was different from our own: not separate individuals linked together, but related persons developing individuality within the group. Helen Lynd commented on our Western folkways ". . . it is a special version of life which regards society as external to the individual, mother love as something 'given to the child,' emotional 'needs' as something that must be felt and 'met,' the social group as a series of links rather than a continuum."[8]

The Chinese social world, especially among the more formally educated, differed sharply from the contemporary Western one in the wider range of significant others in the extended family and in its strong sense of continuity between father and son, ancestors and self, the dead and the living. "I am of the 81st generation," announced Alfred Sze as the natural observation with which to begin his life history.[9] While this example is hardly representative, a five generation consciousness of ancestors was common.[10] Hu Shi, asked to write his credo, found it natural to begin with his father: "My father, Hu Ch'uan, was a scholar and a man of strong will and administrative ability." He alone among the contributors to a volume of credos felt the inherent appropriateness of this as a beginning point.[11] This feeling for biological continuity established the ancestors and the past as powerful symbolic presences in the now-world of Chinese parents and children. Since these meanings were fashioned by the living for their own purposes, the ancestors could become useful reinforcements for parental intentions; they could embody a past glory that family members should live up to, whose accumulated face (*mianzi*) or merits they must preserve and extend by commensurate achievement and proper behavior. When fatherless, thirteen-year-old Jiang Kaishek (1887–1975) first left his native village, he was admonished by his mother to "maintain the reputation of the ancestors." Her meaning, as Robert Payne notes, was not restricted to the farmers and salt merchants among his paternal ancestors, but referred to a family tradition that linked the Jiangs with Dan, Duke of Zhou, the great innovator who established the Zhou dynasty in the twelfth century b.c. It mattered little to a young lad that hundreds of thousands might claim the same ancestors or that genealogical accuracy was fanciful over such a long time; his dreams and ambitions were linked with the ghostly presence of this ancient giant, whose virtue and energy he felt to be his inheritance.[12] Sometimes the ancestors could be concretely present in the form of written wills and instructions and loom as giants governing the moves of parents and children alike.[13]

This dialogue with dead ancestors, as constructed by the living, was one source of leverage placing the child under judgment and making it self-conscious in relation to the record of the past. But the Duke of Zhou and other past heroes in history and literature were primarily supplementary to the image of an adulthood commanding respect which came from the parents, and particularly the father or grandfather. However aloof and awe-inspiring he might have been, the father was a model for the son's future, an image of a respectful place in society. The son was told this, and he came to sense it in his own search for the connectedness of his pains and joys, the reasons for the prohibitions and exhortations, the logic behind the beating and the loving. *Obey, learn self-control*, he responded to himself, *conform to the ways of the group, and you shall in time have your position of respect, a sense of belonging, the chance to lead and teach others. You shall one day be as your father is, if you learn to live as your father lives and think as your father thinks.*

This inducement to conform and adopt the values of the adults draws its power from the anxiety of not belonging, of losing respect in the eyes of others, of being inconsequential and even ostracized. How can a small child bear this prospect?[14] It could not know that its parents' words only described reality as they felt it and wished it to be, not as it actually was. It could not reach an outside perspective on the parent's values or strip away the layers of interpretation surrounding the "realities" it came to learn. It had no defense before a plea that could bring to bear all the leverage of a mother's love and a son's obligation.

> Your father is dead; you live for him. You are bone of his bone, flesh of his flesh, blood of his blood, soul of his soul. If he is the bud, you are the flower. If he is the cocoon, you are the butterfly. My terrible fear is that you shall not grow to be men, and that all my sacrifices will be crowned only with pitiless disappointment and irremediable despair. I am afraid of being false to my duty as a mother, and thereby unworthy of your father. If you need me, take me wholly.[15]

The intensity of this plea is rooted in the suffering of a mother/daughter-in-law bringing up her sons alone in an extended family. But the meanings expressed here—biological continuity, the obligation to past family members, the need to achieve a standard of worthy adulthood within the human group (*zuo jen*)—do not depend upon idiosyncratic factors. The parental understanding of these temporal and social relationships, linked as it was to ancestors to whom the parents themselves felt bound and accountable, was a massive first reality for children learning to orient themselves within a Chinese environment.

THE LANGUAGE OF *LIAN*

Or perhaps we should say learning to orient themselves within a Chinese-speaking environment. The group achieved power not only through a socialization pact that impressed certain themes on vulnerable youngsters, but also through the patterns of the Chinese language itself. Early twentieth-century Chinese, as any other language, labeled the world in certain ways; acquiring the language, especially in the abstract areas most distant from perceptual experience, meant coming to see oneself within certain interpretive schemata. Such schemata seemed opaque and self-evident from within the Chinese-speaking group, until wider awareness and bilingualism began to make them transparent as particular Chinese folkways. In the context of social interaction, the language of *lian* or "face" or "public reputation" was particularly important because it interpreted the "outer" social world to the self and gave the individual a set of coordinates by which to measure behavior. More than an interpretation, *lian* posed the very nature of social existence as a moral order that embraced all the members of a civilized group. Loss of face was not viewed as a punishment inflicted from the outside; it was a state of being, intelligible through a shared vocabulary of what constituted decency.[16]

As described in a pioneering article by Hu Xianjin in 1944, *lian* was a quality so basic that it was noted primarily in its absence. Its most common formulations were negative: loss of face (*diu lian*), to have no *lian (mei you lian)*, not to want *lian (bu yao lian)*. In these expressions, as indicated in Table 2.1, the fall from decency was marked by degrees, with each successive category implying greater humiliation and social isolation.[17] The emotional impact of the loss of *lian* could "come to constitute a real dread affecting the nervous system of the ego more strongly than physical fear."

> A single lapse is punished by ridicule and comments on loss of face, repeated offenses arouse strong disapproval and cause the withdrawal, psychologically speaking, of the community from ego. The consciousness that "loss of face" means that the confidence of society in his character is impaired, and places him in danger of being despised and isolated, usually acts as a strong deterrent in the individual.[18]

To possess *lian* was simply to be a "decent human being," a person who had self-respect as well as respect in the eyes of others. It implied moral integrity, that is, the ability to perform dependably in one's roles and to make an accurate estimate of one's own power and station in life. It was a quality which the poorest low status person may have had and which even the wealthiest official must have had if he were to be respected in the moral eyes of the community. Unlike its counterpart term *mianzi*, which referred to an external accumulation of prestige, influence, power, position, and wealth, *lian* pointed to an inner sense of worth that was maintained or lost as a whole. It was an "indivisible entity as experienced by ego, although felt more or less strongly."[19]

Learning to be Chinese in part meant acquiring this emotional sensitivity to *lian*. Our words "shame" and "guilt" are inadequate to express the inner feel of the emotional state involved, for neither the anxiety of being "out" or "wrong" or "exposed," nor the comforts of being "in" and "right" find exact counterparts in our language. This sensitivity was acquired by a dual process of overt training in group ideals of loyalty and unity and by using shaming techniques to inculcate a high moral anxiety if the group's norms were violated. In one recent study of grade school children of Taiwan, parents and teachers were found to provide children with an individual identity and ideals defined in terms of the group, i.e., family, school, and nation.

TABLE 2.1
States of Social Respect and Social Disapproval

States of social respect and social disapproval, as mirrored in the usage of *lian* or "face." Descriptive of the fit between the self and others in the human environment and therefore a minimal definition of what it meant to be human from a Chinese perspective.

having *lian*	bo-lian / *hou-lian*	diu-lian	bu-yao-lian	mei you lian
A decent human being; self-respect & a good reputation in the community	(thinskinned) and (thickskinned)	(to lose face)	(not considering *lian*)	(no feeling for *lian*)
Dependable performance in social roles; accurate estimate of one's power & station in life	Overly sensitive to social disapproval, or relatively obtuse to social conventions	Humiliation and some social isolation from breaking conventions or over-estimation of self in bragging or boasting	Deliberately exploiting & hurting others; not considering *lian* in one's actions.	The worst insult, directed at outcasts beyond the norms of the group, and therefore unpredictable, dangerous, even inhuman
Behavior within range of conventional behavior & tolerated deviance; five relationships primary	A light floating person as opposed to a reliable heavy person	May recover face if caused by inexperience or ignorance		Criminals and traitors
Being self-cultivated & having self-control or not; in its fullest development, the effortless conformity to virtue of the sage; no inner-outer tension; perfect accord with *li* or propriety				Foreigners or *wai guo ren* (lit. "outside country people") evaluated as they accept & participate in Chinese cultural conventions

Source: From Hu Xianjin (Hu Hsien Chin), "The Chinese Concepts of Face," *American Anthropologist* 46, (January–March, 1944): 45–64. On outgroups, see Richard Wilson, *Learning to be Chinese*, pp. 109–111.

They came to think of themselves as "we children" and "we Chinese." Negatively, the fear of being isolated, exposed, or left out was heightened by generous use of punishing techniques that conveyed rejection, ostracism, and the withdrawal of love.[20] Parents, fearing that the acts of unsocialized children would loosen wagging tongues and create social ostracism, exercised "great vigor and wit" in shaming their children:

> . . . [the parent] is horrified at the prospect of his child ever becoming shameless. To be shameless is to be uncontrollable, and hence an outcast from both the family and the culture. When the Chinese child experiences shame and humiliation, he wants to disappear from sight, to fall through the floor, to shrivel up and be inconspicuous, to hide his face, indeed, to feel the loss of his face.[21]

Like the concept of *bao* or "reciprocity" explored by sinologist Yang Liansheng,[22] the concept of *lian* holds promise as pinpointing a basic orientation of the self within the distinctive Chinese behavioral environment. It has, however, been understudied, and the verdict is not yet in. There has been insufficient participant observation to determine whether this concept only reflects categories within Chinese language and thought or whether it describes actual emotional response patterns. In a major study of formalized social behavior designed as participant observation of an upper class Chinese family in New York City, Leon Stover studied the question of "face," but focused exclusively on the term *mianzi*. In this narrowed definition, "face" becomes a power-oriented interaction game played by elite Chinese. Peasants, he argues, could acquire "face" in theory, "but like the power potential behind it, peasants had it at the zero point."[23] Some ordinary working-class Chinese, such as Ning Lao Tai-tai in *A Daughter of Han*, did, however, know "face" as a strong sense of personal morality. When she was forced to work outside the home because of the nonsupport of her "opium sot" husband, "face" caused her to have a distinct set of preferences about what kind of work she was willing to do and where she would do it, whether as a beggar in certain parts of town or as a servant in a Chinese or Western household. Under no circumstances would she become a prostitute. The opinions of invisible ancestors and unborn successors seemed to matter to her as much as those of her neighbors or fortune tellers, for she saw her duty as being a link in a great family chain. "No one can drop out without breaking the chain. A woman stands with one hand grasping the generations that have gone before and with the other the generation to come. It is her common destiny with all women."[24]

A crucial question is whether the concept of "face" as *lian* can be generalized as a system that once spanned divisions of class, sex, and region. It certainly did not eliminate specialized emotional states that were class-based supplements to that conception of a correct fit between the self and others.

For illiterate peasants, "others" included a population of demons and gods, and the emotional and moral vocabulary of sin and guilt before supernatural agencies. In the *shan shu,* or popular religious books, researched by Wolfram Eberhard, 38,000 gods watched day and night for transgressions and violations. The sense of wrongdoing and remorse was presumedly widespread among the lower classes for whom these books were written. Among the educated this world of sinfulness was left behind; there were instead crimes against the natural cosmic order and failures to live up to the code of honor and noblesse oblige by which they had been taught to measure themselves.[25]

MISSING PIECES: THE COUNTERFACTUAL/THEORETICAL MOOD AND A SEPARATE ADOLESCENCE?

It is intriguing to speculate that the power of the group may lie as much in elements that were structurally absent from the Chinese socialization experience and language as in those that were there. Developmental theorists, attempting to construct a chart of universal human development, have argued that actualizing developmental potential is contingent upon the environmental matrix within which the child grows up; some sectors of development (motor, cognitive, interpersonal, affective, verbal-speech, moral reasoning, etc.) may be accelerated or stimulated by a particular environmental matrix, while others are retarded. The importance of the matrix as stimulus appears to increase after the first six years of life; the more advanced qualitative changes in functioning are more dependent upon this environmental catalyst than upon physical maturation.[26] Breaking free from the hold of the conventional world can be translated into breaking out from earlier stages of development into higher ones.

Alfred Bloom has creatively applied these ideas to our understanding of value change and social control in Chinese society.[27] He has argued that the Chinese language, which furnishes the structures for abstract thought, does not contain the counterfactual/theoretical mood (if such and such were the case, then this or that would happen or would have happened). This mood "calls for an examination of the might-have-been, the granting of temporary reality to a state of affairs one knows did not occur, in order to treat that state as a basis for examining the consequences one hypothesizes would have been engendered by it, had it in fact occurred."[28] The implications of this absent general grammatical structure extend into the thought worlds of unilingual native speakers, although just how is unclear. Bloom hypothesizes that if the hypothetical-deductive mode of reasoning is underdeveloped as a result of this absent grammatical structure, then other developments that require this mode as a necessary prerequisite will also be underdeveloped in

Chinese life. In particular, following Piaget, he cites the development of scientific hypothesizing, theory construction and experimentation, and the development of a facility for building and evaluating abstract theoretical systems in general. Most pertinent to our discussion, he suggests that the ability to depart from "the use of traditional prescriptions and models as guides to moral behavior and evaluation" was influenced by this language/thought characteristic.[29]

The idea that this characteristic tightened the hold of tradition within Chinese life for most Chinese actors (prior to exposure to Marxist categories, science, and Western everyday thought and language in the twentieth century) is reinforced by Bloom from another direction. He correlates a qualitative leap already established in the theories of late childhood cognitive development by Jean Piaget and in moral development by Lawrence Kohlberg with a similar, and interrelated, leap in sociopolitical thinking processes. The development of "social principledness," as Bloom calls this developmental sector, is a matter of going from unanalytical adherence to the demands of existing social and political authorities to a personal, analytically-derived conception of what values a sociopolitical system should seek to maximize, coupled with a continual critical evaluation of existing social and legal conventions. The Hong Kong sample that Bloom used in his cross-cultural comparison of social principledness tested out significantly lower than sample groups in France and the United States. The reasons for this difference remain conjectural; Bloom suspects that it is related not only to overall levels of economic development and traditional cultural practices, but also to the capacity for abstract, hypothetical-deductive thinking. Moral reasoning and cognitive development as well as social principledness were arrested in the Chinese case at a low level of abstraction. Morally, the child emerged from pre-moral stages to see and obey the conventional system, but it did not go beyond to learn to question and evaluate this system and envision others. Cognitively, the child learned to detach itself from the perceptual world, but did not grow past concrete operations to hypothesizing and theoretical postulating. And on the level of social principledness, the child developed an abstract notion of responsibility that locked it into "an unquestioning acceptance of conventionally defined values, and an unanalytical response to conventional authority. . . ."[30]

The picture that emerges from Bloom's studies is that there was, and in some ways still is, a modal developmental profile for unilingual Chinese adults, a common leveling off at certain interrelated stages of development. The environmental matrix did not stimulate individuals to higher developments; in fact, traditional cultural practices retarded such developments. This nonhappening logically leads to a consideration of the time of the life cycle when these developments were theoretically arrested, i.e., adolescence. Kenneth Keniston has argued that the nature of the adolescent experience in different cultures, subcultures, and historical eras has had a direct bearing on different modal developmental profiles. In an admittedly bold conjecture, Keniston hypothesizes that in societies where adolescence as a separate experience does not occur, many of the psychological characteristics which we consider the results of that experience will be very rare: "a high degree of emancipation from family, a well-developed self-identity, a belief system based upon a reexamination of the cultural assumptions learned in childhood, and perhaps, the cognitive capacity for formal operation."[31] The lack of an adolescent experience apart from the family—the condition of life for all but a handful of Chinese young people until the twentieth century— certainly reinforced the continuity of values across generations and held the individual closer within the embrace of the group. This factor must be added to Bloom's conjectures as another environmental variable influencing cognitive, moral, and sociopolitical thinking processes.

These Bloom/Keniston hypotheses remain to be convincingly demonstrated in the Chinese case. It is hoped that this line of investigation into modal developmental profiles will proceed along the entire spectrum of developmental capacities and not just cluster on the ones that seem to cast Chinese actors in an underdeveloped role. Western emphasis upon cognitive development over interpersonal and affective learning should not be exported in cross-cultural studies. There is also a danger of making the differences appear greater than they are. No society, past or present, has had a majority of its people rank high on Kohlberg's scale of moral development; we are, as a species, still underdeveloped by this standard.[32] The differences on Bloom's scale of social principledness (on the range from 0 to 1, low to high, the Hong Kong mean was 0.18, the French 0.47, and the American 0.43), while statistically significant, may not be enough to establish qualitatively different levels of cognitive organization. The significance of this minority that thinks differently is also difficult to assess: when and under what conditions does this minority, acting as a leaven in the mass, become capable of altering overall sociopolitical organization and policies? How large must that minority be? Lastly, how can we observe and pinpoint where behavior—encompassing feelings and thoughts as well as words and deeds— really belongs on the levels of moral reasoning or social principledness, when many of the responses are internal and invisible to us? What appears on the outside as "unquestioned acceptance of conventionally defined values or an unanalytical response to conventional authorities" may on the inside not be unquestioning or unanalytical. Thinking/speaking may be thought of as interdependent, for example, as a mode of reasoning predicated on certain grammatical structures, but the pair can also be thought of as discontinuous processes, for thoughts do not necessarily result in speech and writing. This is a theoretical problem that I shall discuss in the next section.

The hypotheses based upon structurally absent features should not deflect us from appreciating that individuals probably stayed within the kinship circle because their basic perceived social needs were met there better than through alternatives, real or imagined. In the formulation of anthropologist Francis L. K. Hsu, the satisfying of human needs for status, security, and sociability within the family and clan weakened any outward drive into private escapes or extrakinship groups.[33] A child quickly learned that it had a status relative to others and what degree of emotional involvement and obligation was necessary to navigate successfully through the family network. This interaction within the group was well-defined in customs, rules, and regulations. *Bao* or "reciprocity" built a hope of mutuality into these rules, stipulating that "every act of receiving means an obligation to return," even if equivalence was measured out over long periods of time. The restricted lives of young people and the suffering of women could be compensated for by the prospect of real authority and privileges as mature adults or honored elders. There was a cost of diminished individual freedom in this arrangement, but also a gain in individual security. Identity for most was automatic within the all-inclusive membership of the family; "I am my father's son," as Hu Shi's credo implied.[34] Indeed, active participation in Chinese family life made one a part of a meaningful drama which through ancestor worship transcended the here and now. This participation schooled one in exacting sociological interaction that required a dense social knowledge of the other actors, sensitivity to interpersonal signals and cues, and considerable emotional self-control. A skillful performance demanded great attentiveness and knowledge and had as its intangible reward contributing to the harmony of the whole living group as well as having practical advantages in mutual support and help.

This system, Hsu has argued, did not produce many visible dissidents nor many who were willing to fight hard to realize new ways they had to offer.[35] The logical recruits to movements for change—the misfits and the ambitious—were effectively neutralized within the system. Was one living up to the ancestral name? Did one have sons to continue the family line? Was one's "face" exposed through breaking with customary practices? Those vulnerable to social ostracism typically reacted by making greater efforts to conform in every way possible. Exceptional individuals who were more ambitious and talented tended to compete along traditional lines in order to become illustrious sons of the kinship group. Their competitive efforts led to bigger funerals, temples, and graveyards, ostentatious weddings, feats of filial piety, extensive genealogical records, and larger families under one roof—changes in scale, but not in kind.[36] While all this seems demonstrable in West Town, Yunnan, and other village studies, it is also true that too little investigation has been directed at the limitations of the hold of the group upon individiuals, and thus our overview is distorted.

THE INNER/OUTER SPLIT

One way to avoid becoming too attached to our sociological generalizations and modal personality creations is to reimmerse ourselves in individual reality, the irreducible human actor through whom, by whom, and for whom all human sciences exist. How else can we refine our analyses beyond gross cross-cultural comparisons and get beyond the recurring image of the Chinese as near-pathological, as having an "overly compliant, self-doubting personality," and prepared to do "whatever is necessary to maintain a sense of safety and security within the group"?[37] Perhaps it is not so much a refinement that is necessary as a shifting of our focus to the micro-level, so that we can see elements of the picture that the macro-preoccupation has hidden from us.

Take, for example, the personal document "My Inner Self" (Appendix A) that was created in the course of the Research in Contemporary Cultures project at Columbia University during the years 1947 to 1951. It recounts early childhood and youth experiences as remembered by a Chinese woman who lived the first fifteen years of her life in a port city of China during the Nationalist era, her father having some prominence as a public official during those years. Subsequently, she lived briefly in an overseas Chinese community before coming to the United States, attending college, marrying an American-born Chinese, and joining the Columbia project as a graduate student. Her document was generated by group discussion about what "inner life" means to the Chinese.[38] Although atypical in some respects—her multicultural exposure, her bilingual and extensive schooling—she spent her childhood and youth in an extended family setting (mother, father, grandfather, grandmother, elder sister, younger brothers, other relatives, and friends) dominated by a conservative-sounding father. Several general issues about growing up Chinese can be explored through her account.

She did indeed act in ways to encourage system stability. Despite considerable rivalry with her sister, the ideal—and a good bit of the substance in their schoolwork—was mutual help. She was willing to compensate for her sister's feeling less attractive and intelligent by deliberately praising her sister's character. She was prepared to let her parents' judgmental attitude towards her own character go unchallenged for many years for the same reason. After a disillusioning experience with her grandmother, she let adults have their way by not being open with them and not putting herself in situations where self-disclosure might be hypocritically betrayed again. To this extent, she acted consistently with the success-in-creating-harmony orientation, rather than a truth-in-honesty orientation. "Truth" had to be applied empirically to situations and thus could involve dissemblance, outright lies, and tolerance of illusions in the surface interactions as the partial and legitimate means of creating and keeping the peace.[39]

Within this orientation there was much stimulation for the development of individual ego awareness. After the experience with her grandmother, her introspection became intense, and she had frequent "debates with my inner self." This process heightened her knowledge of who she was as a particular person, as she differentiated her needs and perspectives from those of others. What she actually did or said came to be one part of a repertoire of possible responses to situations, which included her own inner thoughts and feelings as well as the conscious assessment from which words and acts selectively followed. The awareness of complex behavioral interaction—encouraged as well, no doubt, by the nuances in the language for such interaction, such as the language of *lian*—sharpened the ego's understanding of the self-group interface. Once she outgrew the response of an undifferentiated tantrum, her approach to the sibling rivalry with her sister involved consideration of many dimensions: the overt deeds and words of her parents and sister, the underlying motives and needs that their words and deeds seemed to convey, the ideal action that group harmony enjoined upon her, her own need for self-respect, her obligations as younger sister and filial daughter, the decisions on how much to disclose of herself overtly and how much to withhold and deal with internally. Her "inner-newsreel"—a universal consequence of human self-consciousness but one still marked by distinctive cultural styles—made her an amateur social psychologist.[40]

The courage to be independent must be reevaluated within this complex behavioral environment. Does it take more courage to make a fuss and risk "losing it" as we might say (or "losing face" as Chinese might say), or to remain in control and be temperate? Is it impossible to be "independent" and at the same time act in accord with what group solidarity seems to require? Must independence always be reflected in overt behavior, or is independence a quality of mind that can have various expressions, sometimes invisible in outer behavior? Does external compliance imply lack of ego autonomy and a self-doubting personality? How much courage does it take to swallow bitterness (*chiku*) or to look like a fool without contesting that appearance? How much ego mastery is involved in successfully detaching sentiment from action, individual feeling from social performance? Learning to act responsibly within the group involved much more than taking orders or following dictates; it meant an ongoing dialogue between self and various others, a continuing exploration of boundaries for self-expression in feelings, thoughts, speech, and deeds.

Conformity to group expectations had to be learned and most Chinese children, like children elsewhere, were imperfect learners. What they did learn was to give up the illusion of the omnipotence of infancy, when the world seemed to exist for them and their needs, and to take on a larger world in which their needs had to be negotiated with others who were powerful and not always moral or praiseworthy.[41] For the young girl in "My Inner Self," this larger world meant the disillusioning experience with her grandmother, the teasing and judgmental attitude of her parents, the sparring and outright fighting with her elder sister (". . . I doubt my parents ever knew half that went on behind our closed doors . . ."), the experience of being manipulated and used by others as well as the thrill and guilt of participating in "wanton" mischief with her peer group. Each generation of children had to learn from hard and varied experience what was expected from them; "the group" and "tradition" were not simply filters that restricted experience, but viewpoints, sometimes minority viewpoints, that emerged through real life encounters. Life proceeded in all its untidy fullness and contradictions, no matter what the moral blueprint and its interpreters/enforcers said. The language of *lian* in fact relied upon falls from grace. These slips were noted and recorded, like the categories of sin grouped in circles in Dante's purgatory and hell.

Although many different kinds of messages came through to children struggling to navigate and/or thrive in that larger world beyond the dependency of infancy, one message appears to have been particularly clear: compensate for group restrictions imposed on your outer behavior by building up an active, private inner life. The prescriptive quality of interaction rules based on generation, age, and sex made it very difficult for a young person to weave spontaneous feelings, hopes, wishes, and decisions into the desires of authoritative others, so the "real self" inside split off from the social self that others saw. This inner/outer division is a universal phenomenon, but this natural division intensified into an inner/outer split in the Chinese case due to the authoritarian style of kinship and kinship-based institutions.[42] The informant, shortly after writing her personal document, remarked to the convenor of the discussions, "I have been thinking more about this inner life and do you know, I have lost it since coming to America . . . I have no need for it any more. Here you can come right out with what is in your mind."[43]

The informant's sharpened sense of her inner self was created through certain experiences of revelation, two of which are shared in her account. The first, at age three and a half, took place during a vaccination in a doctor's office, when she saw through her mother's pretense. The event revealed to her that the actions of significant others could be contrived and inappropriate. The child found her mother's efforts to distract her foolish, even though she played along consciously, as in a game. This situation was similar to a child's discovery that one can lie to others and get away with it; parents aren't omniscient, the child says, for they cannot see through my pretense. The inner self becomes the hidden, secret self that others cannot see and see through, the self behind the self that is acting consciously and visibly in front of others. The second experience, at eight years of age, did not reflect such a universal dimension of human social interaction, but posed for the growing child the specific predicament of the Chinese organization of family life. Chinese rules governing the appropriate behavior of children were strict and although younger children might be excused or dealt with more leniently, children after the age of six were made to understand that they were not legitimate partners in a negotiation process. The decisions of traditional authority figures were supposed to end arguments.

> "Children should not open their mouths indiscreetly," my father said to me sternly. "How could you have eye trouble at your age!" I felt terrible inside, I wanted to say, "Why not?" Yet I could not find the words to

express my feeling, so stirred was I by what seemed to me a frame-up. I stammered, "But it was the truth," only to bring sterner remarks from Father. I bolted from the room.

An innocent remark to her grandmother had become a *cause célèbre* because the grandmother apparently chose to present the remark in a critical fashion to her son and he, taking the criticism upon himself, displaced his anger onto his indiscreet daughter. She, in turn, felt anger and calmed herself by "a discourse I had with myself." Through such experiences she became a "quiet child . . . full of observations, feelings, and thoughts, but lacking in speech and action. Externally I was passive, internally I was seldom inactive."

The difference between these two experiences of revelation is instructive. The discovery of pretense or pretentiousness in others, like the discovery of one's own power to convey illusions by lying and pretending, is an enlarging experience. Seeing through her mother's pretense gave the daughter insight into the forms and possibilities of social interaction. But in having her words manipulated by her grandmother and her negotiating power snatched away by her father, she learned to put restrictive boundaries around her interaction with adults and to cultivate her own internal resources. It was the unpredictable and unanswerable nature of parental prerogatives that caused this sharp inner/outer split. What had she done wrong? Disobedience was monitored so closely that virtually anything, if it struck an authority figure wrong, could become "indiscreet." Questioning authority was itself counterproductive and indeed fresh evidence of the very "crime" at issue.

Alternative courses of action did exist, although she chose not to exercise them. First, she could have displaced her anger upon other persons, creatures, or objects within her control. The "unpardonable incident" with her bachelor relative is illuminating in precisely this context. As Father's children, she, her sister, and "little auntie" were protected in their mischief-making by the father's authoritative status. To criticize them was to criticize the father, who had responsibility for them, and this lower-status relative, unlike the grandmother, hesitated to do that. "With a forced smile on his flushed face," he had to beg the brats to stop putting beauty marks on his calendar pictures of seminudes. A second alternative would have been to seek solace and support from others. Instead she chose the hard and lonely path of self-cultivation, a highly valued path within the traditional culture because it was revered as the moral way of the sages. She sought to control her reactions, to exhibit patience and tolerance and understanding, to examine her own feelings and motives, and eventually to overcome the inner/outer split by bringing her inner sentiments into harmony with proper external behavior. It may have been some solace not only that sages sometimes looked like fools but also that Confucius himself was seventy years old before he reportedly claimed to have been able to do the right thing with natural ease.[44]

The inner/outer split, seen from the perspective of the individual growing child, has implications for the nature and hold of tradition. "Tradition" as a body of norms, values, and knowledge is easily reified into a monolithic structure; rather, tradition accrues bit by bit as features of it are encountered and appropriated. Tradition was a world of possibilities, embodied first of all in people and only secondarily in books and artifacts. The psychological mechanism that transferred these diverse possibilities from adult to child was identification, a process that was selective, incomplete, and even contradictory, as in the case of sons of the educated who often came to inhabit one world with their nurses, another with their mothers, and a third with their fathers. Tradition meant diverse interpretations of the world, drawing on plain-speaking bits of peasant folklore, popular religious beliefs, conflicting schools of classical learning, social criticism, and religious skepticism. Was going to school a way to fulfill one's human capacities, a way to attain prestige as an official, or a way to harness children? Was foot-binding a way to perfect one's female nature or a device perpetuated by men in order to restrain women? Was praying to spirits and propitiating demons a praiseworthy, prudent act or a superstitious practice?[45] Individual identity was never a mere replica of society, but reflected the diverse strains within it that had been concretely encountered and appropriated.

Appropriation itself did not necessarily mean internalization, for children might give the behavior as part of a social drama but retain reservations about the sense or fairness of what was required. The inner/outer split thus introduces a huge question mark into our theorizing about Chinese behavior; the relationships between deeds, speech, thoughts, and feelings must be assumed to be discontinuous. To what extent did filial sons want to be what the social drama required them to be? The widespread equation of individual desire and social expectation in much social psychology, via the internalization of cultural norms through the superego, has blunted exploration of permanent and unresolved areas of conflict within various systems and obscured the varieties of experience and behavior found within them.[46] There were undoubtedly Chinese lads who internalized exquisitely the filial norms; but many others were "filial sons by default," held in this role not so much by the voice of the superego as by the overwhelmingness of concrete situations which offered them only disastrous alternatives. When the situational configuration changed, prescribed meanings and roles could lose their hold; alternative meanings and roles were always there, retrievable in the shadows.

The hiddenness of the "real" thoughts and feelings raises some intriguing questions. Are Chinese actors, as Leon Stover asserts, disinterested in this hidden realm, even shunning it?

> The probing of motives is repugnant to Chinese sensibilities. The Chinese want to know *what* the other person is going to do (as a matter of predictability), not why he does it (the unpredictable element) . . . One need not look into these matters in any case. The Chinese make it a conscious policy to keep action apart from feelings.[47]

Or, as Donald J. Munro argues, are the Chinese intensely interested in this inner realm as the budding place for action because of the nature of thoughts/motives as "promptings to action"? The probing of thoughts and motives has hardly been repugnant to the sensibilities of moral philosophers or rulers, both imperial and contemporary, who have taken it upon themselves to foster correct thoughts and weed out incorrect ones.[48] The concept of the inner/outer split allows us to suggest that the contradiction here is only apparent and that both viewpoints are resolvable in the somewhat uncomfortable fact that the inner sphere of the individual was, and is, an unreachable and uncontrollable reality. In the give and take of ordinary social interaction, the denial of the importance of motives was perhaps born in the desire to safeguard one's own inner self from prying inquiry by the group, to protect the private sphere by formally denying its importance. The problem for moral philosophers and rulers was not that "what truly is within will be manifested without" but that what came out in overt behavior was not what they hoped for as moral philosophers or wanted as rulers. Was the effort to probe motives and thoughts a recognition that outer conformity did not mean internalized commitment, that much publicly manifested action was a mask, that an explosive or evil potential lay concealed within the members of an authoritarian society?

UNCONVENTIONAL BEHAVIOR THROUGH THE BACKDOOR

The inner/outer split appears to have been a psychological fact within Chinese society. The hold of the group thus stopped somewhere near the threshold of individual minds. Certain secondary customs, or roundabout ways of satisfying psychological needs, acknowledged this boundary and the private territory inside persons; in so doing, these customs created a backdoor, or semi-institutionalized way to give expression to the unconventional or "deviant" underside of individual and social reality. These customs existed at the macro level of the entire society—especially in the elite characterization of a unified society—as well as at the level of villages, families, and individuals.

At the macro level of the society as a whole, as Leon Stover has argued, the fiction of the moral leadership of the educated Confucian elite over the entire society was allowed to persist, even though peasant communities were self-regulating and even anti-center or anti-elite in their orientation. This fiction was useful to the elite, for they functionally appeared to have something to offer peasant communities in exchange for the taxes and resources they extracted from them. It is less clear how it was useful to the peasant communities, except that they were at least left alone, provided they delivered their taxes and kept the peace, or treated only to the moral indoctrination of the Sacred Edict. Their separate and varied tradition-sanctioned ways of life could continue undisturbed beneath the veneer of uniformity provided by upperclass Confucian culture.[49] This arrangement permitted a society-wide outward acceptance of authority and moral leadership by the cultural center while acknowledging in practice the reality of two separate subcultures. Stover finds a similar fictive gloss in such elite-defined terms as "friendship" among peers and "contentment" among peasants. In each case the terms tell only an idealized part of the story and conceal underlying realities that he argues are more accurately defined as "formalized informality" for friendship and "sactimonious husbandry" for contentment.[50] The outer, more-idealized impression is held out for public viewing.

At the level of villages, some types of unconventional behavior were tolerated and even expected. As recorded by Margery Wolf in *The House of Lim*, the dominant clan in one Taiwanese village had a tradition of pride in being apart, in innovating, in leading. Eccentricities were simply felt to be inherited in these strong individuals, and it was taken for granted by villagers that their behavior would be somewhat unpredictable. Yet there were limits: the clan elder could spend hours idly with foreigners as long as this appeared to be an alternative outlet for the release of inner strains and desires, much the same as spending time with prostitutes or gambling, but not if this contact began to draw him away from the village and its established ways.

> In the closed life of a Taiwanese village, the usual quirks of a man's personality are accepted in the same way as a crippled leg: that's just the way he is. But even the slightest suspicion of a more basic peculiarity—a man who questions the premises his neighbors call fact—leads to doubt and distrust. Because of the long hours he wasted talking with us, some of Lim Chieng-cua's neighbors wondered at his patience, others grew suspicious of his motives and ours, and the more acute were uneasy at his obvious enjoyment of profitless discussion . . . I hope his neighbors concluded after our departure that the hours Lim Chieng-cua wasted with us were only a modern variation of the hours he wasted in the company of his mistresses.[51]

Most salient in the premises of village morality appeared to be the maintenance of the basic roles of parent, neighbor, friend, and provider. Knowledge of the bonds of human relations was the core of traditional teaching; as revealed in the language of *lian* it was believed to distinguish men from beasts. Disregarding these bonds was thought not only to be subversive to tradition but to be a monstrous crime as well. On the other hand, if in one's public performance an individual was, or appeared to be, subservient to these conventional moral expectations, he or she could be forgiven much in private life. For example, in the particular Taiwanese village cited above, it was interpreted as a filial act for a poor daughter to sell her youthful body as a prostitute and thus help support her parents; prostitution held little community respect as a vocation, but a prostitute might gain community respect as a filial daughter.[52] Situational constraints, such as an option-limiting poverty that could create strong conflicts among values (the prostitute as filial daughter), were considered in village morality.

The unconventional behavior traditionally permitted to scholar-officials in their private lives may be interpreted in the same way. It was acceptable as long as it was part of a rhythm between dedication and release, work and leisure and did not threaten to undermine their public performance. In a contemporary version of this phenomenon, a "modern" social reformer could become more palatable to traditionalists on Taiwan if he were conventional in his interpersonal relations, i.e., filial to his parents and faithful to friends. When Hu Shi, for example, is cited by traditionalists as being in some ways very Confucian, this is usually what they mean. He is widely respected for enduring his unhappy marriage and being devoted to his mother.[53]

In these varied ways some straying of individuals beyond the normal boundaries of conventional behavior was known to happen and was not automatically condemned. Francis L. K. Hsu has postulated that these secondary customs, or "safety valves," were built into Chinese social life at precisely those points where unqualified insistence upon primary cultural demands and regulations would have produced unmanageable psychological and external conflicts. He cites in particular the institutional and architectural arrangement of family divisions under one roof, which allowed mature sons within an extended family some scope for economic decisionmaking, self-expression, and conjugal intimacy. The importance attached to form, particularly to grandiose funerals for deceased parents, also worked to appease the guilty consciences of sons for less than devoted filial behavior.[54] The emphasis placed on dutiful public performance in certain key roles also took pressure off individual performance in less primary roles. In minor roles, such as mother-son, brother-sister, and grandparent-grandchild, affection and intimacy were permitted as well as in major roles at certain times and places, such as between father and son during the infancy-toddler period and between husband and wife in the privacy of the inner room.

Another important area of secondary custom was in the socialization of talented young male children, whose precociousness earned them not only praise but immunity from normal expectations and an enlarged scope for self-assertion. Young Shu Xincheng relates in his autobiography how he acquired the appelation "prodigy" (*shentong*, lit. good-spirit child) for his exceptional study achievements. The underlying belief was that an unusual spiritual force resided in him, and a *shentong* could for this reason become an object of awe and respect in the village. At age fourteen Xincheng was emboldened to write and post a long essay condemning the "despicable behavior" of a local deity. His parents deeply believed the claims of a local literatus that this image possessed divine powers. The youth's attack stirred up the entire town like a storm, but no one dared dispute him directly. "That

I had the gall to act in this way meant that I must have other spirit powers supporting me secretly. Thus my parents did not even reprimand me seriously."[55]

With or without imputed supernatural assistance, many children in the late Qing period developed into stereotypical *taochi* or "mischievous" children. The various meanings attached to *taochi* (undisciplined, annoying, willful, obstinate, intrusive, assertive, disobedient, boisterous) express precisely the traits that many contemporary parents would associate with a young child struggling to emancipate itself from dependency, trying to be a "self" and to possess a personal sphere. They describe the opposite of that model good child (*guai haizi*) who, as Lu Xun noted in 1934, was obedient, composed, self-effacing, respectful, and industrious.[56] That the *taochi* child could emerge and even thrive within the filial system was due to some permanent cracks within the extended family system, such as the tardy impact of paternal disciplining, the delegation of authority to teachers, the interventionist style of the father, and the supporting network of mothers, nurses, grandparents, sisters, and kindly males. In combination, these openings guaranteed a steady stream of "poorly" socialized children who could not easily be bent to the will of the group. And many parents themselves had ambivalent feelings about bending them. Unconventional activities, especially immoral behavior, could not be openly condoned, but parents were often secretly pleased with the uncommon vigor and intelligence of their children. A sharp-witted lad with bright eyes could usually rely on a coalition of supporters to exert influence in his favor.[57]

THE TRADITIONAL IDEAL AS A CRITIQUE OF THE NORMS OF CONVENTIONAL "SMALL MEN"

The complex interplay between cultural demand and psychological needs illustrates that breaking the hold of tradition and the group meant, in part, drawing for leverage upon secondary customs or counter tendencies within the larger tradition. It also could mean drawing upon formulations of ideal behavior that went beyond the standard of the "decent man," described in the language of *lian*. As intimated in the document "My Inner Self," the morality of a sage was a support and comfort to a young person experiencing a binding fit between self and group. And indeed, as is argued by some twentieth-century defenders, the Confucian philosophical tradition was meant to be a living, creative force in society; it should not be evaluated primarily through the historical forms with which it appeared so thoroughly intertwined, such as the imperial monarchy or the hierarchical family system. The striving for *ren*, or "human heartedness," required fresh moral visions and new institutional forms appropriate to a given time and place.[58] Sagelike men who fully developed themselves and the potential of their situations would always be few; their very scarcity, however, pointed to the failings of the many rather than to the impracticality of the ideal. In this perspective, the "normal" orientation of ordinary men can be seen as the retarded development of human potential; it was certainly not reflective of the standard of ideal moral striving.

In the document "Elder Hu's Self-defense" (Appendix B), the nonconformist stance of the "superior man" (*junzi*) is vividly illustrated in a concrete life situation and contrasted with the "small man" (*xiaoren*) mentality. The document is found in Hu Qiuyuan's autobiography, *Collected Fragments of Early Writings (shao zuo shou can ji)*; it describes the situation of his father, who had taken over responsibility for an innovative local school and railway, but was then imprisoned for default when higher authorities claimed the ventures without asssuming local debts. In the summer of 1930, when nineteen-year-old Hu Qiuyuan returned to the village of Huangpi, Hubei, his father, was facing another crisis and another possible prison sentence. Relatives and friends argued the indignity and uselessness of his going to prison and urged him to leave Huangpi and to retire in the face of the public clamor over the case. In this self-defense, as reconstructed by his son, the elder Hu kept turning the arguments back upon them and in the process redefining "shame" and "respectability."[59]

The elder Hu portrays the small man as, above all, a weak individual who drifts with the prevailing tides of opinion and rumor. The small man is attuned to conventional definitions of crime and shame that he assents to out of fear or self-effacement before authority ("emperors, demons, and gods"). His life is organized around the motives of profit-loss, fame-shame, and status, and he has no ability to go beyond these to the discrimination of truth and falsehood (*shi fei*) and the discernment of correct moral behavior. He is anxious to preserve appearances and to avoid undignified situations. He is likely to nod his head towards the Will of Heaven as a ready explanation for both difficulties and successes. He cannot stand up to the world and penetrate the conventional face of things in his environment because he has failed to anchor his ego firmly in something other than the small world he knows. He has no independent stance—economically or intellectually—with which to face the world and so is doomed to exist as a reflection of conventions, authorities, and fashions. He is the "decent man" who lives within the inherited or prescribed definition of the personal and nonpersonal world.

In contrast, the social type of the superior man is revealed as an unconventional person, distinguished above all by the personal stamp he places on the world about him. He defines shame and crime and sin not solely by convention and appearance but by the context of the acts and the truthfulness of the charges. If truly wrong, he feels under judgment before a weak child as much as before a strong official or powerful deity. He has a long-range view of reputation and shame, and trusts in the considered judgment of posterity, not in the instant judgment of community approval or condemnation. He is not intimidated by the powerful or by the threat of ostracism and isolation, nor is he afraid that "even falling leaves may break open one's head"; he even anticipates the unfamiliar and strange. He accepts neither himself nor conventions at face value and recognizes the need to re-examine the integrity of his own views as well as to penetrate the falsehoods, injustices, and delusions of life around him. Put into contemporary developmental terms, the superior man of tradition, as personified in this portrait of the elder Hu, represented the highest levels of individual moral reasoning and social principledness.

A major inner struggle of those breaking free from convention and exposing their "face" was how to handle the shame that others might thrust upon them. "I can be shamed [by others], but cannot be made to shame myself." How could the individual become invulnerable to the barbs and stares and gossip? How could one conquer the resentments that seemed bound to arise, especially if self-reflection confirmed the correctness of one's stand? There were two approaches, and elder Hu's self-defense employs them both. One was to inflate his own self-image and denigrate the opposition as mere "wolves, a pathetic lot." Hu tried to establish his superiority by satirizing the abilities of his tormenters, calling them poor calligraphers or mere clerks and assuring himself that he could do better. "My not doing so is a matter of intent, not ability." By such defenses, he could keep his equilibrium and endure the shame that "small men" inflicted on him. This is similar to the traditional superior man, who worn down by the perversity and unreasonableness of lesser men would say, "This is a man utterly lost indeed! Since he conducts himself so, what is there to choose between him and a brute? Why should I go to contend with a brute?"[60]

The second approach—reversing the perspective on who or what was shameful—was a more profound response, for it went beyond the calculus of ability and righteousness that still characterized the first approach. It embodied the recognition that shameful acts contained a double revelation: as society exposed the social failings of the individual, the limited nature of social mores was also revealed to the individual. Were those who perpetuated the act shameful, or those who suffered from it? "Who will say that beating [the buttocks of] people is dignified, but being beaten is disgraceful?" In the experience of shame—of being out of step with society—lay the possibility of identification beyond the morality of the particular social group and its prescribed rules. It permitted the discovery of other standards with which to measure oneself and one's society and could liberate one into a larger historical and human perspective. That larger awareness itself, while it may have left one more isolated and unprotected in the particular social milieu, also gave such persons a certain sturdiness through being able to "discern and ally themselves with men and values over wide ranges of time and space."

The sense of kinship with past sages and the sense of knowing and living ancient truths may have more than compensated for the loss of the comforts of a righteous well-adjusted life.[61]

Helen Lynd has constructed a suggestive typology of personal growth on the basis of this need and/or capacity for seeking larger identifications. Her distinction between "normal" persons and "restless" persons is closely related to the traditional distinction between the small man and the superior, or unconventional, man. Normal people tend to find continuity in their lives by acting upon what superiors and significant others have taught them they should or should not do. They are conscious of behavior in terms of transgressions that are culturally defined and redeemable and in terms of roles that assure them a well-defined life in the group. Restless persons, however, form their identity more in terms of an evolving ego-ideal than a prohibiting superego. They discover their own lines of direction, but at greater emotional cost. Experiences of shame lead to revelations of the innermost self and of the central dynamics of the society.[62]

LU XUN AND THE DOUBLE-EDGED POWER OF SHAME

Lu Xun exemplified in his life and his works one who had come to live on this restless axis, measuring himself by his own internally evolving standards. In the autobiographical preface to "Outcry" (*Nahan*), Lu Xun recounts several experiences through which he came to shed earlier views as outmoded, provincial, unworthy, or uninformed. He came to seek broader identification based on more universal criteria, which in turn exposed whatever failed to live up to them, be they aspects of his own behavior or that of his fellow Chinese. He was keenly aware of the double-edged power of shame either to submerge the individual into the conformist crowd or to sharpen individual insight into society's claim and how that claim might be, or should be, contested. The "small men" of the village wine shop, the Ah Q's of China and the world, knew shame as a prod to conformity. Not even the young and the disabled could be shaken out of their familiar righteous worlds; Lu Xun's early pessimism about social change in China was grounded in this assessment, as this scene from his short story "Medicine" makes clear.

> . . . the greybeard walked up to the man in brown and lowered his voice to ask, "Mr. Kang, I heard the criminal executed today came from the Hsia family. Who was it? And why was he executed?"
>
> "Who? Son of Widow Hsia, of course! Young rascal!" Seeing how they were all hanging on his words, Mr. Kang's spirits rose even higher. His jowls quivered, and he made his voice as loud as he could. "The rogue didn't want to live, simply didn't want to! There was nothing in it for me this time. Even the clothes stripped from him were taken by Red-

eye the jailer. Our old Ch'uan was luckiest [for he got a bun soaked in blood for his consumption-ridden son], and after him Third Uncle Hsia. He pocketed the whole reward—twenty-five taels of bright silver—and didn't have to spend a cent . . . Third Uncle Hsia is really smart. If he hadn't informed, even *his* family would have been executed, and their property confiscated. But instead? Silver! That young rogue was a real scoundrel! He even tried to incite the jailer to revolt!"

"No! The idea of it!" A man in his twenties, sitting in the back row, expressed indignation.

"You know, Red-eye went to sound him out, but he started chatting with him. He said the great Manchu empire belongs to us. Just think: is that kind of talk rational? Red-eye knew he had only an old mother at home, but had never imagined he was so poor. He couldn't squeeze anything out of him; he was already good and angry, and then the young fool would 'scratch the tiger's head' so he gave him a couple of slaps."

"Red-eye is a good boxer. Those slaps must have hurt." The hunchback in the corner by the wall exulted.

"The rotter was not afraid of being beaten. He even said how sorry he was."

"Nothing to be sorry about in beating a wretch like that," said Greybeard.

Kang looked at him superciliously and said disdainfully, "You misunderstood. The way he said it, he was sorry for Red-eye."

His listeners' eyes took on a glazed look, and no one spoke . . .

"Sorry for Red-eye—crazy! He must have been crazy!" said Greybeard, as if suddenly he saw light.

"He must have been crazy!" echoed the man in his twenties . . .

"Crazy!" agreed the hunchback, nodding his head.[63]

In his first-person reminiscence, "A Trifling Incident," Lu Xun reveals how he too could identify with being caught up in the web of conventional, protective reactions. One evening in Peking a rickshaw in which the narrator was riding accidently knocked over an old woman. It was disgusting, he thought, that the old woman should pretend to be hurt; the rickshaw puller deserved the mess he was getting into for helping her to the nearby police station. His own impulse was to "go on" and avoid trouble.

> Suddenly I had a strange feeling. (The rickshaw puller's) dusty, retreating figure seemed larger at that instant. Indeed, the further he walked the larger he loomed, until I had to look up to him. At the same time he seemed gradually to be exerting a pressure on me, which threatened to overpower the small self under my furlined gown.
>
> My vitality seemed sapped as I sat there motionless, my mind a blank, until a policeman came out. Then I got down from the rickshaw.
>
> The policeman came up to me and said, "Get another rickshaw. He can't pull you anymore."

Without thinking, I pulled a handful of coppers from my coat pocket and handed them to the policeman. "Please give him these," I said.

The wind had dropped completely, but the road was still quiet. I walked along thinking, but I was almost afraid to turn my thoughts on myself. Setting aside what had happened earlier, what had I meant by that handful of coppers? Was it a reward? Who was I to judge the rickshaw man? I could not answer myself.

Even now, this remains fresh in my memory. It often causes me distress, and makes me cry to think about myself. The military and political affairs of those years I have forgotten as completely as the classics I read in my childhood. Yet this incident keeps coming back to me, often more vivid than in actual life, teaching me shame, urging me to reform, and giving me fresh courage and hope.[64]

The unconventional reaction was to confront his shame, to forego the easy labels "ridiculous, pointless, troublesome" and to turn inward after the moment of the glassy stare. The secure, even smug, relationship between the self and others dissolves in such moments; the self-image is shaken and the world never looks quite the same again.[65] What turns the unconventional reaction into a promise for social change is using the insight gained through such experiences to break outward, from feelings to thoughts, from thoughts to words, from words to actions. Breaking free meant breaking through the "meaningful necessity" of the group drama and the group face.

Through such apparently minor incidents as this one or the news slide-show in Japan during the Russo-Japanese war, Lu Xun was driven to plumb his inner depths and to reassess his "self" in society and society in him. His life was a restless dialectic of growth in understanding and ego-assertion that knew no boundaries. In a prose poem written after the March 18, 1926 incident, in which several of his students at the Women's Normal School in Peking were killed and wounded, Lu Xun presumed to have insight into the meaning of creation itself. The creator was playing a game with mankind, using time and forgetfulness and a daily fare of "sweetened bitter wine" to make humans wish to live on, ignorant of the truth. But this would change.

A rebellious fighter has arisen from mankind, who, standing erect, *sees through* all the deserted ruins and lonely tombs of the past and the present. He remembers all the intense and unending agony; he gazes at the whole welter of clotted blood; he understands all that is dead and all that is living as well as all yet unborn. *He sees through the creator's game.* And he will arise to save or destroy mankind, these loyal subjects of the creator.

The creator, the weakling, hides himself in shame. Then *heaven and earth change color in the eyes of the fighter.*[66]

He who has made the world look different has already changed it.

APPENDIX A: "MY INNER SELF"*

My inner self is my real self, my consciousness of awareness of being. It is a self not easily revealed to others and guarded unto myself as a basis of my secured well-being, especially in a society where truth is arrived at empirically, not scientifically.

A typical example of this inner self as revealed in experience is the following. I was eight at the time. My grandmother had just returned from America to join the family consisting of my parents, grandfather, elder sister, younger brother, and myself. Up to then my feeling toward Grandmother had been one of innocence and eager acceptance of her as a new experience in my young, sheltered life. The slightly American ways she brought with her, her comparatively positive approach toward life (in comparison to my grandfather, who spent his old age in naive philosophical bliss), her ability to help my sister and me in our Chinese, her introduction to us of Chinese juvenile literature (such as *Monkey*), and her readiness to tell us the history of the family (my grandfather and mother were the quiet type, my father was busy with his career, spending very little time with us children)—all these created a favorable heroine image in my impressionable mind.

One day she remarked casually that at her age she needed glasses. Innocently I told her that probably my eyes were not so good either. "Why," I said, "the other day when I was walking into the bathroom (which had a window facing the door), I saw rings in the air coming toward me." (Scientifically, this phenomenon is attributed to the movement of the impurities in the fluid in the eyeballs.) She did not say anything to the remark and I forgot about the incident.

A few days passed. I entered the dining room one morning and found my grandmother having breakfast with my father. The conversation was about glasses, and observing my entrance into the room, my grandmother repeated what I had told her about my eyes.

"Children should not open their mouths indiscreetly," my father said to me sternly. "How could you have eye trouble at your age!" I felt terrible inside, I wanted to say, "Why not?" Yet I could not find words to express my feeling, so stirred was I by what seemed to me a frame-up. I stammered, "But it was the truth," only to bring sterner remarks from Father. I bolted from the room.

My inner self was my best friend at such trying moments. I did not go to Mother, nor did I tell my sister, who was my closest companion. I felt *ch'i* (filled with air or anger), which was only calmed down after a discourse I had with myself. To me it was truth sacrificed by the fact that it was uttered by a

---

*Reprinted from *The Study of Culture at a Distance* (document RCC-CH 689, Informant 45F, pp. 157–162) edited by Margaret Mead and Rhoda Metraux by permission of the University of Chicago Press. Copyright 1953 by the University of Chicago.

child. As for my grandmother, I thought her double face most hypocritical. I took it as a warning not to be too open with her, or any other adult, again.

Such experiences helped to make a quiet child out of me, full of observations, feelings, and thoughts, but lacking in speech and action. Externally I was passive, internally I was seldom inactive. Everything I observed, I "think over in my heart" (*hsin li hsien*—"heart within think"). Such thinking, however, was seldom translated into speech or action, partly because of the pressure from adults that children should not speak freely, and partly because of the feeling that the battle is already won in your heart and exposure of it only makes a small person out of you. This premeditation and reflection may be partly responsible for the pungent speech I developed in my teens, speech that was cutting and cold and somehow seemed uncontrolled by internal thoughts. Of course there must be other reasons for this sarcasm, as we shall see later in my relationship with other members of the family.

The earliest incident in my life in which I remember my inner self playing a part occurred when I was about three and a half years old. The doctor was giving me a vaccination while my mother tried to distract my attention with an alarm clock. I knew exactly what was happening. I was not frightened by what the doctor was doing, and I thought it foolish of my mother to attempt to distract me. However, I pretended that I was interested in the clock, whereas all the time I kept an eye on the doctor.

My elder sister and I were constant companions when we were young. Our parents were careful not to show partiality between us. As a matter of fact, they always tried to give more consideration and attention to the child in the less favorable position in order to help her along. This we understood very well and as individuals we even co-operated with our parents.

I understand my sister was a demanding baby and very much attended to by both my parents. When I was born the novelty had worn off, I was given to the care of a wet-nurse—a fact which my parents talked about in teasing moods and which in turn made me feel rejected for many years to come. That must have accounted partly for the tantrums I used to have before five, curable only at the touch of Mother's hands. Before I was five, I had much childhood sickness, and as a result was kept home much of the time. I was then the envy of my sister. In later years, as our individuality developed we had our complaints of parental partiality, but these were complaints known only by our inner selves and very seldom expressed.

Our work, whether for home or school, was shared in good spirits. The one who was better in one subject helped the other without condescension, and the other accepted the help as freely as it was given. We never went to bed until the work of both was finished, and we took it as a duty to check on each other's homework. Many a time our teachers in the American school which we attended from the sixth to the eighth grades found we made similar mistakes or had the same ideas—actually those were mutual mistakes and ideas. This mutual help is no doubt one of the dominant features of Chinese home life, but here I wish to write of the consciousness of *myself* as a participant in such a society.

I usually helped my sister in her English lessons, sometimes even to the extent of rewriting a whole composition. But that was never made known to others. Our report cards were compared by our parents; no praise was ever given to the one with the higher marks, and whatever weak mark one had called for a general lecture for both. I knew my parents sensed that my sister was slower in her work. This, however, they attributed to good sense and steadiness. They somehow always maintained that my sister knew what is right and wrong, while I was temperamental, and that knowing what is right and wrong gives character to a person, and that a fast mind is secondary to character. I often held debates with my inner self over this observation of theirs. I conceded that my sister had a strong mind, but I doubted if I lacked character of my own. No doubt I betrayed my feeling through the sarcastic speech I developed in this period, but in general I decided that the best way to correct such an attitude of my parents was through time and fortitude on my part. I figured that if I should make a fuss of the situation (and this is not possible in a hierarchical family like the Chinese), it only would prove the opposite of what I wanted to prove. It would show narrow-mindedness, which I considered a base character. "The sage looks like a fool"—I was bent to be that kind of sage. Furthermore, I was happy to see that through this debasement of myself, my sister felt less inferior to me. What I did well in achievements she made up in her superior feeling in character. This attitude of my parents persisted through our high school and college years. I had never attempted to correct it as I felt it preserved better feeling all around. So far as I myself maintain inner security afforded by my inner self—in other words, as far as I know the reality—my equilibrium is not disturbed. And so far as they like to hold onto a conception which makes them comfortable, I have no objection.

In the first Chinese girls' school we attended, a few boys were accepted in the lower grades. There was one boy in my class who sat next to me and who did many errands for me. My sister and I belonged to a gang which included my mother's stepsisters and brothers. One day the subject fell on boy and girl friends, and my sister told the group that the boy in my class was my boyfriend. Actually it was not so, but I was embarrassed by the teasing that ensued. Inwardly I felt very bad about my sister, whose act, to me, spelled betrayal and lying to gain group acceptance at my expense.

Our maternal uncle was like an elder brother to us. He was entering college and was full of fun and spirit. He invented games for us, told us historical stories, helped us in our homework—in fact we always felt he was more approachable than our overworked and much absent father. In his treatment of us sisters, it was apparent he had a partiality for me. I did not like the idea at all and so always tried to give my sister the benefit whenever possible. Many of Uncle's college friends became friends of the family; they too, to my annoyance, were attracted to me. I knew physical attraction is not man-made, and I felt God had done injustice to my sister. In time I developed some guilt feeling from this and compensated for it by being extra nice and sympathetic to my sister.

My sister had aimless tantrums until she was at least fourteen, and I was usually the victim of those fits. I never talked about those incidents, except sometimes to tease her when we were alone, and I doubt my parents ever knew half that went on behind our closed door. One time she gave me a punch so hard that I was out for a few seconds.

Relatives often lived with us. We rented two three-storied houses in a row in a lane. One of them was occupied by the family, the other was used partly as an office but chiefly as quarters for the men relatives who worked in Father's office. One of them was a young bachelor who was very fond of me. He used to greet me with kisses, a practice which was very modern considering the fact he was from the village, and which was discontinued as I grew older. When we were seven and eight, our parents were away for a whole year, and in that period my sister and I saw much of him. On Saturdays my sister usually made me ask him to take us to the movies. That presented great conflict to my inner heart. I wanted to go to the movies, but I also felt it inhuman of us to ask him to take us, considering the meager salary he made. The greatest guilt felt, however, sprang from the fact I felt my sister was making a prostitute out of me. I remember the relief I felt when our parents came home and took care of our week-end entertainment, but it was not completed until this relative moved out and got married.

My sister, a stepsister of my mother whom we called "little auntie," and myself were week-end companions. Our alliance was considered by me anything but holy. Under the domineering leadership of our "little auntie" we formed a gang with her younger brothers and sister and did many wanton things. With the group I felt perfectly happy, but with her and my sister, I often felt uneasy. My sister and "little auntie" were of about the same age and they teamed up very nicely. I was taken into this inner circle merely because I was part of a sisterly pair, and even then the two often teamed up to tease me (as in the case of the boy friend incident).

One unpardonable incident I remember was their mischief toward the relative described above. That relative had in his room many calendar pictures of seminudes. One Sunday we barged into his room in search of excitement. He was practicing calligraphy, but we would give him no peace. We tried to get him to tell us stories; he was not a good storyteller. We wanted to drag him out to play with us; he insisted on practicing calligraphy. Disappointed, we were on the verge of leaving when the two older girls decided to take it out on his treasured pictures. With pens in hand, they began to make beauty spots all over the pictures. Our relative, who at first dared not oppose us, as we were Father's children, had to beg them to stop, with a forced smile on his flushed face. I stood by while this went on; I did not want to have any part in it. I had no aesthetic liking for the pictures, but I had respect for another's property and did not think much of fun through destruction. I pleaded with the girls and only succeeded after much effort. They had so much fun from their deed that they forgot to make an issue of my pleading for the young man, and for that I was thankful.

APPENDIX B: "ELDER HU'S SELF-DEFENSE"*

If as soon as I hear that someone doesn't like me I must move to Wuchang, and then someone else doesn't like me and so I go to Nanjing, and then someone else doesn't like me, how can I avoid going abroad? Although the world is large, if it goes on like this there will eventually be no place to rest my body. I have already retreated to this village, and there is no other place I can retreat to. I will go out to stroll when I please, and I will not be intimidated into fleeing. They are not emperors, and they cannot force me. If we have broken the law or done some shameful thing, then we should be afraid even before a three-year-old child. But if we have committed no crime nor disgraced ourselves, then we need not fear heaven, earth, or spirits, let alone emperors. This matter really should not be considered very important, and there is nothing to fear. These friends and relatives only know that even falling leaves may break open one's head. They do not know that if one does not consider strange things as unusual, their strangeness disappears. We must know . . . [the limits of] our virtue and our strength, and not provoke disputes. . . . [But] we shouldn't fear people without reason or be excessively afraid of doing things. . . .

I do not consider it dignified to sit in prison and to present oneself in court, but if one has committed no crime, then there is no shame connected with it. The first Chinese to sit in prison was King Wen, and no one considered it shameful. Some friends and relatives say if you have to sit in prison, go sit in the large prison in Nanjing. You should not be seized and handled here like a chicken. That's no different than saying that the beggars in Nanjing are a bit more dignified than the beggars in Hankou. This expression reveals an impure heart, and hankers after fame and profit. At the end of the Eastern Han, some people wanted to sit in prison in order to become famous, even to the point of wanting to be killed in order to become known as virtuous men. These are "martyrs" seeking fame, who are really like greedy men dying of wealth, or ambitious men dying of power. It is no better than this. I am certainly not seeking fame or profit, and do not want to sit in prison for any purpose. I am being forced to sit in prison, and I have no

---

*Hu Qiuyuan, "Fuchin zhi xun" (Father's Teachings), *Minju Chao (Current Democracy)*, 10 (Number 15): 15–19.

strength to resist them, that is all. I am only being true to myself, seeking to quiet my heart and to act virtuously [lit. "reach the *li*"]. We should know that for a man to act in this world he can only look for the resources in himself. He can really only ask about the rightness of things, and inquire into his own conscience. I do not concern myself with profit and loss, glory and shame. One must also take a long range view, counting on the judgment of posterity. Confucius said, "States not acting according to the Dao yet rich and honorable, and states acting according to the Dao yet poor and humble, are both humiliating." This phrase, broadly interpreted, says everything. No matter whether one is an emperor or bandit, acts done without regard for the right way are shameful.

In the Ming dynasty, many eminent persons had their buttocks beaten by the eunuchs, and who will say that beating people is dignified but being beaten was disgraceful? One must consider the "why" in all matters. If we meet misfortune and do evil in order to meet our family's needs for food and clothing, this is a crime that must receive due punishment. On the other hand, death is too kind for one who is corrupt and immoral, grasping for power and fortune, ruining the country, and endangering the people in order to increase his reputation and wealth. Those who struggle for power and profit but reap humiliation instead of fame, or appear foolish instead of clever, have only themselves to blame. Lastly, those who strive to reach the highest virtue (*ren*) have no resentments to voice and no shame to reveal.

If we are not wrong but are insulted by others, this is what we call undeserved disaster. To become angry and feel hurt are normal human feelings. But one must examine his own views and see how well one lives up to his own words. One must look at things in a detached manner. If fame, wealth, and honor come from undeserved sources they will not last. This is truly the gateway to catastrophe. On the other hand, common people wading in the mud may outlive kings and princes. "The net of Heaven is loose, but there is no gap." If you think this way, you may quiet your heart and harmonize your feelings. Why should we bother about the small, short-term gains or losses?

One must also boost his self-image a bit. If you regard those who attack, vilify, and insult you too highly, you will feel it is unjust. But if you know that they are only wolves and foxes—a pathetic lot—you will be able to endure your sufferings [lit. "endure your shame"]. "Han Xin rewarded the favor of one bowl of rice given him by a washing lady." "Han Xin never paid back the insult of having to crawl between the legs of a butcher." [From the *Shi Ji*] Why? This [latter] was not worth taking seriously. [The Buddha] believed it was his personal calling to bear insults and suffer wrongs for mortals. We ordinary people need not think this way. If one is not tested, one should not seek trouble. Those of us coping with this present-day world must first of all anchor ourselves firmly, second be cautious, and thirdly proceed slowly according to the way of justice. All else—success or failure, achievement or disappointment—will come in its course. We can only give our best efforts and await the verdict of Heaven. . . . [We can only] live with integrity in order to feel guiltless, exhausting ourselves in seeking inner peace and moral action.

I have already said these things to the relatives and some friends, but they never understand. When they speak out, they all say that I am provocative. Because I'm not thinking of leaving, they say there's trouble. What kind of words are these? These friends and relatives naturally are decent people, but they are also "yes men." Some of them even listen to the propaganda of those people [his enemies] on the streets who say that they only want me to leave Huangpi and can help me find work elsewhere. These words are not only nonsense but insulting. I eat only my own rice. Each grain is earned by bitter toil and tastes good and sweet. I also have some small talents, and each time after the family resources were exhausted I was able to restore them. Because they [his enemies] don't have this small talent, or wouldn't value this kind of talent, they can only pick up a signboard, look for some position of influence, and live off other people. And what great talents do they have? To play with words and writing is a small skill. Their accusing petitions and vilifying broadsheets I understand were composed by their best strategist. Conscienceless and senseless, they are not up to middle-school standards. What kind of work can they find for me? I wouldn't want the most lucrative job among them. If I had wanted those things I would have found a higher position much earlier than they. My not doing so is a matter of intent, not ability. Actually these relatives and friends do not understand the principles of things and do not understand insulting words when they hear them. If someone says insulting things, they have no way of preventing him. If you smile instead of listening, it doesn't become an insult. They take in the insulting words of others, and even want to convey them to my ears. This is to fall into their trap, to do their bidding, and use my friends and relatives to surround me, intimidate me, insult me. I can be shamed but I cannot be made to shame myself. Since they are not outsiders but friends I must ignore it. If I say they are helping others to intimidate me, they will certainly not be convinced. But this kind of yes man is none other than those Confucius called local hypocrites (*xiang yuan*). I would call them "pig's intestine." They cannot stand up, and they cannot comprehend principles. Since they cannot distinguish truth and falsehood, they also cannot understand profit and loss. They only fear this and that. You can go tell them that I only believe in Heaven and fate. . . . If fate decrees that I should die, fleeing will not keep me alive, and if fate decrees that I shall not die, no one will be able to kill me! Only because decent men are useless do bad men acquire power. From the conditions in this little village, one can see a microcosm of all of China. If the macrocosm is like this, there isn't much individuals can do. But spirit can both expand and contract. If the principles of the good man spread, then those of the small man contract. In whatever time or place, we can only stand on our principles and let correct principles slowly spread and pernicious ones slowly contract. At the very least one must not permit one word or act to spread the small man's principles. Doing this is what we call "changing customs" or "turning back the trend." To do these things we must measure our strength. This is then the meaning of "grasping the opportunity and exhausting one's effort"—the only path that you will be able to follow.

NOTES

1. Lu Xun (Lu Hsun), *Selected Works* (Beijing: Foreign Languages Press, 1956–60), I, pp. 2–3; Cao Juren, *Lu Xun Pingzhuan* (Hong Kong: Xin Wenhua Chuban She, 1956), p. 74; William A. Lyell, Jr., *Lu Hsun's Vision of Reality* (Berkeley: University of California Press, 1976), pp. 73–75.

2. Lu Xun, *Selected Works*, I, pp. 31, 10.

3. Not only does Ah Q have no name, but the names of the two families in the story—Zhao and Qian—are the first two names in the common children's text, the *Hundred Family Surnames*. In addition to textual evidence, there is further evidence for its general incisiveness to be found in the reactions of people who read the story in serialized form in a Beijing literary supplement, not knowing its author. Many readers thought they were being personally satirized, and that the author must be someone who knew their innermost thoughts and needs. Cao Juren, *Lu Xun Pingzhuan*, pp. 72–73.

4. Lyell, *Lu Hsun's Vision of Reality*, pp. 233–37, 244–46.

5. Hu Shi (Hu Shih), *Sishi Zishu* (Hong Kong: Shijie Wenzhai, 1957), p. 32.

6. Talcott Parsons, "Social Structure and the Development of Personality; Freud's Contribution to the Integration of Psychology and Sociology," *Psychiatry*, 21 (November 1958): pp. 321–40.

7. Peter Berger and Thomas Luckmann, *The Social Construction of Reality: A Treatise in the Sociology of Knowledge* (Garden City, N.Y.: Doubleday, 1967), pp. 134–35.

8. Helen Merrell Lynd, *Shame and the Search for Identity* (New York: Harcourt, Brace, and World, 1958), pp. 158–59.

9. Sao-ke Alfred Sze, *Reminiscences of His Early Years, As Told to Anming Fu* (Washington, D.C.: [N.D.], 1962), p. 1.

10. Hugh D. R. Baker, *Chinese Family and Kinship* (New York: Columbia University Press, 1979), pp. 88–91.

11. Hu Shih, "My Credo and its Evolution," in Clifton Fadiman, ed., *Living Philosophies: A Series of Intimate Credos* (New York: Simon and Schuster, 1931), p. 235.

12. Robert Payne, *Chiang Kaishek* (New York: Weybright and Talley, 1969), pp. 47–49; Pinchon P. Y. Loh, *The Early Chiang Kai-shek: A Study of His Personality and Politics, 1887–1924* (New York: Columbia University Press, 1971), p. 4; Chéou-kang Sié, *President Chiang Kai-shek: His Childhood and Youth* (Taibei: China Cultural Service, 1954), pp. 3–5, 37.

13. Hu Shi's father, for example, wrote a will to his wife and each of his sons just two months before he died. In the will to his wife he stressed three-year-old Hu Shi's intelligence and the need for him to pursue studies. He said the same in the will to Hu Shi himself. Hu Shi felt that these wills exerted considerable influence on his later life, especially when these pieces of paper led his older half-brothers to accede to their father's wish and help him progress in his studies. Hu Shi, *Sishi Zishu*, p. 17.

14. Hannah Arendt in *Between Past and Future* (New York: Viking Press, 1961), has captured the inequality of the situation in which the small individual confronts the group.

. . . the authority of a group, even a child group, is always considerably stronger and more tyrannical then the severest authority of an individual person can ever be. If one looks at it from the standpoint of the individual child, his chances to rebel or do anything on his own hook are practically nil; . . . he is in the position, hopeless by definition, of a minority of one confronted by the absolute majority of all the others. There are very few grown people who can endure such a situation, even when it is not supported by means of compulsion; children are simply and utterly incapable of it. Richard W. Wilson, *Learning to be Chinese* [Cambridge, Mass.: MIT Press, 1970], p. 32.

15. Sheng Cheng, *A Son of China* (New York: W. W. Norton, 1930), p. 125.

16. Wilson, *Learning to be Chinese*, pp. 29–30, fn. 28.

17. Hu Hsien Chin, "The Chinese Concepts of Face," *American Anthropologist*, 46 (January-March 1944): 45–64. See Table 2.1.

18. *Ibid.*, pp. 54–55.

19. *Ibid.*, p. 50.

20. Wilson, *Learning to be Chinese*, chapter 1. One must be cautious in interpreting these observations as typical for late Qing China. Before the Western impact there was no sense of "nation"; Chineseness was lived and Chinese did not think of themselves as citizens. And there was no extensive peer group experience in schools before the twentieth century; the group focus was then the multifunctional family clan or village neighborhood.

21. Lucien Pye, *The Spirit of Chinese Politics: A Psychocultural Study of the Authority Crisis in Political Development* (Cambridge, Mass.: MIT Press, 1968), pp. 95–96.

22. Lien-sheng Yang, "The Concept of 'Pao' as a Basis for Social Relations in China," in John K. Fairbank, ed., *Chinese Thought and Institutions (Chicago: University of Chicago Press, 1957), pp. 291–309. Also Francis L. K. Hsu, "Eros, Affect, and Pao"* in Francis L. K. Hsu, ed., *Kinship and Culture* (Chicago: Aldine Publishing Company, 1971), pp. 453–58.

23. Leon E. Stover, "Face and Verbal Analogues of Interaction in Chinese Culture: A Theory of Formalized Social Behavior Based Upon Participant-Observation of an Upper-Class Chinese Household, Together with a Biographical Study of the Primary Informant," Diss. Columbia University 1962. See also Leon E. Stover and Takeko Kawai Stover, *China: An Anthropological Perspective* (Pacific Palisades, Cal.: Goodyear Publishing Company, 1976), pp. 202–07, esp. p. 207; and Leon E. Stover, *The Cultural Ecology of Chinese Civilization: Peasants and Elites in the Last of the Agrarian States* (New York: New American Library, 1974), pp. 242–63, esp. p. 248.

24. Ida Pruitt, *A Daughter of Han: The Autobiography of a Chinese Working Woman* (Stanford: Stanford University Press, 1967), p. 239.

25. Wolfram Eberhard, *Guilt and Sin in Traditional China* (Berkeley: University of California Press, 1967). Eberhard's intent is to correct the notion of China as a "shame-based" culture and to argue that both shame and guilt are present as internalized moral concepts, the former particularly for the literati, the latter for the common people. His conclusion that China was a "stratified society with one guilt-based value system," however, seems unwarranted. Because shame and guilt operate "in essence . . . in the same way" as internalized moral concepts—as a code of propriety or as sin—does it follow that the whole system is guilt-based now instead of shame-based? The controversy over shame and guilt cultures is largely over in the West, as it is becoming clear that the shame/guilt distinction is one of our peculiar "folk-psychological" concepts. To concentrate on these terms and their "equivalents" in China—"propriety" (*li*) as the sense of shame or "sin" (*zui*) as the sense of guilt—is not as useful as the effort to reconstruct the primary emotional states that prevailed in the culture. In this case *lian* seems to have escaped his conceptual net.

26. Kenneth Keniston, "Psychological Development and Historical Change," *The Journal of Interdisciplinary History*, II (Autumn 1971): 329–45; reprinted in Robert J. Lifton, with Eric Olson, eds., *Explorations in Psychohistory: The Wellfleet Papers* (New York: Simon and Schuster, 1974), pp. 149–64; the reprint is used in the references below.

27. Alfred H. Bloom, "The Role of the Chinese Language in Counterfactual/ Theoretical Thinking and Evaluation," in Richard W. Wilson *et. al.*, eds., *Value Change in Chinese Society* (New York: Praeger, 1979), pp. 52–64, and "A Cognitive Dimension of Social Control: The Hong Kong Chinese in Cross-Cultural Perspective," in Amy Auerbacher Wilson *et. al.*, eds., *Deviance and Social Control in Chinese Society* (New York: Praeger, 1977), pp. 67–81.

28. Bloom, "The Role of the Chinese Language," p. 57.

29. *Ibid.*, p. 63.

30. Bloom, "A Cognitive Dimension of Social Control," p. 69.

31. Keniston, "Psychological Development and Historical Change," p. 162.

32. This is particularly true if we consider Kohlberg's stages 5 and 6 (the contractual legal orientation and the conscience or principle orientation) as the yard stick for measuring high in moral development. In Kohlberg's study of middle-class urban boys in three nations (United States, Taiwan, and Mexico), stage 6 was rare and the least common among 16 year olds in all nations; stage 5 represented a common achievement, however, among the U.S. sample. In two isolated villages in Turkey and the Yucatan, stages 5 and 6 were completely absent in the group. If stages 4, 5, and 6 are viewed as alternative types of mature responses, then a higher level of general moral reasoning would obtain. See Lawrence Kohlberg, "Stage and Sequence: The Cognitive-Developmental Approach to Socialization," in David A. Goslin, ed., *Handbook of Socialization Theory and Research* (Chicago: Rand McNally, 1969), pp. 383–85.

33. Francis L. K. Hsu, *Clan, Caste, and Club* (Princeton: D. Van Nostrand, 1963), pp. 162–70.

34. Baker, *Chinese Family and Kinship*, pp. 11, 15–16, 47–48, 69, 104–5.

35. Hsu, "Eros, Affect, and *Pao*," p. 473.

36. Hsu, *Clan, Caste, and Club*, p. 163. Hsu's diagram of the Chinese Orientation on p. 163 attempts to illustrate that, in ideal life as well as in actual life in society, the outcome was conformity and the strengthening of kinship units.

37. As a recent example that contains some of this recurring imagery I would cite Carolyn Lee Baum and Richard Baum, "Creating the New Communist Child: Continuity and Change in Chinese Styles of Early Childhood Socialization," in Richard W. Wilson *et. al.*, eds., *Value Change in Chinese Society*, pp. 114–15.

38. Margaret Mead and Rhoda Métraux, *The Study of Culture at a Distance* (Chicago: University of Chicago Press, 1953), pp. 157-58.

39. This distinction is made explicitly in the document; see also Stover, *China: An Anthropological Perspective*, pp. 202–3, and the related discussion of the "situation orientation" of the Chinese in Hsu, *Clan, Caste, and Club*, p. 164 ff.

40. Ernest Becker, *The Birth and Death of Meaning: An Interdisciplinary Perspective on the Problem of Man* (New York: The Free Press, 1962), pp. 68–71. Becker defines the "inner-newsreel" as the passing in constant review by the ego of the symbols that give us self-esteem, that make us feel important and good.

41. Boyd R. McCandless, "Childhood Socialization," in David A. Goslin, ed., *Handbook of Socialization Theory and Research*, pp. 797–8000. McCandless lists several areas of power that adults possess in childbearing: power in the physical sense to overwhelm children, power in the area of knowledge or omniscience, power in the area of social and economic influence, and power in the area of virility or generativity.

42. The pervasiveness of the kinship model throughout Chinese society is explored in Baker, *Chinese Family and Kinship*, Ch. 7.

43. Mead and Métraux, *The Study of Culture at a Distance*, p. 158.

44. This claim is reported in Book II of the Confucian Analects, as translated and annotated by Arthur Waley in *The Analects of Confucius* (New York: Vintage Books, 1938), p. 88. It reads as follows:

> The Master said, At fifteen I set my heart upon learning. At thirty, I had planted my feet firm upon the ground. At forty, I no longer suffered from perplexities. At

fifty, I knew what were the biddings of Heaven. At sixty, I heard them with docile ear. At seventy, I could follow the dictates of my own heart; for what I desired no longer overstepped the boundaries of right.

45. Each of these areas was a locus of vigorous debate within the traditional framework. For example, on footbinding and the conflicting rationales and viewpoints in Qing China, see Howard Levy, *Footbinding: The History of an Erotic Custom* (New York: Bell Publishing Company, 1967), Ch. 1 and 2.

46. For this point and other pitfalls in social psychology, see Reinhard Bendix, "Compliant Behavior and Individual Personality," in Neil J. Smelser and William T. Smelser, eds., *Personality and Social Systems* (New York: Wiley, 1963), pp. 55–67.

47. Stover, *The Cultural Ecology of Chinese Civilization*, p. 244.

48. Donald J. Munro, "Belief Control: The Psychological and Ethical Foundations," in Richard W. Wilson *et. al.*, eds., *Deviance and Social Control in Chinese Society*, pp. 14–36.

49. Stove, *The Cultural Ecology of Chinese Civilization*, Ch. 5.

50. *Ibid.*, Ch. 9, and pp. 258–62; also Stover, *China: An Anthropological Perspective*, pp. 207–12.

51. Margery Wolf, *The House of Lim* (New York: Appleton-Century-Crofts, 1968), pp. 141–42.

52. *Ibid.*, pp. 102–3.

53. Y. C. Koo, Interview in Taibei, Taiwan, July 11, 1969.

54. Francis L. K. Hsu, *Under the Ancestors' Shadow: Kinship, Personality, and Social Mobility in Village China* (Garden City, N. Y.: Doubleday, 1967), pp. 247–53.

55. Shu Xincheng, *Wo he jiaoyu* (Shanghai: Jung Hua Book Company, 1945), pp. 45–47.

56. Lu Xun, *Selected Works*, IV, p. 83. "Thoughts on a Child's Photographs."

57. Jon Saari, "The Passage to Modernity: The Early Years of a Disinherited Generation of Chinese Intellectuals," Diss. Harvard University 1973, Ch. 4.

58. Tang Chun-i, "The Reconstruction of Confucianism and the Modernization of Asian Countries," in *Report: International Conference on the Problems of Modernization in Asia* (Seoul, 1965).

59. The translation here is made from a reprinted version of the work in *Minju Chao* (Current Democracy), a Taiwan periodical. The excerpt in Appendix B is from Hu Qiuyuan, "Fuqin zhi xun" (Father's Teachings), *Minzu Chao* 15 (Number 10), pp. 15–19.

60. The latter passage is the words of Mencius summarized by Lien-sheng Yang in "The Concept of '*Pao*' as a Basis for Social Relations in China," in Fairbank, ed., *Chinese Thought and Institutions*, p. 305.

61. Lynd, *Shame and the Search for Identity*, p. 234.

62. *Ibid.*, pp. 230-31, 234.

63. Lu Xun, *Selected Works*, I, pp. 30–31.

64. *Ibid.*, I, pp. 50–51.

65. Helen Lynd has expressed this with insight in *Shame and the Search for Identity*, p. 46.

> Sudden experience of a violation of expectation, of incongruity between expectation and outcome, results in a shattering of trust in oneself, even in one's own body and skill and identity, and in the trusted boundaries or framework of the society and the world one has known. As trust in oneself and in the outer world develop together, so doubt of oneself and of the world are also intermeshed.
>
> The rejected gift, the joke or the phrase that does not come off, the misunderstood gesture, the falling short of our own ideals, the expectation of response violated—such experiences mean that we have trusted ourselves to a situation that is not there. We have relied on the assumption of one perspective or *Gestalt* and found a totally different one. What we have thought we would count on in our-

selves, and what we have thought to be the boundaries and contours of the world, turn out suddenly not be the 'real' outlines of ourselves or of the world, or those that others accept. We have become strangers in a world where we thought we were at home.

66. Excerpted from "Amid Pale Bloodstains," *Selected Works*, I, pp. 358–59. Italics added.

3 RELIGIOUS CONVERSION IN NINETEENTH-CENTURY CHINA: FACE-TO-FACE INTERACTION BETWEEN WESTERN MISSIONARIES AND THE CHINESE

Nishan J. Najarian

"Go ye into all the world and preach the gospel of Christ to every creature."[1] This much controverted passage in the Gospel of Mark provides a theological legitimization for the Christian missionary movement. The Church's response to this view of the world in the New Testament was the institutionalization of Christian missions to evangelize and convert the non-Christian world to Christianity.[2] In order to accomplish this mission the Christian enterprise mobilized a missionary movement and enlisted hundreds of men and women into missionary careers.

In this work I intend to examine, in terms of a general theory of interpretation, the social phenomenon of the missionary as "stranger"[3] and the typical face-to-face relationships a missionary encountered, developed, and interpreted during the course of his everyday experience in a Chinese setting. The missionary as "stranger" is a sub-type of the category of "religious stranger." In this study the "religious stranger" is an adult male claimed to have received a "Divine Call" to enter a career in religious proselytism in an alien environment—China—and commissioned by and delegated to represent a religious agency in evangelistic endeavors. Unlike other "strangers," the "religious stranger" was a member of an exclusive profession, with membership believed to be ordained by God. My focus in this essay is the Protestant missionary in China during the years 1845–1900.

Since my purpose is a sociological analysis of the reality of a missionary's everyday encounters with the Chinese—more precisely of the knowledge that guided his actions in carrying out his mission—I am interested in the process of religious conversion as a feature of the missionary's typical face-to-face relationships.

The term "religious conversion" is used here in a very general sociological way to stand for the whole series of shifts in an individual's self-attitude and reference groups[4] in a direction that is discontinuous with earlier commitments.[5] The conversion of non-Christians to Christianity entails a decision to change from the familiar to the unfamiliar. This process of change brings with it a certain rupture with the past. The need for breaking with the established order arises either from inner feelings of worthlessness or from the pressures of external, pre-eminently social situations contributing to the individual's feelings that life is meaningless.[6] The individual's attempt to resolve his feelings of conflict and his condition in life by changing to a new set of beliefs, attitudes, values, and reference groups can thus be described as a conversion if the change involves "relatively permanent commitment to antithetical values."[7] An important element in the conversion process is the displacement of the primary reference group (family, friends, peers, teachers, political and religious leaders) by another set of significant others (missionaries, other converts) "whose sympathetic support is apparently a crucial part of all conversion."[8] In the conversion process, the role of the missionary is seen as an intervening variable in the convert's shift from participation in his primary group to participation in the missionary's community.

In sociological terms, the phenomenon of religious conversion among non-Christians occurred in the context of the foreign missionary enterprise which the Christian Church launched to deal with the Church's problems of religious control of non-Christians. Religious conversion represented God's will to dominate the sinful world by enjoining non-believers to be converted to the "one true" religion—Christianity. Basically, missionaries were employed by the Church to persuade non-believers of the instrinic merits of their messages and in this way drastically alter the beliefs, attitudes, and values of non-Christians to those of Christianity.

One methodological approach in sociology for examining the social interaction between missionaries and Chinese is the interactional model, a synthesis of symbolic interactionism and its variants, phenomenology and ethnomethodology.[9] This combined approach provides a context in which to examine more closely the missionary's impact on the Chinese. Specifically, I will ask how the missionary proceeded in his attempt to convert the "millions of unsaved" Chinese. What tactics did he employ to achieve his objectives? It seems reasonable to propose that answers to such questions must depend upon an appreciation of the dynamics of two diverse cultures. Also it seems reasonable to propose that although extremely stereotypical relationships did exist between missionaries and Chinese, there were situations in which the relationship between missionaries as strangers and Chinese as "hosts" were less stereotypical.

Instances of social interaction collected from the data reflect missionary perceptions and interpretations of face-to-face encounters with the Chinese. In recording their experience during the conversion process, missionaries appraised situations and people according to the "meaning" they themselves attributed to such "things," in contrast to the meaning which "others" attributed to those same "things," and therefore their appraisal was one-sided. Consequently, the data indicate how the missionary felt about his role and how he perceived Chinese attitudes toward his role; how he felt about the Chinese and how he perceived the Chinese felt about him; how he interpreted his actions and those of the Chinese and how he perceived the Chinese interpreted his actions and those of "other" Chinese; and how he defined situations and how he perceived the Chinese defined situations. In certain instances the Chinese point of view of "things" is presented. Accordingly, there are two sets of subjective meanings given to the interactional process; that is, the missionary's point of view on the one hand, and on the other hand the Chinese point of view. Since a great portion of the data in this study is presented from the missionary's point of view, I have developed categories which define and classify how missionaries perceived social interaction during the conversion process.

In order to present a detailed and accurate description of the missionary's point of view of the situation, I will seek to reconstruct and analyze by means of a set of interpretative categories such historical materials as biographical and autobiographical works; correspondence; diaries; newspapers, journals, and pamphlet articles written by missionaries, Chinese, and non-missionary foreigners; mission board archive records; missionary reports; mission conference minutes and reports; and mission board policy papers.

Study of missionaries as agents of change in the face-to-face interactional encounters within a Chinese social world will be useful in four different but complementary areas of social theory and research. First, the sociological interpretation of the "meaning" of relationships and events in the missionary's life can serve to demystify that world. Second, the socio-historical picture of China's recent past can be examined in a sociological framework. Third, Chinese response to propaganda, persuasion, and changes that derived from outside Chinese society may become clear once their behavior is related to the values, motives, and actions of missionaries. Fourth, the interpretation of face-to-face interaction, communication, persuasion, and domination between culturally alien groups remains one of the most important and pressing sociological issues.

The analysis that follows this introduction begins by describing the Chinese setting and the Chinese attitudes toward the missionary. It then goes on to examine the three issues raised earlier: (1) how the missionary organized his actions to effect salient responses for conversion; (2) what kind of cognitive responses he did effect; and (3) what strategy he employed to pursue the convert into making a decision for conversion. A very general and theoretical model analyzing missionaries' interpersonal encounters and conduct allows us to delineate the many and varied conversion experiences into two meaningful categories—"induced incentive" and "induced conflict." Moreover, the model I employ here describes three theoretical conversion stages associated with the missionary role, making it possible to systematize the conversion process along a continuum from unlocking to shifting and relocking.

THE CHINESE SETTING AND THE MISSIONARY

The missionary to China was faced with fixed Chinese sets of attitudes towards "outsiders." Traditional Chinese society was fairly self-contained. Confucianism was one of the chief instruments by which those in authority maintained control over the community, and many relationships were prescribed in order to regulate the harmonious functioning of society by defining each person's role and status. Confucian tenets were the principal means of legitimizing and limiting political leadership. Taoist and Buddhist religious superstitions and myths offered explanations for man's mystical relationships with the supernatural. The concept of "sin" appears in Chinese folk religion and folk Buddhism as a violation of a moral code which was somehow set "and was applicable to and valid for the world of the gods as well as the world of man."[10]

Confucian bureaucrats were completely uninterested in salvation; Taoist magic and Buddhist sacramental and ritual grace survived as the faith of the folk. The three beliefs constituted the political, social, and religious structure of the Chinese world order and reality. The syncretic disposition of the Chinese religious "community," undergirded with ancestor worship, constituted what Weber termed *Gemeinde*, "the organization of religion at the collectivity level which became an 'aspect' of the organization of society in other functional respects, notably the political, but also of kinship and the like."[11] Moreover, political, religious, and social processes were closely integrated, often in a single set of institutions, values, attitudes, and practices. "This integration, even if imperfect," notes Edgar Schien, "gives continuity and stability to the person and operates as a force against being influenced, unless the change which the influence implies is seen to be a change in the direction of greater integration."[12] Any element of change, especially from the outside, posed a major threat to the Chinese sense of stability, sensibility, and continuity. Lacking the understanding and appreciation for the superiority of Chinese culture, any agent of change was considered a barbarian. There is an old saying in the Book of Rites—"When you enter the frontiers, inquire respecting the prohibition; when you enter into a country, inquire into its custom"—the wisdom of which Westerners in general have seemingly ignored, consequently arousing hostile feelings and attitudes among Chinese. The Manchus also had a saying pertaining to strangers: "The man who comes from a strange locality is contemptible; the thing which comes from a strange locality is precious."[13]

Indeed, the stranger in China was an unknown element whose appearance provoked rumor, curiosity, and animosity. The missionary Arthur H. Smith relates his experience in the following commentary:

> It is in travelling in China that the absence of helpful kindness on the part of the people towards strangers is perhaps most conspicuous. . . . . No one will inform him that the road which he has taken will presently end in quagmire. . . . When the traveller has been plunged into one of the sloughs with which all such roads at certain seasons abound, and finds it impossible to extricate himself, a great crowd of persons will rapidly gather from somewhere, "their hands in their sleeves, and idly gazing," as the saying goes. It is not until a definite bargain has been made with them that any one of these bystanders, no matter how numerous, will lift a finger to help one in any particular.[14]

Direct information, idle gossip, or tales of power and benevolence, often determined the reception accorded many missionaries.

> . . . The most damaging of all, however, were the stories which represented the Christians as living in promiscuous intercourse. Some of the things that were said were stupid and absurd, but that did not in any way affect the credence that was given to all and every report about foreigners. A peculiar kind of pill was in use among the Christians, which whoever swallowed forthwith all sense of shame forgot.[15]

The emotional response to strangers is captured in the terms of the Analects: "qing kuei shen e yuan ji' "—the literal translation of which calls for respecting the supernatural spirits, but keeping your distance from them. Its application to foreigners meant that one should be respectful on the surface, but keep inner feelings from them. An expression dating back to the earliest days of Sino-Western contact, "*yang guizi*" was spoken as an insult and typified much of China's attitude toward strangers from the West. It was the customary form of speaking of a westerner, which was frequently heard by early missionaries and traders, and is casually translated as "foreign devil."[16] Literally, it means "ocean sons of the devil." It was not surprising that Chinese looked with distrust and suspicion upon the "*da bizi yang guizi*", the ocean-borne devils with red hair, big noses, and blue eyes from across the seas. Chinese artists have always depicted the devil with green eyes. What could be more natural for them than to assume that the fair-skinned, hairy, big-nosed, blue- and green-eyed foreigners who interrupted their accustomed way of life were devils? So thoroughly did the term permeate the language that through the years it almost lost its connotation of insult. A missionary of modern times relates the story of a trip into the countryside near his station. He stopped for a snack by the roadside, and unwrapped his food. A farmer came by and, upon invitation, shared the missionary's lunch. As they departed, the farmer bowed low and said, *"xiexie ni, yang guizi xian shang"* (thank you, Mr. Foreign Devil).[17]

There were other Chinese designations for the stranger worthy of note. A more popular and unflattering name for western strangers was *"fangui"* (uncivilized devil).[18] The following terms were less innocuous: *"wai zhongren"* or *"wai guoren"* referred to a person from outside the country, a foreigner; *"wai ren"* was an outsider, applied also to a Chinese who was not from the same province; *"keren,"* a guest who came to visit for only a short period of time, a Chinese who was not a member of the sib or clan; *"sheng ren,"* an unknown person, someone not known well enough to be fully accepted but who after careful observation for a period of time might become accepted as a member of the group (applied to Chinese and non-Chinese); *"lao fan,"* a neutral term or polite term for a non-Chinese stranger who was respected.

Most of the literature describes a Chinese conception of missionaries as "outsiders" coming from a lower form of culture and demanding that the Chinese renounce the old ancestral culture which would bring about the disintegration of Chinese civilization. As seen through Chinese eyes, the Christian missionary was the uncivilized devil or king of the uncivilized world who could not be reasoned with. Their fundamental attitude toward foreigners has thus been translated:

> . . . the barbarians are like beasts, and not to be governed on the same principles as citizens. Were any one to attempt controlling them by the great maxims of reason, it would tend to nothing but confusion. The ancient kings well understood this, and accordingly ruled barbarians by misrule. Therefore, to rule barbarians by misrule is the true and best way of ruling them.[19]

Into this Chinese frame of reference entered the missionary in the role of proselytizing agent, with the objective of changing individuals and ultimately a whole society. The missionary came with materials, money, knowledge, privileged legal status, and magical arts which some Chinese associated with prestige, prosperity, and power. The following remark arose from the then-general belief that missionaries were masters of magical arts:

> Ku announced to his wife he was going to visit the foreigners who had sold him the book Mark's Gospel. "What!" replied his wife in consternation: "you are already mad; the foreigner will make you tenfold more a madman." The proof of this magical power lay in the fact that when any Chinese who hated foreigners came into close contact with the missionary, their hatred disappeared and they actually began to speak well of the foreigners. To one who dared then to speak well of the for-

eigner it was at once retorted, "You have drunk the foreigner's magical medicine."[20]

To a relatively small number of astute missionaries it became apparent that to facilitate conversion it would become necessary to secure information about the character of Chinese society. Nevertheless, many held views about Chinese mentality, custom, and the structure of Chinese society which led them along a certain course of action for conversion. To initiate the process of conversion, their first tactic was to denigrate what was sacred in the Chinese tradition—ancestor worship—and attack what was familiar in Chinese mores. From a Chinese point of view, they were insensitive to local customs and prone to pass moral judgements; they were quick to identify China's endemic dirt, suffering, and idolatry and thus challenge the semi-divinity of the emperor and undermine the Confucian system of public order; they failed to understand the nature and implications of ancestor worship and filial responsibility; and they prohibited converts from participating in village religious festivals and theatricals, which was perceived as a condemnation of the communal structure of rural China.[21]

One young Chinese Christian student criticized the work of Christian missionaries with extreme candor:

> I think the missionaries, in spite of their good will, noble devotion, and unselfish work, have done more harm to China than good; . . . Consciously and unconsciously, purposefully and indifferently, directly and indirectly . . . missionaries make misrepresentations and thereby cause the Western people to form misunderstandings. . . .
>
> The missionaries, generally speaking, are confined within the low parts of China's citizenship and morality. It has been, furthermore, their interest and habit to see the dark and gloomy side of China. The truth is that the "missionary attitude" in China has been largely "egotistic fault-finding," almost never wholesome criticism. When they write home, they usually draw pictures of worse things than they have seen, and often give bad interpretations of good things. When they come home, they tell the people of abnormal and unusual cases that they know of. Of course the purpose of the missionaries is to appeal to the missionary sympathy of their own countrymen. They want to arouse and revive their missionary spirit and work up and stir up missionary enthusiasm. I do henceforth ask for a fair and square answer to my honest and sincere question, "who is responsible for the misconception of things Chinese in this large Western part of the world?"[22]

In Beidelman's terms, "the need to missionize makes sense only if one has a basically negative, evolutionary view of the culture one is trying to change."[23]

And yet, these early missionaries by virtue of their faith held out the promise that acceptance of Christianity would result in a greater sense of self-fullfillment, "greater integration," and acceptance into a new social group. In spite of what may have appeared to be obvious values that these innovators offered in the form of skills, well-being, and perhaps prestige, it seems the ties of traditional life prevented most Chinese from accepting this new religion, at least at first. Moreover, the Chinese did not seek out the missionary because they had a profound sense of sin and salvation. On the contrary, "the Chinese had no sense of sin," notes Paul Varg, "for the simple reason that he actually lived up to the ideals set before him thanks to the social control exercised by the family, clan, and guild."[24]

The Chinese came to listen to the missionary more out of mere instinctive curiosity than from the motivation to be saved. The reason listeners appeared to pay attention to street-chapel preachers may have had no connection with any sublime aspirations; instead, the interest may have depended entirely upon the tendency to be curious about anything exotic and novel. Though some missionaries misinterpreted the initial interest of the Chinese, others knew very well that crowds listened out of sheer curiosity. Charles Scott wrote of his experience:

> . . . for dinner I bought of a peddler hawking them on the nasty dust-blown street cold *hwoa shao* (coarse-flour native biscuits) and some peanuts. As I munched, the whole village gradually gathered to watch the manipulation of the foreigner's jaw, to comment on his buttons, to marvel at his coloured glasses on top of another pair, and to discuss with animation the price of everything about him. After meal time on the road usually afforded an excellent opportunity for an informal preaching of the Gospel; for the curious will assemble to see the outlandish foreigner outlandishly eat."[25]

Nevertheless, the missionary capitalized on the Chinese sense of curiosity for Christian witness.

COGNITIVE CONVERSION TYPES AND THE MISSIONARY'S ACTIONS

Every contact was an opportunity for the missionary to "sow the seed" of his religion. Once the missionary initiated situations to open the way for him to get his message before his "heathen" audience, it was crucial to him to convey a message which would persuade his auditor to make a decision to become a Christian. To this end, the missionary had stock religious words and phrases which he used repeatedly in preaching the Gospel to non-Christians and in his strong pleas for a regenerate life.[26] By calling the non-believers "lost," "wicked," "sinner" and by showing them their "unfortunate," "doomed," and "evil" condition, the missionary hoped to make them more ready to come and accept his "way," his salvation, his mode of living, his rites and beliefs, his values, and his *Weltanschauung*. To use the language of religious sentiment, the convert "comes out of a life of sin and enters a life of grace." Stated in sociological terms, the missionary's "modus operandi" was directed toward inducing the prospective convert, through the art of "repetitive suggestion," to change from one social group to another.

I use the term "repetitive suggestion" to characterize the technique used by the missionaries to evoke a definite response on the part of the non-Christian, resulting in his joining this "exotic" religious group for which the missionary was the leader. The individual was continually invited to visit a place where there were long speeches, instructions, and certain peculiar exclusive ceremonies—most mysterious of which were baptism and holy communion—and was required to promise compliance with the missionary's code and that of his Book—the Bible. All the strategies and agencies employed by the missionary—medical work, preaching, itineracy, schools, literature translation, distribution of tracts, industries—were by nature a form of repetitive suggestion organized to induce a change in the non-believer's beliefs and attitudes about himself and Christianity. The missionary's strategies deliberately established face-to-face encounters with his listeners in order to subject his audience to continuous and prolonged suggestive techniques, the content of which was an appeal to accept Christianity. "Quantity as well as quality counts in giving effectiveness to a suggestion," reported one missionary. "And neither 'repetition' nor 'the multiplying of points of contact' are overlooked in the missionary's procedure."[27] Missionaries recognized the importance of intensive interaction on a concrete, daily, and hourly basis between missionary and recruit.

There are numerous missionary accounts describing the day after day, week after week preaching, praying, worshipping, healing, Bible reading, and spreading of literature among non-believers in the attempt to exert a personal influence in the Chinese to convert. Such religious acts on the part of the missionary fall under the head of "persuasion," in the sense that persuasion is the art of "repetitive suggestion," and "religious cosmogonies are designed, in the last analysis, as exceptionally thoroughgoing modes of persuasions."[28]

Leang Afa reveals in his memoir the impact missionary persuasion had on his friend Le, who was Dr. Milne's teacher of the Chinese language. On a trip to Malacca, Le and Dr. Milne stayed in Dr. Morrison's house for two months, while they waited for their ship to depart.

> During that time Dr. Milne took frequent opportunities to converse with him, and importuned him to read the holy Scriptures and to worship the living God. "I was surprised," says he, "and thought it exceedingly strange that he should wish me to do this; and I was much dis-

pleased; there was no other way, however, but to comply with his wishes."

. . . Dr. Milne, in the mean time, was constant in maintaining family prayer, with the reading of the Scriptures, every night and morning, and also public worship every Sabbath day; but though I read the words of the Bible, and heard him explain their meaning, yet I did not understand the sense of the one, or comprehend the reasoning of the other. Though I yielded in some measure to the wishes of Dr. Milne, yet I disliked exceedingly to read the Bible and worship God; and as I saw that he used no gilt paper, incense, candles, or images, I could not comprehend what kind of deity he worshipped, and therefore I did not wish to join with him.[29]

However, over a period of time Le did come to see the "light" and made a decision to become a Christian.

What is implied is that the missionary directed all his efforts to confronting Chinese non-believers with a series of intense and continued exposures to the Christian message, sometimes at the displeasure of the auditor. Nevertheless, the tactic of intensive and extensive interaction in the form of repetitive persuasion offered missionaries the opportunity to reinforce and elaborate their message to any Chinese who showed an initial, tentative, or curious interest in the Christian religion. The technique of repetitive suggestion appeared to offer missionaries the most effective method by which they oriented their meaningful actions to lead individuals to make a radical decision to convert to Christianity.

Encounters on the open road, in the street chapel, the marketplace, and the dispensary exposed the missionary to a variety of situations requiring his ability to negotiate the interaction, so as to conveniently advance his message of the Gospel.

For the preacher has to get in his message edgewise, so to speak, and he must have the ability to sing and speak and hold his own against every conceivable variety of noise made by men and women, barrows and babies, and boys and dogs and donkeys and all else that goes to make up the strident doings of the village street.[30]

Frequently, the audience was suspicious of the missionary and afraid of the tract which he attempted to hand them. The more experienced missionary, who had become a "pro" at his job by studying the customs and behavior of the Chinese, knew how to present himself so as to convey an impression of benevolence, decorum, and a conciliatory manner in order to gain his listeners' confidence and disspell their suspicions. The following account illustrates how the missionary negotiated his role in a manner which opened the way for him to gather a small group who listened to his explanation of the Gospel:

There is one hour of the day which is often best for evangelistic work. When the men have returned from the fields, eaten their supper, and had their bath, especially in the spring and summer evenings. . . . Very often things will take some such course as the following: The missionary, who, if possible, should be accompanied by two or three earnest and sympathetic native assistants, may begin by friendly inquiries about the state of their crops and such local topics as may be of interest at the time. They will then probably ask where he comes from and where he is going, and the more straightforward and explicit his answers to these questions are the better. He may then ask them if they know why he has come to their village. . . . many good-natured guesses will be made as to the object of the visit. "Probably to shoot birds," someone will say, or someone else, "To do business"; and after putting aside several of these guesses, someone who had heard something of our mission work perhaps explains that the missionary has come to teach people to do good; or some explain that he has come from some Christian chapel in the neighbourhood. The missionary may then take up the most of the talking somewhat as follows: "My home is a long way from . . . ." By this time some exclamations will be made of wonder at a foreigner being able to speak their language. . . . "When I first came to Swatow I could not speak your words because I had not learned them, just as you cannot speak mine, but I invited a Chinese graduate to teach me, and now I suppose you can understand me. I am not a merchant, and have not come to do any business. . . . Neither am I an officer sent by our Queen, nor have I come to shoot birds. I belong to the mission in Swatow, but we have a great many chapels over the country, and I am on my way to visit some of them. In passing through your village I thought you might like to hear what people mean by worshipping Shang-ti. If you would like to hear about it I shall be happy to talk to you; but if you are too tired with your day's work, I will not trouble you." By this time there will probably be many calls to go on and let them hear all about it, and the missionary goes on: "When I came into your village I noticed that you all gathered round to look at me because my clothing is not like yours. The colour of my face is not the same; as I said to you, my language is not the same; and you see a great deal in me, as I see a great deal in you, that looks new and strange. But after all, although my home is a long way off and you live here, we have a great deal in common. How is it that I, who am a foreigner, and you, who are Chinese, have bodies so much alike? And how is it that although I never saw you before I can know a great deal about you simply by knowing my own people and my own heart? It is because we are all made by the one God who made heaven and earth and all things. . . ."

In this way one reaches readily the great central ideas of our Christian teaching, and is able to present them to the people without the previous irritation or unnecessary offence which would be treated by discussions on the question of idolatry . . . [and remove] from their minds the impression which has often been lurking there, that we are teachers who overthrow religion and are reckless of morality."[31]

There were many situations in which a missionary was at a peculiar disadvantage in interpreting initial responses in face-to-face encounters:

> Several years ago a missionary in China was preaching in a country chapel to a large crowd mostly made up of "raw heathens." Few of the crowd showed any interest. But one man at the back of the assembly showed from the beginning of the talk an extreme interest in the speaker. He moved from his seat at the back to one nearer the front. The missionary noticed him and began to center his remarks upon this man. The man moved again, when a vacancy occurred, to the very front of the crowd, all the time appearing to drink in literally every word as it fell from the preacher's mouth. At the end of the sermon the missionary invited inquirers to remain. This man remained and the missionary went to him first, because of the intense interest that the man had been manifesting.
>
> "Yes, I want to ask you a question," answered the Chinese, to a request for some expression from him, "I have been watching all through the service that gold tooth in your mouth, and I would like to know if it grew there, or how you got it, and whether it is real gold."[32]

The missionary took advantage of the Chinese setting to establish conducive situations to generate face-to-face encounters. Street preaching seemed to attract the curious attention of men going to work, of women on their way to market, and of children playing in the streets. The environment made it convenient for the missionary to develop the arena which afforded him the greatest opportunity to engage the Chinese in his long and continuous preaching and story telling. Missionary explanation for this situation seems to lie in two facts. First, missionaries claimed there was a paucity of leisure interest for the Chinese.

> Apart from the theatre, which being in the open street or temple is free to all, or an occasional game of chess, which again is a recreation only for the few, there is little left to relieve the monotony of their sordid life. There are no clubs . . . no lectures, no politics, no elections, no concerts, except the equal of an occasional ballad-singer. What is a man to do by way of amusement unless it be to "have a gamble" occasionally.[33]

Secondly, the use of Bible stories as narratives, a favorite Sunday school and pulpit device, evoked interest regardless of content. Yah Phou Lee recounts in his early childhood in China this Chinese characteristic:

> The Chinese are passionately fond of stories and storytelling. On the public streets and squares, professional storytellers congregate from

noon to midnight, going over the achievements of a hero or portraying the despair of a lover. . . .

All classes indulge in this favorite pastime. The dignified scholar relishes a good story as much as a child in the lap of a fairy tale. Story books in the language can be counted by the tens of thousands.[34]

Whether the missionary be regarded as a story-telling magician, a solemn mendicant, or a proselytizer, his "stories of the Bible are everywhere listened to with pleasure. The heathen are keenly interested in them."[35] It is such use of leisure which appears to have brought many a Chinese convert into the mission church.

To some missionaries preaching presented a problem. In January 1867, Young J. Allen of the Methodist Episcopal Mission, South, acknowledged his deficiency in being able to relate to his Chinese listeners through sermons. He found conversation "very useful in communicating scriptural truth—enabling one to understand and be understood."[36] Again in March he noted that "personal contact alone seems to effect the change in their minds towards Christianity."[37] On March 19 he reiterated the need for personal contact, but added this pessimistic note:

How discouraging is the result of the past and how dark as yet the future. Yet we toil on and are spent in the Master's service. He hath promised, commanded and we question not the one nor refuse obedience to the latter.[38]

One reason that Allen attributed to his discouragement and lack of success in preaching was that his congregation at the city chapel was mostly "loafers, pleasure seekers, etc., about the street." The number of attendees was also dependent largely upon the weather.[39]

Missionaries reported that early recruits to Christianity came from those already dissaffected from traditional society, such as the poor, the illiterate, the individual unhappy with his life or status in his social group who concluded that his present social group could offer him no solutions for his condition.[40] Such an individual was a good candidate for conversion because his loyalties to his primary reference group had grown weak. One missionary's observation of this fact was noted in 1847 in the *Missionary Advocate*:

. . . I have often thought that the poor and ignorant people in China, who cannot read at all, are far more likely to receive the gospel than the learned scholars, for they have not got their minds so preoccupied with false notions as the latter, and though they are more superstitious and ignorant, they are not so proud and unwilling to receive new doctrines.[41]

"Very frequently," wrote Dr. King Eng Hu of Fuchow at the close of her first year (1895) in the women's hospital, "I hear the patients say, 'Truly my own parents, brothers, and sisters could never be so good, so patient, and do so carefully for us; especially when we are so filthy and foul in these sore places. Yes, their religion must be better than ours.' "[42]

The missionary not only offered solutions to improve life's conditions but also gave the convert special recognition as a member of a new reference group. "The convert is not only reborn," state Kurt and Gladys Lang, "he is given a new identity and a sense of selfhood anchored in new group affiliations from which he can return only with the greatest difficulty. His defection is complete; the convert burns his bridges, or, as the Chinese put it in their thought reform program, 'cuts his tails.' "[43]

William Soothill lamented the fact that it was rare for a noble or wealthy man to join the Christian ranks, for "he is too firmly tied to earth, to his wealth, his comfort, his standing with his fellows."[44] Missionaries seldom had the opportunity to reach any who were above the rank of the lowest literary graduate (*xiu cai*), and even these only with comparative infrequency. The missionary Arthur H. Smith concluded that probably "ninety-five percent of our auditors are farmers, small tradesmen, coolies and loafers."[45] Any willingness on the part of the upper classes to avail themselves of missionary teachings were predicated on the condition that such teachings were not to be exclusively Christian, but to embrace as well the useful arts and sciences.[46]

The missionary faced certain difficulties in leading his listeners to make a decision to become converts. One of his major problems was how to adapt his Christian message so as to have some meaning to his non-Christian audience. This problem arose from the fact that the missionary took as the primary source for his preaching the "revealed Word of God" as found in the "Sacred Books"—the Bible. "The great difference," one writer remarked in the *Universal Missionary Journal*, December 1880, "between preaching to the heathen and to those who are not wholly unacquainted with Christianity seems to be in this, that in the former case the Bible is the goal and end and in the latter the starting point."[47] It was the missionary's job to interpret the contents of the Bible, an unknown book strange in style and unheard of in doctrine, and to do everything he could to make the heroes, incidents, localities, style, doctrines, and parables not only intelligible but acceptable to the Chinese.[48]

The missionary frequently experienced much embarrassment in the effort to communicate his message in a language somewhat devoid of words and phrases adapted to convey Christian sentiments. Some forms of thought possessing peculiar significance to the Christian mind often lost all their importance when the missionary tried to put them into Chinese. There was also a notable sense in which the symbol system used by the missionary was essentially different from the symbol system familiar to the Chinese listener. For example, Jesus was symbolized as the "Great Shepherd" leading his flock of

"lost sheep," a symbolic term for "sinners," to safety, or to salvation. However, in China there were millions of Chinese who had never seen a sheep,
and, while in the North and Northwest some had seen sheep, the sheep and
the shepherd had anything but the sacred connotation found in Scripture. In
fact, the Chinese regarded the sheep as the most stupid of animals, and the
shepherd held a degrading position in society, similar to that of the swine-
herd. Yet another illustration can be found in the symbolic idea of the relationship between the vine and the grape, which missionaries used to
demonstrate the importance of the relationship between God and man, and
the fruits or benefits of such a relationship. In Central and Northern China,
the vineyards were plentiful and grapes were widely used for eating, but not
for making wine. Consequently, winepresses and their operation, as well as
wine itself, in the Christian acceptance and usage of the term and symbol
were nonexistent for the Chinese.

Young Allen provides an example of a missionary who changed his
preaching tactic in order to become more interesting, appealing, and con-
vincing. In early 1867, he observed that when he incorporated Chinese proverbs into his sermons, there appeared to be a greater response to his message.
Allen was convinced that the use of such expressions in the context of his
sermons helped "to break down the very system which the [proverbs] have so
long supported."[49] Also, he shifted the content of his sermons from a mere
exposition of Christian dogma to attacking Chinese ideas, for "striking at
the root or fundamental principles of their faith and revealing the absurdity
thereby to their minds has vastly more influence than any dogmatic efforts. . . ."[50] He also discovered that "we are compelled to consider subjects
in their fundamental relations, not, however, because the Chinese mind requires it, but because that seems a more comprehensive and intelligible mode
of conveying truth to their minds. . . ."[51]

Nevertheless, these difficulties in preaching to the Chinese were recognized by at least some missionaries at the Shanghai Conference of 1877 and
1890.[52] The most serious aspect of the problem rested in the fact that the
missionary was faced with the task of translating his stock of religious
words, which had no Chinese equivalent, in one of two ways:

> . . . either to transfer words, and give mere sounds, or to select the word
> nearest in sense and give it a new shade of meaning. The former is con-
> trary to the genius of Chinese and to the object which we have in view in
> helping the people understand the revealed will of God. We cannot, as
> the Buddhists, transfer Sanskrit sounds into Chinese, nor as the Roman
> Catholics, (in some cases) transfer Latin ones. It is far better to endeavor
> to find the nearest Chinese equivalent and use it in a modified sense. This
> is the plan pursued by missionaries generally, as by the translators of sci-
> entific works. The same plan is followed in diplomatic and commercial
> intercourse; e.g., in the Chinese terms for "consul," "telegram,"

"steamboat" etc. Not only is it important that the translator should be acquainted with the term which will best express the idea he wishes to render, but it is equally important for the preacher to remember that the popular understanding of a term is somewhat different from that assigned to it in his Bible and associated with it in his mind.[53]

Regardless of whether his auditors had completely understood him or accepted his doctrines, the missionary was committed by his mission to employ tactics that induced the conversion experience. I use the term "induced" to refer to any conscious or unconscious effort or action introduced by the missionary which prevails upon, persuades, suggests, influences, or causes the Chinese to make a decision to convert to Christian norms and values. Applying induced tactics with the Chinese, the missionary engaged the "heathen" in two distinct types of face-to-face interactional conversion experiences, typified as conversion through either "induced incentive" or "induced conflict."

The "induced incentive" conversion type is characterized by the prospective convert's conscious decision to respond and to be receptive to the missionary and to his doctrines in order to position himself to take full advantage of the various economic and social rewards as well as certain "protections" offered by the missionary's mission and church. Association with the missionary was perceived by such recruits as an essential means toward very practical ends (education, employment, food, shelter, legal protection, status, etc.). Since the prospective convert was intent upon satisfying his personal interests or needs rather than responding to a spiritual or moral restlessness, his determination to negotiate his position with the missionary, so as to secure certain of these social and economic advantages, created very little, if any, internal conflict or crisis.

In the second type of conversion experience, "induced conflict," internal conflict is the primary response the missionary strives to create. The role of the missionary is oriented to making his actions produce conflict within the recruit; and, secondly, to offering a resolution of the conflict in such a way as to direct the recruit into a new reference group (missionary-convert). Religiously speaking, the missionary's aim was to introduce to the recruit his present incompleteness or wrongness ("sin") as a non-believer, and then to proceed to present to the candidate the positive ideal of salvation and peace followed by profound emotional release, which is his "promised" reward. The struggle with "sin" almost exclusively engrosses the convert's attention, so that conversion is "a process of struggling away from sin rather than of striving toward righteousness."[54] This type of conversion may also be called a "sudden change of role." Often the change is sudden and dramatic; however, such conversion has also taken place gradually and over a period of time.

INDUCED INCENTIVE CONVERSION:
COGNITIVE NEGOTIATION OF POSITION

In this type of conversion process, interaction between the missionary and recruit was determined by the missionary's ability to make available material and status incentives as inducements for conversion. Charles A. Robinson reports that "cases are to be found in all parts of the mission field in which converts have been induced to make a profession of their Christian faith in the hope that they might secure for themselves material advantages, and in some instances the responsibility for arousing this hope lies with the missionaries." He continues with the observation that "the principles, however, of endeavoring to attract converts by the offer of such advantages is one which has now been abandoned by all non-Roman missionary societies." "Experience shows," Robinson concludes, "that missionary work prospers most and the best types of Christian character tend to be produced when the convert to the Christian faith has to face at least a mild form of persecution."[55]

Converts readily admitted to the fact that their motives in embracing Christianity were due to reasons other than spiritual. One missionary recalls an informal discussion on the subject of religion with a company of native Christians of Huairuan. The conversation turned on the motives which had led to their conversions.

> To one man it was frankly the hope of material betterment; to another, the reaction from the failure of an effort long continued to attain Buddhahood; to a third it was the influence of the unselfish lives of the missionaries, notably their work in healing the sick. An old boatman dated his conversion from a sermon on the flood which he said he could verify from his own experience, since he too had lived through the flood.[56]

Still others regarded the missionary's religion as a more adequate protective technique against bodily harm, social annoyance, and magico-religious uncertainties.

> It was at a time of drought in China. "While they were all thus praying to the idols everywhere," says Timothy Richards, "I prepared some yellow placards with only a few words on each, saying that if the people wanted rain, the best way was to turn from dead idols to the living God and pray unto Him and obey His laws and conditions of life. . . . The result was very striking . . . deputations of elderly men would come to the inn, go down on their knees and beg me to tell them how to worship and pray to the living God."[57]

The Chinese had no objections to trying any new magico-religious practices for the protection they promised, provided they did not controvert their previous ones too ominously. The missionary held up his religion as offering unequivocal protection from all evils of the world. Such an inducement was attractive to anyone who held the world of spirits in fear. Soothill once reported that "when Ah Nyang Pah first came amongst us, it was not love of God, but fear of evil spirits that brought him."[58]

The following missionary account of Mrs. Ma records the safety, security, and certainty the missionary perceived that she felt in finally allying herself with the missionary's God. Her husband, being a seafaring man, often made long voyages, during which time the care of the family became her responsibility. She was a very religious person who would pray to her idols for comfort.

One day she was invited to attend a Christian service. "To worship God" was to her a very vague expression. She had the general impression that she would be asked to abandon all her social customs, to reject her ancestors, and to adopt the worship and customs of the despised "barbarians."

> Mrs. Ma was undoubtedly led by an invincible hand that day when she walked to the meeting, for Christianity was a profound mystery to her. Although she did not comprehend all she heard, her impressions were favorable. She carried away one thought, to which she clung with irrepressible delight, and which became the germ-seed in her life of new ideas. It was contained in a line of one of the hymns, and it said that God was the giver of houses and clothes and food. This touched her with irresistible force. Twenty years after the event, when she was telling the story, she said, "These were the first words that led me to God." They were so practical. She had been struggling all her life with poverty. She was then living in a tumble-down shanty, and how to pay the rent, or where to go when she was turned out of it, she did not know. Here was a revelation to her. The idols never promised that. This was her first step toward the new life.[59]

The recruit's elemental motives for material gains, protection, or status led him or her to make a very direct, deliberate, and conscious decision to accept the inducements proffered by the missionary and his religion. To the missionary it mattered not which inducements attracted the Chinese to his religion, just so he got them coming to church, and kept them coming. Once the prospective convert indicated a nominal interest in the new doctrines, the missionary directed all his efforts to developing a personal relationship with the recruit until the individual was ready to make a commitment "to him and his group and 'the cause' of Christianity."[60] At the outset, the commitment to his new religion might be slight and misunderstood, but the individual had taken a course of action which displayed to the missionary an element of hope for a firmer commitment through involvement with the missionary's community.

Soothill's report graphically illustrates the complete gap in Chinese understanding of the ways of his new religion.

> . . . Four men from Pi-lien, Crystal Lily, who had been cured (from opium) in our small refuge, returned home, resolved to start a branch church in their village of 3,000. . . . Not one of these could read correctly, and, even had he been able to do so, his ignorance of Christian terms, and of the meaning of Scripture teaching, would have made his exposition at least quaint, probably heterodox enough to have had him excommunicated from every Church in Christendom. Neither had any one of them prayed, or heard prayers, before his entry into the refuge, where he had remained less than ten days, much of the time in physical weakness and considerable distress. Indeed, the very word we use for prayer, 'tao-kao,' was, in their ignorance, perverted to 'pao-kao,' "practical information."[61]

Since such conversion was opportunistic and came about through the process of induced incentives, the commitment to the missionary's religion and norms was one of compliance, involving no indications of a religious experience. The convert felt that he had "found a new ritual for relief, protection and help, and that he must submit to the new group in order to get thoroughly satisfying results."[62]

"I suspect every Chinaman who applies for baptism—everyone," said the missionary Dr. Robert McKay to a visitor. "There may be quarrel between him and his neighbors, or a rich man may be oppressing him, or there may be a lawsuit pending, and he thinks that by joining the church he will get help from the foreigner, or at least he will see that one of his members gets fair play, and the advantage, if there is any."[63] In South China, where clan-fights were frequent, it wasn't uncommon for a whole village to present itself for baptism in order that it might have foreign support in carrying on its feud against a neighboring village. This system of baptism "en masse" was strongly discouraged by most Protestant missionaries.[64]

The original inducements attracting the non-Christian to the missionary covered a whole range of incentives, from relief from physical pain, pleasing his employer or teacher, getting rich through the westerner's knowledge, satisfying the desire to solve some philosophical or theological problem, even the learning of Christianity's weaknesses so as to attack it the more effectively, learning English in order to gain status, to mere curiosity. The utilization of such incentives on the part of the missionary is illustrated by the case of an educated Chinese addicted to opium, who tried to persuade the missionary Soothill to treat him. Soothill tells of the incident in this way:

> I told him I was inexperienced in this sort of work, but he was persistent in submitting himself to my tender mercies. Assured that faith was the

best cure I urged him to prayer, and, in order to support his physical strength, dosed with quinine as a tonic three times a day. He suffered, of course, but in ten days was free from his twenty years' thraldom, and being a man of strong will, and having given himself to God, he has remained free ever since."[65]

Even among the Chinese it was commonly asserted, with great boldness and persistence, that the missionary induced the people to embrace Christianity. In 1880 Li Hongzhang, the noted statesman of China, stated to Timothy Richard, "your converts gather round you because they and their friends are in your service and have their living thereby. Withdraw the pay of these native agents and there will be no more Christians."[66]

The full effect of this observation regarding the rewards associated with conversion is revealed in figures compiled by *The Missionary Review* in 1878. According to their findings the ratio of converts employed in the different missions in Fujian Province indicates the following:

> The London Missionary Society had in mission service and pay, 7.33% of their converts
> The Reformed (Dutch) Presbyterian of America, 2.53%
> The Presbyterian Church of England, 3.35%
> The Presbyterian Church of Canada, 8.84%
> The American Board of Commissioners, 21.14%
> The American Methodist Episcopal Church, 7.33%
> Church Missionary Society of England, 11.25%[67]

While recognizing the importance and absolute necessity of training Chinese pastors and workers to assist in the Church's mission to evangelize all of China, some missionaries also recognized the problem associated with this practice. At the first General Conference of the Protestant Missionaries in China held at Shanghai, May 10–24, 1877, the Reverend T. P. Crawford of the American Southern Baptist Conference raised the question, "Can any of us believe that one in fifteen of these semi-converted, money-loving Christians has been thus moved to preach the gospel while not one in a hundred is so moved in western lands?"[68] Mr. Crawford then continued with these remarks of concern:

> Unfortunately for the native converts this employment business, this foreign money always before their eyes and clinking in their ears, begets a spirit of the opposite kind. . . . Thus pecuniary gain becomes the sole end of their religious profession. The motives of the sincere are gradually corrupted, and designing men of the baser sort are led to seek connection with the church. The result is to bring Christianity into contempt before the people and weaken, if not destroy, its saving efficacy.[69]

A Chinese scholar of the old system of education declared to Dr. Maurice Price in 1919, "The Chinese look at everything from the point of view of securing profit, personal profit, bodily profit. Foreigners think officials do much for reputation—the Chinese think they do all for profit ('li')." The scholar claimed that he never knew a Chinese to come into the church because of persecution. "Chinese all come to the missionaries for the profit they can get out of it."[70] This apparent Chinese characteristic of seeking profit extended to the practice of recruiting converts for a reasonable fee.

> While I was at Fuhchau, Mr. Gibson, the missionary, introduced me to a literary character, who had been for some time a hearer. I suppose he thought he would like to do a good stroke of business, and he volunteered his services to produce native converts at the reasonable rate of a dollar a head. He was evidently under the impression that we undertook nothing unless a profit was made, and I suppose he thought that the missionaries would have such a liberal percentage upon the converts that they could afford to give him a dollar. I need not say that this proposition was not accepted.[71]

The unconverted looked upon the mission-paid agent as openly making a profession of religion only as a means to seek and obtain employment. They regarded him as insincere in his profession and teachings; serving men, not God. The effect of this problem upon the Chinese agent's listeners often resulted in his hearers tauntingly saying, "If your foreign missionary will pay me six dollars a month, I can preach as well as you." Or, some repeated the familiar adage, "Eat his rice, speak his words." Such a reputation was, perhaps, well-deserved, since some of the mission-paid agents engaged in their work with the idea of "no foreign dollars, no work for Jesus." A case in point was the first Methodist class-leader in Fuhchau, who refused to continue his task when he discovered there was to be no pay.[72]

Although these general facts are beyond dispute, the missionary did not deliberately set out to "buy" converts, nor did he condone the foreign pay system as a direct inducement to win converts. His ultimate objective was to establish Christianity in a viable form in native churches, with Chinese helpers performing the necessary duties to maintain a congregation. However, the fact that missionaries were willing to pay them for their services proved to be a strong inducement for some Chinese to abandon their traditional alliances for new ones. The Reverend Nathan Sites, in addressing the missionary body at the 1877 Shanghai Conference, called attention to the illfated effects of this practice, in these pungent remarks:

> Again: The foreign pay system induces in the agent a want of zeal and earnestness in his work. It renders him indifferent about developing

his native ability, or giving to his work the entire strength of his mind, or the full energy of his will. All along these years, we have seen preachers on ready mission pay, sitting down at ease in their stations, indisposed to toil and suffer, that they might win souls.[73]

While the results of this system greatly distressed some missionaries, others resigned themselves to the reality of the situation with the attitude "we would like it to be different if it were possible, but it is impossible." And still other missionaries accepted the facts of everyday life in China with the attitude "Notwithstanding, every way, whether in pretence, or in truth, Christ is preached: and I therein do rejoice, yea, and will rejoice."[74]

It is significant that one of the leading inducements accounting for willingness to convert to the missionary's religion was legal protection. There are numerous accounts of how the Chinese, harassed by clan or family disputes or oppressed by men in power, sought recruitment into the Christian church in the hope of securing the support of missionaries against their enemies. The Reverend R. H. Graves noted in his article, "To the Progress of The Gospel," ". . . we know very well that instances have not been few of Chinese desiring to make a profession of Christianity merely because they hope to have the powerful influence of foreigners on their side in some litigations. Whole villages have offered to turn Christian in this way."[75] This was a repeated theme:

> . . . In nine cases out of ten the real truth is, that the so-called convert being now associated with a movement which seems in his eyes a vigorous and promising one, has presumed on the strength of this alliance to pay off some of his old grudges or to carry matters with a high hand towards those of whom he had been formerly in fear.[76]

Those Chinese outside the Christian movement became irritated to the point of permanent hostility directed toward the "meddling" foreigners who protected their converts by using their "privileged" position to overturn the administration of law by the Chinese magistrate. Some of the missions sensitive to this Chinese feeling adopted policies against such "favors" or inducements such as:

> First, those desiring interference on the part of the missionary in things that are wholly beyond his province, and in these he will refuse from the first to meddle. Under this head come family disputes and law cases, with all the forms of political interference. This duty is so carefully observed in China by most Missions that candidates are not received, even to the catechuments, while they have any connections with a lawsuit.[77]

In China, the ruling of the Wesleyan Methodist Church in its *Book of Disciplines* reads as follows:

> Members and enquirers must understand that position in the Christian Church does not alter the status of a Chinese subject. A man who, according to Chinese custom, has not the right of entry to a Yamen or the power to send his card to the Yamen in ordinary cases gains no such right or power because he has become a member or enquirer.[78]

Although certain missions had either an implicit or explicit policy, the question of legal protection for Chinese Christians remained a very perplexing problem for the missionary, especially since whatever course of action he took would affect his relationship with the Chinese.

> If on the one hand we decline to entertain them, we are liable to the charge of unkindness, of being indifferent to their interests, of want of sympathy with them in their trials, which are sometimes very great. Sometimes the parties who thus fail to receive the aid they expected become disaffected, and sometimes worse consequences ensue.
>
> Suppose on the other hand the missionary takes up these cases, suppose he interferes in all the petty quarrels and law suits in which the native members may be concerned.
>
> The results are equally unsatisfactory. Much valuable time is consumed, that might be employed to better purpose.
>
> Then again this course does not always promote the best interests of the church.[79]

It would be impossible to determine the number of Chinese who became nominal Christians because of the inducements, either to earn foreign money or to obtain foreign support in village quarrels or in lawsuits.

One of the most clearly specialized kinds of incentives satisfying the need for prosperity, recognition, status, and power was the drive to obtain schooling at the hands of the missionary—purchased if it could not be obtained free. The demand for English brought eager parents with their children and ambitious youngsters to mission schools simply because the foreign instructor was known to provide the best teaching in the foreign language, and the foreign language was desired as a means to remunerative employment with foreign trade companies, in government, in native stores, telegraph offices, or within the missionary community.

> In considering the place of English in the schools today, it is to be remembered that there has been a strong demand for this subject on the part of Chinese students, and it has been believed by many that, unless the missionary schools supplied this demand, there would be serious risk of losing many of those who would otherwise come to them.

. . . Some of the strong men among China's rulers have been prepared for their position by such a course of study, and when a high official does not know English he finds it necessary to surrround himself by those who have obtained it.[80]

In 1882 T. P. Crawford revised his wife's school curriculum requiring all instruction to be in English because "her students had always come for mercenary reasons anyway, and because it made more sense to teach them English and lose them to treaty-port business than to educate them only in Chinese and have to put up with their cries for mission employment. The change would also supposedly attract more respectable patrons, who would pay more."[81]

In such cases, status was often the inducement to send children to the mission schools, especially among the upper-class Chinese. The distinctive attitude of the highly privileged class toward Christianity consisted of an absolute lack of feeling for the need to convert. They approached what the missionary had to offer with what was substantively an opportunistic and utilitarian doctrine of conventions appropriate to the elite. In their minds, learning English and western science and technology represented an instrument of power. In the missionary's mind, offering a thorough education was a proper and healthy inducement to parents to send their children to school. To make this inducement effective, the education was designed to prepare a young man for a successful career which was available and seemed desirable to the parents and friends of the pupils.

Although for the non-Christian youth the incentive to attend the foreigner's school was a means by which he might attain an honorable and successful career, the missionary established schools in order to instill the Christian religion, and so bring about the conversion of the pupil. More importantly, the missionary envisioned that these educated converts would assume a prominent and influential role in society and in the church. As the Reverend C. W. Mateer put it, "If we are going to displace Confucianism in the minds of the people and wrest from its educated men the position they now hold, we must prepare men, educated in Christianity and in science, who will be able to outshine them."[82]

Special importance is attached by a number of writers to the fact that schools are a means of reaching classes who can be reached in no other way. By means of schools where English has been taught, the sons of officials, literati, merchants, and gentry have been attracted. In this way they have been brought under the influence of Western ideas and Christian ideals. One writer says: "In China, girls' schools occupy a peculiar place as a means of bringing the women to Christ. The women cannot attend our public preaching nor read our books as the men can. Unless they are reached as girls, it is difficult to bring them under the influence of the Gospel." Elementary schools often prove a means of getting access to homes otherwise inaccessible.[83]

Chinese thinking did not include education for daughters or wives. The position of women in Chinese society is best captured in the following remark: "She must remain stagnant so long as she allows her daughters to be made household drudges and denied the right and opportunity to cultivate and cherish an interest in things beyond the four walls of their homes."[84] Even faithful Christian Chinese men were horrified at the idea of a school for women. No self-respecting women would think of being seen on the streets going to the missionary's compound for a few hours' schooling each day or of receiving a foreigner into her home in order to learn to read and write. "It will spoil her," affirmed the men. Since there were no appealing incentives the missionary could offer to induce husbands to expose their wives to Christian education, missionaries turned their efforts to offering incentives to parents of young girls, with the expectation that they would send their daughters to the mission day or boarding schools. The parents of many of these potential female students were extremely poor. "The offer of a good noonday meal, of free tuition and books, and, in addition, a daily portion of hair oil to make glossy their raven locks, were inducements not to be withstood."[85] Also, many young girls decided on their own to enter mission schools with the hopes that they would find the opportunity to secure a well-paying position either in church work or some other kind of work through the assistance of the missionary. For this reason alone many converted to Christianity and joined the church.[86]

The missionaries viewed the education of females as an integral program in the total evangelistic enterprise of the church. They anticipated that female schools, where girls might be trained in Christianity, would turn out Christian wives for Christian young men, who would establish Christian families. The Reverend Dr. Wentworth, of the Methodist Episcopal Mission, prepared on behalf of the mission an appeal on this subject, in which he said:

> Girls converted in Christian schools, and returning into the bosoms of heathen families, will carry with them the results of Christian instruction, and sow the seeds of Gospel truth in the minds of their children, and thus insensibly promote the spread of Gospel truth in quarters where no other influence could possibly be brought to bear. Christian school girls make Christian wives and Christian mothers. This it is that makes all Churches so anxious to get the educating of as many youth as possible within the influence of Bible truth. Chinese girls will form no exception to the general rule. The female heart is as religiously inclined in China as in any other quarter of the globe.[87]

As the educational program for boys and girls took on a greater importance in the total evangelistic enterprise, missionary wives and female missionaries played an increasingly significant role in the missionary movement. In many situations, after the missionary established schools, his many other duties required him to turn over the running of the school to his wife or to a female missionary. Moreover, in order to establish relationships with the female segment of the Chinese population, it soon became obvious to the missionary that female missionaries were more effective in developing face-to-face relationships with Chinese women.

In concluding this discussion of conversion experiences of the "induced incentive" type, it has been implied that underneath the missionary's sublime methods of bringing Chinese to Christ, Protestant missionaries throughout China held out certain obvious non-spiritual incentives to attract non-believers to Christianity. The face-to-face relationships developed during the conversion process were dependent upon the practicality of the incentives the missionary had to offer. Perceiving the Chinese to be a very practical people, the missionary offered very practical inducements—food, shelter, employment, status, protection (the proverbial "rice bowl")—which were of direct personal benefit to the prospective convert. The non-Christian's decision to take advantage of these inducements was contingent upon the value he placed on them, rather than upon the value he placed on the missionary's doctrines. In many reported instances, converts refrained from idolatrous practices and other activities that the missionary had condemned, more for pragmatic reasons than out of a need for salvation.

Once a face-to-face relationship was established, the missionary used the incentives as a means of perpetuating successive encounters with the recruit. In this manner the missionary was able to negotiate the relationship, exposing the recruit to the repetitive message of the Gospel in order to implant a strong and permanent spiritual commitment to Christianity. The relationship established in the "induced incentive" conversion experience, the missionary and the convert "achieved" the results expected by each. The cognitive negotiation of the relationship by the missionary resulted in his "winning" a convert, and the cognitive negotiation of the relationship by the recruit resulted in his taking advantage of those incentives which enhanced his position in life.

INDUCED CONFLICT CONVERSION: PLANNING AND ACTING

In the second type of conversion experience, the missionary directed his total efforts toward inducing the feeling of conflict within the prospective convert. The missionary induced internal conflict by a series of carefully planned tactics that would put Chinese traditional values and norms into conflict by placing negative values on them, and would create feelings of personal dissatisfaction and low self-esteem. Missionaries continually preached and wrote tracts denouncing certain Chinese beliefs, customs, and behaviors: ancestor worship, footbinding, selling of children, opium smoking, concubinage, practices connected with marriage and funeral ceremonies. The Protestant community uniformly opposed all these practices that missionaries considered to be deleterious to Christians.

The missionary took every opportunity he could to condemn severely and repeatedly ancestor worship as an evil practice. Missionaries maintained that worshipping one's ancestors was an act of devotion to the dead, expressed by offerings, prayers, and prostrations before the ancestral tablets, the grave, and the "Song Wang" or Magisterial Deity within whose jurisdiction the spirits of the departed were supposed to be incarcerated. Missionaries preached that ancestor worship was an idolatrous act manifestly condemned by the Word of God as "sinful," and must, of course, be abandoned by every Chinese who wanted to become a Christian. Missionaries exhorted their listeners that for anyone guilty of worshipping idols and rebuking God's commandment to worship the one true God alone the punishment was eternal damnation.

The Protestant missionary body never waivered in its opposition to ancestor worship. At the 1890 Missionary Conference in Shanghai, Dr. William Martin made a case for the toleration of ancestor worship on the following points: it strengthened the bond of family union, stimulated acts of charity, generated feelings of self-respect, imposed moral restraint, and kept alive faith in a future life.[88] At the conclusion of his presentation, the Reverend J. Hudson Taylor responded, "I trust that all those who wish to raise an indignant protest against the conclusion of Dr. Martin's paper will signify it by rising."[89] It was recorded in the minutes of the meeting that almost the whole audience stood in opposition to the propositions put forth by Dr. Martin.

Prospective converts were required to reject not only ancestor worship but also all other evil practices that "hamper, torment and debase these heathen peoples." In his face-to-face relationships with Chinese, the missionary emphasized the cruelty and wickedness of footbinding, selling children, opium smoking, concubinage, and the marriage and funeral practices. The missionary had no qualms in challenging and demanding that these evil practices be rejected as sinful acts.

The consequences the recruit faced in abandoning these traditional values and norms incurred the anger and rejection of his family and of his neighbors. The Reverend Charles Scott tells of the following experiences of a Mr. Wong.

> I entered a room where an old woman lay. She was a Christian and her folks were not. While they had not literally turned her out, they made it manifest that they had no room for her. In each of the end rooms of the

three-roomed house was a "kang" (brick bed). The well members of the family slept in one, and the other, on which the sick woman had been lying, they had commandeered as a nursery for the sweet potato plants. . . .

There she lay in that alleyway on the damp earthen floor, bundled up in her quilts—filthy, ragged, odoriferous—despised and rejected for Christ's sake.[90]

. . . heathen-spirited children of ruthless will and stubborn purpose had, quite contrary to the tenets of Confucius as to filial conduct, turned [their ailing Christian father] out. They had reasoned: "If I cannot bend this old man's purpose to be a Jesus-Doctrine man, I will break him!"

. . . He had been forced out at night and in the winter storm, ill-clad and without food—the climax of the "freezing out" process that the family had for some time been perpetrating upon him.[91]

The missionary considered such sacrifices and persecution in the name of Christ a true affirmation of the convert's faith in his new religion.

The sociological significance of the missionary's actions and the convert's response demonstrate the process of social disintegration of the individual's basic values, norms, behaviors, and his relationship with his reference group. When the individual in Chinese society reacted with doubt, confusion, and displeasure toward traditional values, belief systems, and norms which defined his situation, and intentionally broke the rule of filial piety in order to adhere to the foreigner's "Jesus Doctrine," he made a conscious decision to run the risk of being rejected by his primary reference group. The prospective convert's decision to change radically his life's orientation was re-enforced by the missionary's stressing existing personal conflicts and developing new ones. The consequence of the recruit's decision to convert resulted in his rejection by his primary reference group. The context of meaning for his old behavior, which constituted the "taken-for-granted" experiences of his everyday world, existed in his acts of filial piety. Now, it was predicated upon his willingness to adapt to a new series of behaviors demanding that he desert the authority, norms, and values of his traditional primary group and unconditionally submit to the values, norms, and group organization of a new reference group. This shift from the old to the radically innovative value orientation constituted the social disintegration of the individual's link with his past. The process of social disintegration became complete with the social isolation of the convert by his old reference group.

> A change of religion would be a momentous rupture with the carefully guarded tradition, unless one at the same time attached himself to the people whose religion he adopted; in that case one would enter into the traditions of that people, would be under obligation to venerate its institutions, would accept its protecting deities as his own, and would thereby be protected against the wrath of his own national gods, that is, his ancestors.[92]

The missionary's role in the process of social disintegration was to persuade the recruit that something better was being offered and was attainable by embracing Christianity. "We ought to bear in mind," stated the Reverend Frank Ohlinger at the 1890 Shanghai Conference, "that the only means of getting people to abstain from at least some of their customs is to persuade them of something better."[93] That "something better" was to teach the recruit the new values and ideals of the Christian religion. Missionaries were not interested in embellishing the old by merely adding something new to it. They were eager to eliminate the old values and beliefs and to replace them with the new values and beliefs of the Christian religion which, simply stated, required the Chinese to worship the one true God and no other gods, to accept Jesus Christ as a personal saviour, and to give witness of Christ's love to all those who continued to live in "sin" and "darkness." This traditional, Christian picture of a great, ethically perfect God was the message every missionary conveyed to the Chinese, inducing a sense of inferiority and debasement which the missionary perceived would create a readiness to accept the Christian group relations and group values in compensation for these feelings.

> The foundation of all Christian instruction is laid in the simple essentials of the Gospel. . . . These essentials must be regarded as including in one form or another the knowledge of God, the sense of sin, and the appreciation of redemption. But the good news of the Cross cannot always be the missionary's first message. Without some knowledge of God and His character, men can have no true sense of sin. . . . It is in the light of a dawning knowledge of God that a sense of sin is born, and it is to the man made conscious of his sin, that the story of the Incarnation and the Cross becomes a transfiguring revelation of the Divine goodness. It remains true in the main . . . that it is not usually the acute sense of sin that brings a man to Christ in the mission field, but rather that coming to Christ creates within him for the first time the deeper consciousness of sin. Over all the mission field the great facts of the holiness of God, the offensiveness of sin, the lost and hopeless condition of unrenewed man, and the new hope of eternal life based on a spiritual regeneration, must be taught and emphasized, the truth being from the first imparted in its simplest forms."[94]

By dictating to the recruit what his actions, beliefs, and sentiments should be, the missionary offered the only resolution of his conflict, which was complete conversion and immersion in the Christian church. In return, the faithful convert was promised by the "Jesus-Doctrine" redemption of his sins, salvation from evil, and life eternal.

From a sociological perspective, attempts to alter radically the recruit's behavior for purposes of conversion, resolution, and resocialization involve a four-step process: "(1) radical change, as opposed to ordinary change, requires resocialization rather than ordinary socialization; (2) resocialization requires an intervening process of desocialization, a process in which the efficacy of old values is erased; (3) desocialization occurs when interpersonal relations disintegrate";[95] (4) resocialization occurs when new interpersonal relations are established and the individual is accepted into the new group as a bonafide member.

The following sample testimonies will provide us with a range of "induced conflict" conversion types, as well as illustrate the process of desocialization, resolution, and resocialization.

Peng gives this evidence that he was a sincere idolater. The Chinese have a theory that the gods are especially pleased if one burns his own flesh instead of incense. A steel skewer is thrust through the skin of the arm. To this a heavy candle and holder are suspended so that the flame comes just below the arm. In this painful position the man walks for miles from one temple to another, without giving any trace of pain.

Peng passed through this ordeal more than once. . . . With the development of manhood, however, he felt that his trade no longer satisfied him. He gave it up and entered the army. He was soon on the staff of the Governor. Here he gained an intimate acquaintance with Chinese officials—legal and official—and learned to "read men." A few years later he came with his mother and brothers to Hankow. Through lending money, trading and dabbling in law, Peng made a good living.

Mr. Peng was some time in the town before he found his way to the chapel. But he soon began to attend daily, and evidently was intensely interested. Our attention was soon drawn to him. He sat up in front. He was fairly tall, well dressed and gentlemanly in his bearing.

Mr. Peng had many difficulties to face. Not only were all the ideas which he regarded as certainties in the spiritual world passing away and new truths taking their place, but he knew that persecution awaited a change of faith. His mother would reproach him bitterly, and he loved and revered his mother. Besides, he was making a good living—largely by loaning money to persons engaged in evil practices. But he saw that to go on taking this interest would make him a partner of crime. . . . Step by step he fought his way through these difficulties, at last presented himself for baptism.[96]

Shee's great-grandfather was of the literary class and among his relatives were city elders and officials. He himself had little schooling, being compelled through family misfortune to work on a farm from boyhood. He used opium. Gradually he became a professional story-teller. While at this occupation he learned about Christianity.

. . . At first, however, he had very crude conceptions of the message. He looked upon Jesus as a great wonder-worker, and spoke of him as the great western conjurer. The stories of the four gospels he incorporated with his own. They were new and novel, and he used his liberty to modify and adapt them.

Finally he became attracted by a preacher, Chen, who "denounced sin, and demanded faith and repentance." Shee knew that Chen loved him, but he was of a proud spirit and became openly hostile. These questions occurred to him: "Is this a new religion? What about ancestor worship? Was not this doctrine introduced by the 'foreign devils' who had invaded Chinese life and society?" . . .

Shee had been trying to overcome his craving for opium. The conflict became unbearable: a crisis was reached. He says that in the last awful struggle he closed with his demon enemy in the arms of death. For seven days and nights, in burning hunger, thirst, weariness and excruciating pain, he was pleading with God in prayer. He found he had an added strength. At last the Lord gave deliverance, the light broke in, and the captive of years was free.

From that day he grew in grace, knowledge and power. He was baptized by Dr. W. E. Macklin in Nanjing. Gathering a quantity of Christian literature, he retraced his steps to his old home north of the river. But this time he had a new story to tell. . . .

In many of his old haunts he was visited with reproach and scorn. . . . Proud Confucian students debated with him in cynical pride. But he threw all his native and acquired powers into the new work of God and humanity. With intense fervor and with a force and eye whose expression was irresistible persuasion, he proclaimed the gospel of redeeming grace to those to whom no tidings of Him had ever come. . . .

He has the unreserved confidence of the whole church, native and foreign.[97]

These cases are representative of those Chinese who came into direct contact with the missionary. The essential features in these cases of conversion experience are contained in the words "sin," "evil," and "redemption." Those who repented from "sin" and their "evil ways" to accept the Christian life changed their habits to conform with the social role defined by the missionary. In accepting his new social role the convert was required by the Church to make some visible commitment signifying the break with the old and acceptance of the new reference group. This was accomplished through the Christian rituals of baptism and communion. From a sociological stance, the ritual of baptism represented the relinquishment of previous relationships, and the ritual of communion symbolized the acceptance of a new set of relationships making possible the development of a new commitment and adherence to a new set of values, norms, and beliefs.

The sense of conflict that has been discussed in this section takes its form in feelings of confusion, guilt, displeasure, inferiority, and debasement. In turn, such feelings are to be understood by reference to the central issue of the missionary's plans and actions to provoke Chinese to react against their traditional conduct of life. When we have seen the way in which a spoken encounter can induce a Chinese auditor to oppose and to disengage himself from his old orientation of life and to engage in a foreign orientation of life, and have seen that focused interaction between missionaries and Chinese can result in the phenomenon of desocialization and resocialization, we have some idea of the control missionaries had in face-to-face relationships.

THE COGNITIVE CONVERSION PROCESS AND FACE-TO-FACE CONDUCT

The "induced incentive" and "induced conflict" conversion processes are dynamic phenomena which occurred over time; they consist of several stages, or steps, which I have labeled "unlocking," "shifting," and "relocking."[98] The three-step process suggests a phenomenon of change which was voluntarily regulated by both parties, inasmuch as the rules regarding leave-taking and disbandment of the encounter were determined by each, and the encounters generally took place in an unrestrictive arena.

Our terms can be defined as follows: the first stage, "unlocking," is a period of conflict in which the missionary as the agent of conflict worked on the potential convert to make a decision to dislodge himself from his former allegiances, norms, values, and beliefs. The second stage is a transition period in which the individual was "shifting" from conflict to resolution of conflict. The "shifting" produced a "push-pull" struggle, causing the recruit to wrestle with the decision either to "push" forward toward his new-found orientation or to be "pulled" back to his old orientation. During this stage the missionary took on the role of an agent of change. The third, and final, stage is virtual conformity, or "relocking" the convert into the new group's patterns. The missionary as an agent of resolution offered concrete forms of behavior—repentance and salvation—that placed the convert firmly in his new group's environment.

As defined, the three terms constitute a continuum that delineates the conversion process. In setting out some ideas concerning the stages of the continuum, we will be able to analyze a part of what goes on during each stage, in order to determine the nature of the face-to-face interchange and exchange between missionary and Chinese.

The initial, "unlocking" stage occurred when the missionary encountered his listener. In these situations the missionary's presence evoked a range of responses from the Chinese, including indifference, resistance, counter-attack, and passive cooperation. In order to break through these barriers, it was vital to the missionary that he exhibit certain capacities and certain properties of his role, such as patience, courage, integrity, self-control, forgiveness, love, faith, affableness, humility, and "in the presence of what seemed like unfriendliness or disapproval maintain a certain approachable reserve."[99] The missionary's effort to maintain these standards of character and conduct provided the basis Chinese used for imputing a personal judgement to his role and his religion. Moreover, the missionary's appreciation and demonstration of social rituals and behavior acceptable to the Chinese had an important conservative effect upon their encounters. Consequently, the "facing-off" between the missionary and the potential convert was determined in part by the missionary's reputation, conduct, language, and gestures which affected the process by either attracting or repelling his auditors.

Once interaction was initiated by the missionary (in some instances Chinese did the initiating) and he was able to gain the attention of his listener, it was crucial for him to convey a message which would persuade his auditor to make a decision to become a Christian. To this end he employed well-chosen words and expressions to communicate to his hearer the "sinful" condition of his life, hoping to arouse a deep sense of guilt and conflict. By means of this tactic the missionary hoped to arouse in his listener an agonized feeling of utter unworthiness, combined with an overwhelming sense of guilt and fear of eternal torture and damnation. The missionary directed his entire efforts to "unlock," to wrench, the individual free from his "traditional and sacred" patterns by applying, first, disapproving influences and, then, approving ones through deliberate and repetitive techniques of suggestion, persuasion, and support to stimulate desires, wishes, and needs. The significance of this strategy was evident in the depletion of previous relationships and values, resulting in unlocking the bonds of the collectivity.

The missionary's role in the unlocking process was to create an intolerable, overwhelming sense of inferiority and debasement; he then held out his own group's patterns of belief and behavior as the only means of compensation for that sense of inferiority.[100] The kinds of forces operative in the missionary's interactional strategy were the forces of conflict, disruption, alienation, disorganization, and the promise of relief from them. This strategy played upon the individuals' attitude of submission, with the missionary attempting directly or indirectly to unlock the individual from his reference group's values, norms, sentiments, and beliefs. One missionary recounts the experience in the following way:

> Wang Pao Kevei was born at Fu-sah, ten miles west of Chefoo, in 1826. . . . His mind became so tinctured with the teaching of the Chinese sages that he glorified in being a Confucionist of "the strictest sect."
>
> He was a jealous advocate of ancestral worship. A distinguished ancestry, recording names of men eminent for scholarship and holding high positions in the Government, made him highly prize his birthright privileges.
>
> . . . He resolved to make his first visit to the chapel and there investigate the truth. Much of the afternoon was spent in asking questions and listening. He received a copy of the New Testament. He began to study, learned to pray, came to the church on the Sabbath, and soon became deeply interested in Christianity.
>
> At times intense anguish filled his heart at the thought of what it meant in his case to become a Christian. His kindred and friends would despise him and regard him as an apostate unworthy to live. He contin-

ued, however, to study and pray. Soon the conviction took hold of his mind that he was a wretched sinner, and there was no hope for him but to accept free salvation through Jesus Christ. As soon as persuaded of this, he yielded his whole heart to Jesus, made a public profession of faith, and received baptism.[101]

Unlocking in this context, then, refers to those experiences or events in the encounter which tended to subvert old values in order to introduce new ones. Subjectively, the strategy operated to "unlock" the individual in both the conscious and subconscious levels of old interests labeled as "sin," with new interests identified with "God's way."

When a listener became an inquirer, he was "tagged" by the missionary as a "potential" convert. At this point, the missionary pursued the relationship with greater intensity, focusing upon establishing what Goffman calls "cognitive recognition." The missionary "places" or "identifies" the prospective convert, "linking the sight of him with a framework of information concerning him. . . . such as his name, or a specific configuration of statuses, or a unique personal biography—in brief, his 'personal identity' ".[102] Cognitive recognition was used by the missionary to place the "would-be" convert in the "shifting" stage of the conversion process.

In this stage of the conversion continuum, the missionary plied the individual with positive re-enforcements to maintain the face-to-face relationship, strengthening the bondedness which developed through the cognitive recognition process. To the degree that continuing relationships reinforced old values, the missionary continued to dislodge, disclaim, and displace such relationships in order to facilitate the "unlocking" process.

Once the individual gave indications of his willingness to unlock himself from his reference group's beliefs, sentiments, attitudes, values, behavior patterns, and expectations, he entered the "shifting" stage, which entailed the shifting of his status from one reference group to another. The shift from the old to the new was a necessary transition step in which the recruit re-established an equilibrium offering continuity to his life and relationships. Since the missionary provided information or models to be exemplified, the recruit knew in which direction to change and approximately how long it would take to re-establish a new, stable equilibrium. Although the missionary continued to direct him toward new alignments, the recruit experienced a "push-pull" force during the struggle to unlock the old from the new, and between sentiments of doubt and confidence, guilt and salvation, filiality and unfiliality, and anxiety and calmness. The forces of his family pulled at him to retain the traditional ways, while the forces of the missionary pushed him into new alliances.

The whole structure of the nation, commercial, political, social, mental, moral and religious, is dominated by principles that are antagonistic to the truth of the gospel. Think what it must have meant, then, for this young man [T. T.] Zia to make a decision in favor of the Christian life. On the one hand it was the easy way of "established usage," with the good will of friends and the hope for a peaceful, prosperous life; on the other, he faced the sacrifice of all he held dear. He would be counted a traitor to his country, false to his friends, unfilial to his ancestors, and, harder than all, yea, harder than giving up life itself, was the necessity of disobeying that dear old mother and be branded as an ungrateful son.[103]

During the "shifting" stage, the missionary's relationship with the recruit took on new meaning, for now he was offering new information that told the recruit what belief in the Christian faith meant, what he was joining, what was expected of him, and the time it would take before he was wholly accepted into the church. The recruit was thus placed in a probationary status. Often the nature of the relationship took on the tones of a parent-child relationship. The missionary took on the "father" or "mother" role, instructing the atoning "child" in the proper and "good" ways of life. The recruit was received into this new relationship as a prodigal son—"one who was once lost and now has returned home into the arms of his forgiving father." The inquirer was given explicit information and instructions regarding the requirements of his new role and membership in his new "family."

For example, the individual who became motivated to inquire further into the Christian faith was invited to talk with the missionary. "There alone, or with others similarly minded, he may sit for hours discussing, in a chatty, informal fashion, the truths he wishes to investigate."

> In such meetings, "nine-tenths of our converts receive the rudimentary knowledge of Christian truth. . . . Every professed inquirer is welcomed, his inquiries are fully met and kindly answered, till he becomes perfectly satisfied. . . . During the nine months' probation and instruction following, there are ample opportunities for the fullest investigation into the knowledge, character, and motives of the applicants for baptism. The session undertakes the responsibility of a weekly class for the catechumen. The special doctrines and specific duties of Christianity are carefully taught. . . . At the end of the nine months' probation the candidates are examined by the pastor. Those who are in knowledge and character regarded as satisfactory are accepted and baptized. The others are delayed for months or indefinitely."[104]

By prescribing the directions, requirements, and time the missionary was able to maintain control over the process and the recruit's preparation for shifting his status.

The process of shifting can be regarded as the reclassification of mental, spiritual and in some cases the intellectual experiences which the recruit went through in order to arrive at his new beliefs, attitudes, norms, values, behavior patterns, and self concept. These experiences often resulted in the adoption of a new frame of reference, of new standards for evaluating behavior, and of new associations. However, before the recruit was fully accepted into this new reference group, he had to pay attention to the information provided by the missionary and give evidence of his change of character during a period of probation. It was during such experiences that the recruit received from the missionary a new personal identity and began to shift his allegiances, trying to re-establish his status in the foreigner's community. The shifting process was defined, in large part, by the information the missionary provided the inquirer in their face-to-face encounters. Thus, the missionary calculated the content of his relationships and employed words, actions, expressions, symbols, gestures, and behavior which prepared and supported the inquirer, to ensure shifts with a minimum of stress. Subjectively, the inquirer's experience can be described as "seeing the light," or "here was a revelation," or being delivered from "sin and evil" to "grace" and to a "new life." Once the missionary was satisfied that the inquirer's knowledge was satisfactory and his character in accordance with his profession of faith, he was ready for the next stage of his conversion—to be received into the church as a full member, with all the rights and privileges associated with such status and thus to become "relocked."

If changes in beliefs are to remain stable, the new equilibrium of forces must be "relocked." "This process implies that the new beliefs must be integrated into other parts of the person," writes Schein. "It must be supported and reinforced by the behavior of significant others"[105] (missionary, other converts); if it is not so integrated or supported, the recruit will "shift" out of his situation and return once again to his "old ways." When this reverse shift occurs, it is called "backsliding." The true understanding of "backsliding" is to be found in part in the principle of the natural fluctuations of religious feelings.[106] Generally, the problem is one of deliberate, intuitive, or unconscious deviation from the prescribed course of action. The recruit acts out his "backsliding" behavior by rebelling from and repudiating, the missionary's control. The backslider may neglect to attend prayer meetings, to go to church, to follow the missionary's instructions, or to observe the norms of the group. The following significant account reported in *The Chinese Recorder* provides us with an example of backsliders' behavior:

> A missionary travelling on a passenger boat overheard a conversation between two Chinese on the subject of the price of a Church membership certificate, and it was all too conclusive that in a certain city. . . a regular trade in membership certificates was carried on by the Chinese evangelist in charge.[107]

Put in religious terms, backsliding signifies a failure to resist temptation.

Frequent backsliding results in a return to previous status, or change to yet another. Robert Needham Cust notes, "When a man has changed his faith once, there is always a risk, that he will do it again, and something more; he will become a bitter enemy of his late associates."[108] Backsliding was considered by the missionary to be deviant behavior. This potential for relapsing into deviance placed a premium on the missionary's ability to notice the signs leading to such oscillation of faith, and on his sensitivity to changes in the individual, so that he could adjust his face-to-face relationships accordingly—that is, to get the recruit back into the relocking mode.

However, if the changed attitude toward life and the person's sense of identity were to become fairly constant, coherent, and permanent, although fluctuations appeared, the interpersonal confirmation played a very important supportive role as a relocking force. The missionary's main task was solid integration of the individual into his new-found group, with new values, and with certain a priori guiding norms dominating them. Many of the experiences during a church meeting or prayer meeting tended to relock whatever changes in the direction of Christian attitude had occurred in the convert.

> . . . under Confucian teaching the highest possible duty of man is filial piety, and it is laid down that one of the highest examples of filial piety is the duty of revenge against any one who has wronged a man's father or any of his near of kin. A filial son, it is said, will not live under the same heaven as his father's murderer. . . revenge must be the one object of his life, not to be laid aside until he has slain the wrongdoer or is himself slain.
>
> "An evangelist in Manchuria was the nephew of a zealous preacher, 'Blind Chang,' who was cruelly murdered many years ago. At one of the meetings, this evangelist, in a moment of profound spiritual emotion, declared that he had for the first time come to know the Lord, 'Do you forgive your enemies?' he was asked by a Chinese pastor. For a moment this was more than he could promise. A Chinese friend arose and went to his side saying to him, 'I want to help you; I will do all I can to help you. Forgive them!' Still he could not promise, and many silent prayers were offered for him. At last he said very quietly, 'I forgive them. Pray for these men, all of you, that they may be saved; and pray for me that I may be given the victory over myself and them. I shall first write and tell them of my forgiveness and hopes, and then at the earliest opportunity visit them, and plead with them to repent and be saved."
>
> It may seem little that a Christian man should abandon the thought of taking a bloody revenge, but he was not only giving up the impulse of present passion, but breaking with the traditions of his race, and teachings of a lifetime.[109]

The acceptance by the missionary of the convert's offer of himself as a member of the Christian church qualified him to engage in ceremonial activities (baptism, communion, etc.), which legitimized his conformity to the new group's values, norms, sentiments, and beliefs. The conforming process reorganized the convert's personality, so that he complied enough to satisfy his self-respect and his needs to refer his conduct to the recognition and approval of his new associates. The convert made commitment, involving convictions to what is right and proper, as well as their converse, which "relocked" him into his new role and associations. The following illustration demonstrates the new behavior patterns.

> Ling Fuh Pah described himself before his conversion as "a wild, reckless, foul-mouthed man, always spoiling for a fight. If anyone helped himself to my vegetables, it was woe to him when I caught him. But one day, as I was passing the street chapel, I thought I would go in and hear what this 'foreign' preaching was about, so in I went, and stood amongst the people at the back. I hardly understood it all, but one phrase went to my heart, and I could not rid myself of it. The preacher said, 'it is sin to curse and swear.'
>
> "His conversion was a reality. . . his lips were cleansed, his fierceness tamed, his passions brought under control. One day, he saw a man stealing from his garden. The man caught sight of him, and knowing only the old Ling Fuh, fled in terror; but the old man cried out, 'take it easy, you'll fall and hurt yourself; take a few more. He overtook the would-be thief, who fell on his knees begging for mercy, but Ling Fuh lifted him up, and giving the astonished man greens he had gathered, bade him take them away with him."[110]

At the emotional level the convert received the support and encouragement of other converts, and "the fellowship of believers." At the spiritual level his motives and purposes had been purified and higher ideals aroused, justifying any changes he had undergone. When relocking, or closure, was completely desirable to the convert and the missionary, the ceremony of baptism and communion marked the end of the shifting stage, heralding the completeness of the conversion process and the fulfillment of the face-to-face relationship to this point. The ceremony symbolized having travelled a rough path to enlightenment. The result which seemed to be attained in the relocking process was essentially ascribed by the missionary to the birth of human consciousness on a higher spiritual level, "which leads the person to reach out and feel his life one with the larger institutional and spiritual world."[111] It was particularly important that the missionary as the agent of Christianity provide the institutional means to re-establish continuity and stability for the convert, and establish integrative structures (Sunday schools, choir, committee work, prayer groups) as a relocking force.

SUMMARY

The value of the symbolic interactional approach to the process of religious conversion lies in its emphasis on the peculiar and distinctive character of social interaction between culturally different people. The peculiarity consists in the fact that each party negotiates face-to-face interaction according to his or her "definition of the situation" formed by one-sided, culturally preconceived notions of the "other."

Cultural differences in perspective between the missionary and Chinese and uncertainties inherent in the routine application of role negotiation during the religious conversion process generally made for conflict. Conflict occurred especially when missionaries, on the basis of their definition of the situation, tried in some way to control and dominate values and behaviors of the Chinese people. Consciousness of dominion placed the missionary in a position of superiority, while consciousness of being dominated placed the Chinese in a position of inferiority. There seems to have been no other possibility in the position in which missionaries were placed, given the character of the Mission organization and objectives. Consequently, such a perception of the situation from the Chinese point of view resulted among some Chinese in the building up of certain defense mechanisms in the form of resentment, indifference, or deception and camouflage of intentions. Much of what was regarded as inscrutability was probably nothing more than the artful and adroit accommodation of manners and methods to what the Chinese perceived to be the domination of the missionary. The Chinese, knowing what was expected of them and knowing too what they themselves wanted, used that knowledge to maneuver the situation in securing their objectives, and thus retain a sense of identity.

The missionary aim to place non-Christians under the control of the Christian Church required, first, producing conflict and, second, resolution of the conflict in such a way as to segregate converts into a special community under the influence of the missionary in order to provide a new social environment conducive to supporting a different way of behavior. Sociologically speaking, this aim implies, first, producing such disintegration of traditional values as to eliminate any forces that oppose the missionary or that will not submit to him and, second, requiring those whom he can persuade through social interaction to desert traditional values, norms, and sentiments and to submit unconditionally to his imported group, group organization, and group values.

I should like to suggest that the outcome of the conversion process was primarily dependent upon the actions of the missionary and the cognitive response of his or her auditor, and not upon "some mystical power working in some mysterious manner to bring non-believers to Christ." It was the missionary's personal ability to utilize effectively incentives and conflict which helped determine the success or failure he encountered in persuading the non-Christian to accept something new and alien. The missionary's strategy for conversion reflected his understanding of the value of face-to-face relationships, which he systematically, persistently, and thoroughly manipulated to achieve his objectives. The success or failure of his encounters can be related, for the most part, to the intensity and quality of face-to-face relationships formed between missionary and Chinese.

By looking at the ways in which missionaries introduced incentives and conflict, knowing that the presence of each could manifest itself in a series of salient decisions and actions leading to conversion, we have in some measure understood something about the way in which actions of domination between culturally different people modify behavior and orientations to life.

NOTES

1. Mark 16:15. According to Christian interpretation, the term "gospel" means the "good news," which is that Jesus Christ died for the sins of the world, and all who believe in Him will have eternal life.

2. James M. Buckley, *Theory and Practice of Foreign Missions* (New York: Eaton and Mains, 1911), p. 10. The term "Christian missions" implies forms of action put forth in unusual places and among those without the religion of Christ, for the sole purpose of converting non-believers to becoming believers in Christ and members of the Christian religion.

3. Other examples of stranger sub-types include diplomats, businessmen, tourists, guests, military personnel, immigrants, etc.

4. For our purposes, the usage of reference groups means the source of an individual's value or perspectives, as well as a group whose acceptance one seeks, such as family, friends, peers, teachers, and religious leaders. For a fuller discussion of reference groups and the different usages of the term, see Ralph H. Turner's article, "Role-Taking, Role Standpoint, and Reference Group Behavior," *American Journal of Sociology* 61 (January 1956):327-328.

5. Kurt Lang and Gladys Lang, "Collective Dynamics: Process and Form," in *Human Behavior and Social Processes*, ed. Arnold M. Rose (Boston: Houghton Mifflin, 1962), p. 353.

6. The term "conversion" has two biblical connotations. "Conversion" is used in the Old Testament to denote one's change of attitude toward his faith which would lead the individual to a more exacting attitude toward his faith, as with persons who suddenly feel "called" to become a prophet or a religious leader, like Moses. In the New Testament, "conversion" took on the meaning of abandoning one's faith for another, like Paul's drastic transformation on the road to Damascus. It is the New Testament usage of conversion which is the "popular" understanding of the term. The classic psychological definitions and explanations of conversion remain the ones in Edwin Starbuck's work, *Psychology of Religion* (New York: Charles Scribner's Sons, 1900), p. 21, where he defines the term: "conversion stands for the whole series of manifestations just preceding, accompanying, and immediately following the apparently sudden change of character"; in William James', *The Varieties of Religious Experience* (New York: Random House, 1902), p. 186, we find the following statement: "to be converted, to be regenerated, to receive grace, to experience religion, to gain assurance, are so many phrases which denote the process, gradual or sudden, by which a self hitherto divided, and consciously wrong, inferior and unhappy, becomes unified and consciously right, superior and happy, in consequence of its firmer hold upon religious realities. This at least is what conversion signifies in general terms, whether or not we believe that a direct divine operation is needed to bring such a moral change about."

7. Lang and Lang, "Collective Dynamics," p. 354.

8. Tamotsu Shibutani, "Reference Groups and Social Control"; Rose, Human Behavior, p. 142.

9. Terms like "symbolic interaction," "phenomenology," and "ethnomethodology" are a convenient kind of scientific shorthand for the observer to describe complex arrangements and activities in social life, carrying maximum utility for specifying how the actor or observer negotiates everyday behavior. The most extensive discussions of these methodologies are to be found in the following works: Alfred Schutz, *The Phenomenology of the Social World*, trans. George Walsh and Frederick Lehnert (Evanston, Illinois: Northwestern University Press, 1967); *Collected Papers*, Vols. II and III (The Hague: Martinus Nijhoff, 1964 and 1966); Irving Goffman, *Behavior in Public Places: Notes on the Social Organization of Gatherings* (New York: Free Press of Glencoe, 1963); *Encounters: Two Studies in the Sociology of Interaction* (Indianapolis: Bobbs-Merrill, 1961); *Interaction Ritual: Essays on Face-to-Face Behavior* (New York: Doubleday, 1967); *Strategic Interaction* (Philadelphia: University of Pennsylvania, 1969; *The Presentation of Self in Everyday Life* (New York: Doubleday, 1959); Peter Berger and Thomas Luckmann, *The Social Construction of Reality* (New York: Doubleday, 1966); and Harold Garfinkel, *Studies in Ethnomethodology* (Englewood Cliffs, New Jersey: Prentice Hall, 1967). This is not an exhaustive list, but a sample of works in the field.

10. Wolfram Eberhard, *Guilt and Sin in Traditional China* (Berkeley: University of California Press, 1967), p. 18.

11. Max Weber, *The Sociology of Religion*, trans. Ephraim Fischoff (Boston: Beacon Press, 1963), p. xxxvl.

12. Edgar H. Schein, *Coercive Persuasion* (New York: W. W. Norton, 1961), pp. 117–18.

13. Louis Rochet, *Sentences, Maximes et Proverbes Mantchoux et Mongols* (Paris: Maison, 1875), p. 62.

14. Arthur H. Smith, *Chinese Characteristics* (New York: Fleming H. Revell, 1894), pp. 208–9.

15. W. B. Bentley, *Illustrious Chinese Christians* (Ohio: The Standard Publishing Co., 1906), pp. 246–47. See "Reviews or Literary Notices," *The Chinese Recorder* 3 (February 1871):254–55.

16. Richard Terrill Baker, *Ten Thousand Years* (New York: Board of Missions and Church Extension of the Methodist Church, 1947), p. 11.

17. Ibid., p. 19.

18. The etymological derivation of these terms is very interesting and should be noted. See Dr. L. Wieger, S. J., *Chinese Characters* (New York: Dover Publications, 1965), pp. 253, 112, 286, 317, and 231 for further elaboration.

19. L. N. Wheeler, *The Foreigner in China* (Chicago: S. C. Griggs, 1881), pp. 47–48.

20. John Ross, *Mission Methods in Manchuria* (New York: Fleming H. Revell, 1903), pp. 21–22.

21. Arthur F. Glasser, "Success and Failure in the China Mission," *International Reformed Bulletin* 11 (1975):4.

22. Lin Shao-Yang, *A Chinese Appeal Concerning Christian Missions* (New York: G. P. Putnam's Sons, 1911), pp. 67–68.

23. T. O. Beidelman, "Social Theory and Study of Christian Missions In Africa," *Africa* 44 (1974):242.

24. Paul A. Varg, *Missionaries, Chinese, and Diplomats* (Princeton: Princeton University Press, 1958), p. 28. Also, Eberhard's *Guilt and Sin in Traditional China* is an excellent sociological treatment of the Chinese concept of guilt and sin in premodern society. The study is based on Chinese literary documents.

25. Charles Ernest Scott, *China From Within* (New York: Fleming H. Revell, 1917), pp. 136–37.

26. Kenneth Burke refers to the body of religious words used to persuade men towards certain acts as the "rhetoric of religion." There are certain "religious" words which help form the kinds of attitude which prepare the auditor for such acts. "In this sense, the subject of reli-

gious exhortation involves the nature of religion as a rhetoric, as persuasiveness." The "religious" words used by the missionary in his preaching strongly reflected the persuasive determinism of his religion. See Kenneth Burke, *The Rhetoric of Religion* (Boston: Beacon Press, 1961), pp. v–vi. One critic draws the following comparison in regard to the use of religious words and phrases: "The Protestant missionary in China affects to ridicule the practice of the Romanists for their ceremonial use of a dead language, not realising that, by his own ritualistic repetitions, his retention of a religious vocabulary, and his adherence to archaic words and crude and repulsive metaphors in his hymns and prayers, he is making use of methods that do not essentially differ from those of the Romanists." Lin, *A Chinese Appeal*, p. 247.

27. Maurice T. Price, *Christian Missions and Oriental Civilizations* (Shanghai: Privately Printed, 1924), p. 458.

28. Burke, *Rhetoric*, p. v.

29. Elijah C. Bridgman, "Memoir of the Evangelist, Leang Afa," *Missionary Herald* 30 (October 1834):354–55.

30. Scott, *China from Within*, p. 140.

31. J. Campbell Gibson, *Mission Problems and Mission Methods in South China* (New York: Fleming H. Revell, 1901), pp. 151–57.

32. Maurice T. Price, *Christian Missions*, p. 4.

33. W. E. Soothill, *A Typical Mission in China* (New York: Fleming H. Revell, 1906), p. 94.

34. Yan Phou Lee, *When I Was a Boy in China* (Boston: Lothrop, Lee & Shepard, 1887), p. 81.

35. Price, *Christian Missions*, p. 290.

36. Adrian Arthur Bennett, "Missionary Journalism in 19th-Century China: Young J. Allen and the Early Wan-kuo-king-pao," Diss. University of California 1971, p. 146.

37. Ibid., p. 147.

38. Ibid., p. 148.

39. Ibid., p. 149.

40. Price, *Christian Missions*, pp. 305–6. Also, for a fuller discussion of religious needs among the non-privileged class, see Max Weber, *The Sociology of Religion*, pp. 95–117.

41. "The Religion of China," *Missionary Advocate* 3 (April 1847):1.

42. Margaret E. Burton, *Notable Women of Modern China* (New York: Fleming H. Revell, 1912), p. 43. In describing the Chinese attraction to Christianity, the World Missionary Commission reports: "The brotherhood of man always proves attractive. The sympathy, friendliness, and kindliness of Christianity tend to win those who have never been in such an atmosphere. Patience, love and sympathy are the three great elements of the Gospel which reach the Chinese heart. . . . A Chinese pastor writes: 'The element in the Christian Gospel which possesses the greatest appeal is its manifestations of the spirit of love. It is this spirit appearing in the lives of Christians in the form of mutual sympathy and helpfulness in the opening of hospitals, schools, and other philanthropic agencies, which above all others appeals to the people.' " *World Missionary Commission* 4, p. 154.

43. Lang and Lang, "Collective Dynamics," p. 354.

44. Soothill, *A Typical Mission*, p. 101.

45. Arthur H. Smith, "The Best Method of Presenting the Gospel to the Chinese," *The Chinese Recorder* 14 (September-October 1883):395.

46. Bennett, "Missionary Journalism," p. 131.

47. By "Waterford," How Can a Preacher of Christianity to Chinese Heathens Adapt His Message to His Hearers?" *The Chinese Recorder* 15 (November-December 1884):423.

48. Alexander Williamson, "On the Need of Concise Historical, Geographical, Ethnological and Philological Notes," *Records of the General Conference of the Protestant Missionaries of China* (Shanghai: American Presbyterian Mission Press, 1890), p. 106.

49. Bennett, "Missionary Journalism," p. 150.

50. Ibid., p. 151.

51. Ibid., p. 152.

52. See *Records of the General Conference of the Protestant Missionaries of China* (Shanghai: Presbyterian Mission Press, 1878 and 1890); held in 1877 and 1890, hereafter referred to as *Records of the General Conference.*

53. Rev. R. H. Graves, "On Some Theological Terms," *The Chinese Recorder* 15 (November-December, 1884):425.

54. Starbuck, *Psychology of Religion*, p. 64.

55. Charles A. Robinson, *History of Christian Missions* (Edinburgh: T. & T. Clark, 1915), p. 22.

56. William A. Brown, *Modern Missions in the Far East* (New York: Union Theological Seminary, 1917), pp. 50-51.

57. Timothy Richard, *Forty-five Years in China, Reminiscences* (New York: Frederick A. Stokes, 1916), pp. 97-98.

58. Soothill, *A Typical Mission*, p. 117.

59. Bentley, *Illustrious Chinese Christians*, pp. 199-201.

60. The idea of commitment, says Strauss, "in some acts may be slight, for one's action may be provisional, forced, or indifferently valued; but insofar as a line of action is assessed highly, then involvement is strong. . . . Everyone has had the experience of using some kind of action as a means for a purpose, and then growing so interested in or fascinated with the means that it became of more concern than the original end." See Anselm L. Strauss, *Mirrors and Masks: The Search for Identity* (Glencoe, Illinois: The Free Press of Glencoe, 1959), p. 40.

61. Soothill, *A Typical Mission*, pp. 59-60.

62. Price, *Christian Missions*, p. 375.

63. Edward A. Lawrence, *Modern Missions in the East* (New York: Harper & Bros., 1897), p. 69.

64. Lin, *A Chinese Appeal*, pp. 50-51.

65. Soothill's general treatment of 300 to 400 opium refugees, he describes as "spartan": "Our treatment was as much moral as physical, for, recognizing the hopelessness of permanently liberating these men—whose will power had been so severely shaken by indulgence in so demoralizing a habit—except by the aid of a power external to ourselves, earnest prayer was daily offered, in which they all joined. It was, moreover, expressly urged upon them that the only certain cure was a change of heart, of life, and of companionship, which could only be obtained through Jesus Christ and His Church." See Soothill, *A Typical Mission*, pp. 59-60.

66. Richard, *Forty-five Years in China*, p. 151.

67. "Missionary Statistics of the Fuhkien Province," *Missionary Review* 1 (January-February 1878):85.

68. Rev. T. P. Crawford, "Advantages and Disadvantages of the Employment of Native Assistants," *Records of the General Conference*, 1877, p. 325.

69. Ibid., p. 326

70. Price, *Christian Missions*, p. 277.

71. Mr. Dodds, "China," *Missionary Advocate* 19 (October 1863):49.

72. Rev. N. Sites, "Advantages and Disadvantages of the Employment of Native Assistants," *Records of the General Conference, 1877*, p. 331. The Reverend J. R. Goddard expressed his feelings concerning this problem in the following statement: " 'How much a month do you receive for adopting this religion?' is the question most frequently asked of Chinese Christians. How many offer themselves for membership with this object in view is too well known to all missionary workers, and how many are received into our churches on a fair profession, yet secretly cherishing the hope of employment as their chief motives. . . . So when the question comes up, as it often will, between employing a Christian or a heathen in work for the mission (household servants, workmen employed in erecting, repairing, or furnishing mission houses, chapels, schools, and hospitals, teachers, assistants in hospitals, workmen in printing

offices, boatmen, etc.), or for ourselves personally, we are not free, we cannot be free. . . . Because the one is a fellow Christian, a member of the same great family, we are bound to have special consideration for him." See J. R. Goddard, "Employment of Natives in Missionary Work," *The Missionary Recorder* 16 (September 1885):342–45.

73. Sites, "Advantages and Disadvantages," p. 331.

74. Ibid., p. 335.

75. Rev. R. H. Graves, "To the Progress of the Gospel," *The Chinese Recorder* 15 (May-June 1884):172–73.

76. Gibson, *Mission Problems*, p. 296.

77. *World Missionary Conference* II, p. 89.

78. Ibid., p. 105.

79. Rev. J. A. Leyenberger, "The Treaty Rights of Native Christians, and the Duty of Missionaries in Regard to Their Vindication," *Records of the General Conference, 1877*, p. 411.

80. *World Missionary Conference*, III, pp. 93–94.

81. Irwin Hyatt, Jr., *Our Ordered Lives Confess* (Cambridge: Harvard University Press, 1976), p. 47. A native informant in one of the well-known Chinese cities reported to Price: "Miss _____ had a school here where they taught English and foreign branches. Chinese came for that. When the school dropped English and cut down the number of foreign subjects taught, establishing a normal school taught in Chinese, the pupils lesssened. The attendance decreased greatly. For the Chinese have their own schools to teach Chinese language, history, etc., and think their own normal schools are much better for that than foreigners' normal schools." Apparently this statement, reports Price, was verified by foreigners in the city. See Maurice Price, *Christian Missions*, p. 300.

82. Rev. C. W. Mateer, "How May Educational Work Be Made Most to Advance the Cause of Christianity in China?" *Records of the General Conference 1890*, p. 459.

83. *World Missionary Conference*, III, p. 74.

84. Miss Hattie Noyes, "Girls' Schools," *Records of the General Conference 1890*, p. 216.

85. Mary Ninde Gamewell, *Ming-Kwong "City of the Morning Light"* (Massachusetts: The Central Committee of the United Study of Foreign Missions, 1924), p. 57.

86. I. Hyatt, Jr., *Our Ordered Lives*, pp. 81–84.

87. Rev. R. S. Maclay, *Life Among the Chinese* (New York: Carlton & Porter, 1861), pp. 250–51.

88. W. A. P. Martin, "The Worship of Ancestors—A Plea for Toleration," *Records of the General Conference 1890*, pp. 619–31. Also see Rev. H. Blodget's article, "The Attitude of Christianity Toward Ancestral Worship," Ibid., pp. 631–59.

89. Martin, "Worship of Ancestors," p. 659.

90. Scott, China From Within, pp. 174–76.

91. Ibid., pp. 180–82.

92. Johan Warneck, *The Living Forces of the Gospel, the Experiences of a Missionary in Animistic Heathendom* (Edinburgh: Oliphant, n.d.), pp. 138–39.

93. Rev. Frank Ohlinger, "How Far Should Christians Be Required to Abandon Native Customs," *Records of the General Conference, 1890*, p. 604.

94. *World Missionary Conference*, II, pp. 58–59.

95. Peter McHugh, "Social Disintegration as a Requisite of Resocialization," *Social Forces* 44 (March 1966):355–63.

96. Bentley, *Illustrious Chinese Christians*, pp. 62–63.

97. Ibid., pp. 76–86.

98. See Edgar H. Schein, *Coercive Persuasion*, pp. 117–39, for a discussion of a model for the analysis of coercive persuasion which delineates three stages—"unfreezing, changing, and refreezing"—for the process of conversion. I have selected Schein's model from a variety of

other models because it is a useful schema in my particular approach to the process of religious conversion.

99. S. M. Sites, *Nathan Sites* (New York: Fleming H. Revell, 1912), p. 239.

100. Price, *Christian Missions*, p. 340.

101. Bentley, *Illustrious Chinese Christians*, pp. 181–83.

102. Goffman, *Behavior in Public Places*, pp. 112–13.

103. Bentley, *Illustrious Chinese Christians*, pp. 91–92.

104. Ross, *Mission Methods*, pp. 77–78.

105. Schein, *Coercive Persuasion*, p. 136.

106. Starbuck, *Psychology of Religion*, p. 360.

107. "China," *The Chinese Recorder* 51 (March 1910):209. Rev. J. L. Nevius reported that " information attained by use of Record Book, and assistance of the leaders and helpers, and information obtained from other sources," help identified backsliders. "Those excommunicated for reasons other than scandalous offenses is comparatively small. As many as eighty per cent of these are cases of gradual and at last complete neglect of Christian duties, commencing with giving up Bible study, disregard of the Sabbath, and neglect of public worship. It now appears that most of these persons entered the Church without a clear apprehension of what Christianity, theoretical and practical, is. Their motives seem to have been obtaining a place as a preacher or servant, or pecuniary and in other ways, or getting help in lawsuits actual or anticipated." See Rev. J. L. Nevius, "Methods of Mission Work, Letter V," *The Chinese Recorder* 17 (March 1886):107.

108. Robert N. Cust, *Missionary Methods* (London: Luzac, 1894), p. 83.

109. *World Missionary Conference*, II, p. 228.

110. Soothill, *A Typical Mission*, pp. 103–5.

111. Starbuck, *Psychology of Religion*, p. 354.

4 THE TAIWANESE *TANG-KI*: THE SHAMAN AS COMMUNITY HEALER AND PROTECTOR

Richard C. Kagan and Anna Wasescha

An enormous body of literature discusses the political repression of the Taiwanese under their Qing dynasty masters who ruled from Beijing, under the Japanese who ruled from Tokyo (1895–1945), and under the recent refugees from the Mainland of China (called Mainlanders) who have ruled from Taibei with the claim that it is the capital of all China. The details of this repression are often circumscribed in order to draw even greater attention to economic development under Liu Mingquan of the Qing, the provincial military governors of the Japanese Empire, and the KMT's enlightened economic policies and land reforms of the last thirty years. American scholars and Chinese government officials often use the indisputable fact that the Taiwanese (a population of 14 million out of a total of 17 million) have made considerable economic advances to excuse their conspicuous lack of political and cultural power. Expensive cars, homes, clothes, and entertainment, and the large quantity of costly imports do attest to a high standard of living in Taiwan. The drawbacks to rapid industrialization and careless investment are apparent, however, in the frantic and unnecessarily excessive construction projects, the unregulated nuclear power plants, the high levels of pollution, and the inadequate living conditions of the peasants and working class.

Standing somewhere between the political repression and the economic advantages is the prominent figure of the shaman. Originally coming from southeast China in the early seventeenth century migrations to Taiwan, shamans carried with them the powerful traditions of local political influence and authority.[1] They continue to exist and to hold positions of power and popularity to this day. During the nineteenth and twentieth centuries, while the Taiwanese were being both colonized and industrialized, the shaman's role as protector of the native population took on an all-embracing definition. Previously, the shaman was restricted to the local god of his or her own community. This god was fixed in a locale. Today, shaman masters are itinerant—establishing their temples and disciples throughout the island, under government regulation.

That shamanism in Taiwan is a strong and vital cultural force, with political as well as medical significance, is beyond dispute. That it has greatly increased its appeal since the economic dislocations of the 1960's and 70's is commonly accepted. Its popularity is not because it is a vestige of an antique culture. Shamans are a liaison between the pantheon of gods with their supporting myths and the world of humans with their supporting culture. By linking daily experience to myths and traditions, they provide a perspective on the events of the world. They are a subversive force in a colonized nation like Taiwan because the viewpoint they provide ignores the new set of myths imported by the ruling class. (The two most hypocritical myths from the Taiwanese point of view are (1) that the Nationalists will retake the Mainland; and (2) that the Nationalists uphold the real Chinese civilization of Confucianism.) Thus the political influence the shamans garner by restoring status to the oppressed erodes the power of the KMT. This process of erosion is unintelligible to the KMT elite, who do not subscribe to the old myths. Unwilling to understand and incorporate the methods of the shamans, the new rulers of the island cannot begin to build credibility in their own unifying principles.

Any culture has at its heart myths and archetypes which "are the deepest patterns of psychic functioning."[2] The shaman's primary approach to health care is psychic. On an individual level, that approach is most easily defined by the negative term, non-allopathic. On a collective level, in view of the organized network of shamans and their itinerant lifestyles, the shaman's psychic approach to healing is a strong defense of Taiwanese culture. The greater the KMT attack on the native culture, the greater is the shaman's duty to enhance lost status by revivifying the archetypes.

Because shamanism has been covered up by the Nationalists and suffered from considerable suppression under the Japanese, little documentation of their activities has been published. Suppression of this information has made analysis of their impact on the health of the Taiwanese very difficult.

The Japanese and the Mainlanders attacked the health of Taiwanese society by imposing on it a social order devoted to production, profit, and technology. The resulting damages to the human affairs of the Taiwanese were, in the course of this development, covered over or deliberately excised by the ruling classes. The covering over and excising effort engineered by the occupiers had to be widespread because their attack had been directed at the organizing principles of Taiwanese society, the culture, family unit, and economy. Under Nationalist rule, the Taiwanese language was prohibited in the schools, the community unit deteriorated severely, reported cases of sickness tied directly to polluted air, soil, and water were occurring with alarming frequency, labor conditions were substandard, the press was controlled, and government elections were either suspended or carefully manipulated.

It is significant that the occupying forces utilized allopathic (e.g., drugs and surgery) methods of dealing with human maladies. Shamans, who are by definition non-allopathic, seem to have maintained their sphere of influence by dogged loyalty to their "non-professional" and holistic methods. As healers, shamans take into account everything about and around a sick person—there are no artificial boundaries between an individual and the surrounding universe. Shamans include rather than exclude. Their time is cyclical rather than linear, and their goals are qualitative rather than quantitative. Their world view is self-assuredly independent of and often, coincidentally, diametrically opposed to that of the Mainlander political elite. An examination of the persistent influence of shamans in the community can be a lens through which one can view the qualities and conditions of the Taiwanese struggle for cultural integrity and power.

The 1970's in Taiwan witnessed spectacular political and economic developments. Politically a popular opposition movement emerged which expressed itself in a democratic opposition party. The leaders of this movement were arrested and given long sentences. Internationally, America recognized Beijing as the capital of all China. The resulting process of normalization of relations between the United States and China left Taiwan isolated and its rulers without much hope for a successful reconquest of the Mainland. Economically, however, Taiwan accelerated its success by becoming a major exporter of light industrial goods. Caught between the scissors of political repression (Taiwan is still in a state of martial law) and economic growth, the Taiwanese began to develop their own native response.

During the last decade, shamanistic phenomena have become a major public force in Taiwan. Their activities are extravagant and highly visible. Truckloads of shamans, apprentices, and sympathizers follow the contours of the island from town to town, spending a day in each area. Week-long festivals are staged, during which fully outfitted boats are blessed and dispatched to the underworld by setting them on fire. The costs of these festivals are staggering—the burning of one boat will cost over $25,000 (U.S.). On an individual level, shamans are relied upon for problems associated with health, fate, advice on marriage and business, births, etc.[3]

Even wills are redrawn. For example, one case involved the brother of the deceased. He was not at all happy with the property settlement. He hired a shaman to communicate with his brother's spirit. The spirit amended the will to give the brother a larger share of the inheritance. This was accepted by the whole family. The brother's commitment to this process is revealed by the fact that he lives in Indiana and had to fly back to Taiwan for the spiritual seance. He returned home feeling that it had been a very profitable trip.[4]

No population survey has been made of shamans. The estimate is that 1.5 out of a thousand Taiwanese act as full time shamans. At a minimum level, shamans exist in a ratio of one per two thousand of the rural population, and triple that number in the fishing villages. In addition to their growing numbers is the centralization and organization of new cults. This figure would expand if apprentices and part-time shamans were included. There are also many people who claim that they could be shamans, but have resisted the urge to perform.

The government does have a bureau in Tainan which regulates the two hundred established temples where shamans perform. However, there are many temples which are not official.

One temple's description exemplifies the vitality and integration of the shaman rituals in Taiwanese contemporary life. Hell's Temple is located on a major "religious" street in Tainan. Up and down the street are stores that sell shaman devices—e.g., nail balls, swords, clubs with spikes. Hell's Temple is known for contacting the god of hell. It houses other gods as well, but its main function is to visit souls in hell. These spirit journeys to Hades are routinely convened during the morning hours from nine to eleven daily. On three days of the month large festivals occur when the ceremonies will last all day.

Walking down the street one comes first upon the smell of incense and smoke. The temple itself is large, dark, and very noisy. Attached to the main hall are two wings of small halls and courtyards and a back room. They are always filled with people, offerings of food, small and large statues, eighteen-inch paper cuts of spirit buildings, and a tremendous amount of smoke.

The rituals are performed by Taoist priests and *tang-ki*.* The priests command approximately $140 (U.S.) for a family ceremony. The *tang-ki* are hired only when the family wishes to speak with a deceased member. The *tang-ki* charge for services is probably quite minimal, but the prices were not available.

The seance begins with the priest chanting, ringing a bell, and burning paper charms. During the climax of the ritual a whip or sword might be used. Fruit offerings and paper buildings which represent the spirit's domicile in hell are placed on large tables. The ritual lasts fifteen to twenty minutes.

---

*The Taoist priest is involved in the institutional and textual area of the orthodox religion. The priesthood often enters into a symbiotic relationship with folk religions. Taoism and Buddhism often try to harness the magical and spontaneous nature of the folk religion. In a Taoist temple the priest will supervise and sometimes regulate the shaman's activities. The religious and power relationship between the two groups will not be discussed in this paper.

When people wish to talk to dead relatives, a *tang-ki* will quickly become possessed. The possession is fairly dramatic. Of the ten *tang-ki* observed in Hell's Temple in the summer of 1978, all but one were female. All the Taoist priests were male.

Once the *tang-ki* becomes possessed, a sword is passed to her. She performs a few ritualized dance steps in accepting the sword. However, the ritual may be different each time, depending on the individuals involved. In one case, the *tang-ki*, the priest, and the family circled the table in a continuous line, chanting and lighting firecrackers. To communicate with the dead, family members ask questions or throw divining blocks, and eventually the *tang-ki* will take the sword and slash the paper building, thus freeing the dead person's soul from hell.

At the end of the ceremony the tables are cleared and the crowd slowly disperses. Most of the *tang-ki* come out of possession as soon as they are no longer needed, but a few will remain in a state of trance after the ceremony is over and conduct business in one of the side rooms, offering advice and answering questions. There are perhaps five or six ceremonies going on at the same time.

THE WEN AND WU SHAMANS OF TAIWAN

There are two classes of *tang-ki* that are quite distinct: the scholar (*wen*) and the warrior (*wu*). The scholar, or literary *tang-ki*, resorts to writing his answers in sand or in the air. Often he will work with a spirit writing cult. The warrior has a wide array of weapons which are used to mortify the flesh. The blood from the wounds that are inflicted is considered to be the blood of the spirit whom the *tang-ki* has captured in his own body. The blood is mixed with the ashes of incense and wine, and drunk by the patient.

The following accounts of the activities of *wen* and *wu* shamans in Taiwan were written following a field study in 1978.[5] These descriptions provide the documentation for the analysis of the socio-political significance of the shamans at the conclusion of this article. Although these descriptions are typical, the reader must be aware that one person can perform in both *wen* and *wu* roles. Not only are the divisions between the categories blurred, but the division between shaman mediums and other mediums (e.g., those in spirit writing cults) is unclear.

The *Tang-ki* as Scholar

The Ritual   Mr. Zhou is thirty five years old and has been a *tang-ki* since 1973. He was a successful and prosperous vegetable vendor before his conversion. One day he suddenly became possessed. This was followed by a series of dreams that lasted for two weeks. In these dreams the god of heaven gave him his mission and described the rituals. Mr. Zhou was informed of his duties and told why he was selected to become a *tang-ki*. His mission was to help god's people. He had been chosen to help his people. Mainly he was to teach them to be good and to get along with one another. He projected a great warmth: he had a good sense of humor and was always smiling. He appeared to be a jovial and simple man. He always made two comments to his clients, irrespective of their problem: "It's OK, it's all right," and "Don't worry, I will help you." He was very reassuring and always optimistic.

Mr. Zhou's other dreams were classical shaman dreams of journeys and trances. In one dream, the god of heaven came to him on a white horse and carried him to a river. On the other side of the river was heaven. In another dream he met Jesus. After the initial two weeks of dreams, he became a full-time *tang-ki*. When in his normal state, he did not claim any special knowledge. But while in a trance, he answered questions swiftly and with sure knowledge about religious subjects and the nature of the spirits.

Usually people come to Mr. Zhou's building at 3:00 in the afternoon. When enough people show up he induces his trance. Hanging on the walls of his building are several pictures and plaques expressing thanks for his cures and honoring him as a great *tang-ki*. A certificate from the private Taoist Temple Association is also on the wall. Many statues of gods stand throughout the temple.

Mr. Zhou's gods are the five kings: Li, Wu, Zhi, Fan, and Zhu. He is usually possessed by one of these five gods. Other gods that possess him are Dong Yue Da Ti (Hell's god) and the Buddhist Guan Yin (Goddess of Mercy).

During trance Mr. Zhou usually sits in shorts and a teeshirt at his table in front of the altar. The ceremony begins when his leg starts to shake, as if in a muscle spasm. He clears his throat with loud rasping noises and then makes a swishing sound. Periodically he shakes his head, and frequently he drops spittle to the floor.

When he is fully in a trance, his male assistant (*dou-tau*) hands Mr. Zhou a small glass of tea made from blessed water (water that had been placed before the statue of one of the gods) and the ashes of a burned charm. He drinks the tea, much of which dribbles down his chin. The *dou-tau* then wipes him clean. He drinks tea several times throughout the afternoon in a similar fashion. At the end of the induction, Mr. Zhou slams his fist on the table and announces to the crowd which god he is.

During one visit he was possessed solely by the "little prince," or the youngest of the Wang Yieie. His voice changed as he spoke into a very low, stern, scholarly and authoritative manner. His discourses were punctuated with the slamming of his fist on the table. He did not move from the bench until all his clients were gone.

The usual procedure for asking questions involves filling out birthdate and name, and giving them to the *dou-tau*. The assistant then calls upon people to discuss their problems with Mr. Zhou. Each questioner shows his respect to the god with a small bow and proceeds to discuss his or her problems. Mr. Zhou tends to be hard to understand when he speaks, and the *dou-tau* helps when necessary. Problems are usually written on a charm. Mr. Zhou writes his charms on a yellow piece of paper one by four inches. He uses a brush and writes one or two characters on the paper in imperial red ink. The characters are indecipherable. Mr. Zhou writes the charms with a flourish, using his brush like a conductor conducting an orchestra, slamming the brush across the charms, one after the other, while the *dou-tau* pulls the paper out as fast as Mr. Zhou slams his brush down. Instructions are given for each charm and how it should be used. They might be burned, used for tea, or carried on the person.

Once four or five people arrive, the session begins. About ten to twenty clients (honorable guests) are seen every day. Others simply wander in over a two or three-hour period. The questions put to Mr. Zhou are audible to all present. Most of the clients are female.

During the field study, sessions with fourteen of Mr. Zhou's clients were recorded. One woman refused to be recorded, even after the gods said that it would be all right to do so. She was a woman who was middle-aged and still unmarried. Her reluctance to have her session recorded may have been due to the stigma she felt was attached to her situation as an old maid. The edited transcript of each session is presented below, followed by a few summary comments.

> 1) The problem is that the daughter of this woman argues with her a lot and also has a bad temper.
>
> Answer: "It's OK, it's OK. She is in a bad time (in terms of fate). Mothers should forgive their daughters. Don't blame her. When the dark days pass everthing will be all right. To forgive is the mother's duty."
>
> The next problem is that the woman has lost money from the bank. She thinks someone stole it from the bank and she wants to know where to get it back.
>
> Answer: "This is not my job. I am not a policeman. See the police and I will help them. The thief must be punished. Don't worry, take this charm and burn it in your house. I will help the policeman. (Either he or the woman knows the name of the thief.) We cannot speak behind someone else's back, so I will help the police. Don't worry."
>
> 2) Someone has died and this woman wants to know if she should hire priests to do a ritual for the deceased.
>
> Answer: "This person is dead so don't spend a lot of money to do this."

She answers that the man has been dead for over a year and no ritual has been done and she wants to do something.

Answer (he writes four charms): "On the day of the death burn these four charms in the East, West, South, and North but don't do the elaborate rituals." (He gives the right time and date and writes another charm that should be burned on the grave.)

She works for a rich family, of which the dead man is a member.

"You are very nice to your friends; to travel and help solve problems for others is very good."

She replies that she has worked for them for 10 years.

"When the time comes I will be there."

She asks if they need to burn incense for him.

"No. They can't see me but I'll be there. I'll keep my word."

3) This woman is worried about her son, who is in the military. She wants to keep him safe.

Answer: "This is a good thing. It is for the country that he joins and that is good. I will help." (He gives her two charms for her son to carry on him.)

4) This woman has a sore throat and can't sleep. (Serious.)

Answer: "For this kind of thing you need a doctor. It is not my job. (He gives her five charms.) I will help the doctor. Burn the charm, put it in water and drink it. I will help the doctor to help you, then you will be alright."

5) This woman has a friend who she thinks is sick. The friend has a headache, bad temper, and quarrels with her mother-in-law.

Answer: "She is not a good woman. She can't argue with the older ones. She shouldn't argue with her mother or father. You should try to get the woman to say sorry to her mother-in-law."

The woman says that maybe the mother-in-law has done the wrong.

Answer: "Mothers and fathers need respect even if they are wrong. (He gives her eight charms.) Burn these charms around her body. I will be in her mind to remind her not to argue. (For the bad temper he gives her three other charms to drink.) Because the woman is in a big family and has to work hard, I will help her. This drink will get rid of her headache."

6) This woman's child is sick and after going to a physician there is still no improvement.

Answer: (He gives her five charms.) "Hang these charms on the baby for seven days and keep using the drugs and medicines from the doctor."

7) This woman's baby cries all night.

Answer: "(He gives her nine charms.) The baby should drink three for each of three days and hang five on the baby."

The woman says that the baby has felt tired for several days and has a fever. She feels bad about this.

"Go to the doctor with this kind of thing. I will help."

8) This woman is here for her brother's son who is 19 years old. He was in a car accident and suffered a broken leg. An operation was performed months ago but he still feels pain.

Answer: "This is because of bad luck. (The fate for the year is bad.) So bring him here tomorrow. (He writes charms.) Write his address on the charms and burn them here in the temple now. (He will attempt to change the young man's fate.) It is not because of the doctors that the operation did not work. He must trust the doctors. It is because of his bad fate. I will help him. Keep using the drugs and don't complain about the doctors."

9) This woman's husband has a sore throat and cough.

Answer: "(He writes three charms.) Burn these, put them in water and mix with honey and have him drink it."

10) This woman's son lost some money doing business with some friends.

Answer: "There are other places to take care of this. We have law in this country. If something is wrong there are those who are to deal with it. (He writes her charms.) Write the man's address on it and burn it in this temple. I will make the one who did him wrong change his mind. (The son's friend cheated him.) Friends would not let this happen. They should not wreck a friendship."

The woman criticizes her son's friend.

Answer: "You talk a lot but you are not perfect. Maybe that person is in bad times (bad fate) and needed the money. You should forgive him and do good. I like those who do good. If you go to court it is not good, as it will break a friendship."

11) This young man wishes to know his fate.

Answer: "Young man are you learning of Buddhism, Taoism, and Confucius and you ask me of these things. It is beyond my ability. If you want to discuss with me, that is alright. I am a god, but if I do anything wrong with people you should forgive me."

Young Man: "I want to know if I should go into business or school?"

Answer: "I haven't learned much. I have orders from the king of heaven to help the people solve their problems. I have been here a few years to help people and if I make mistakes you should forgive me."

Young Man: "Please don't say that. You are a god. I just want to know which is better."

Answer: "According to your fate you were born in the time of the five dragons. You must be the second son."

Young Man: "No. The first."

Answer: "If you are the eldest then you have three fires in your fate. Thus you should stay away from fires. You should live at home to help your family."

Young Man: "What is good for me; to read or do business?"

Answer: "According to your fate you should do something for the people."

Dou-tau: "Keep reading."

Young Man: "Is it good to go abroad?"

Answer: "According to your fate you can go anywhere."

12) This woman's leg hurts because of an accident.

Answer: "You are over 60 years old and getting older. To go to the doctor is useless. It is not easy because you are old. I will write you two charms. I will help you and your doctor to cure you. It is not that easy to recover when you are old."

The woman is also worried because her son-in-law is going into business.

Answer: "If he works hard he won't have to worry about anything. (He writes three charms.) Use one a day and burn around your son's body. When he has trouble or a problem he will meet someone who will help him. Tell your son when he does anything he should think of doing good. Patience, kindliness, and friendliness are virtues to use with people. Don't get into trouble with people. (He gives six charms for six days to be burned and mixed in water and the son should wash his face with it.) It will help him show his face to itself. It will help him in his relationships with everyone."

13) This woman wants to know the fate of her past because she has marriage problems.

Answer: "(He burns three charms around her body and one to burn and drop into an urn of water.) Face the water three times and I will see your past. (He burns a charm around himself.) I see a lily flower. It is you before you were born. It is in the East Sea. On the 13th of August a couple of lovers are sitting near you and you don't like that. So you drown them in anger. You owe two human lives. When you were re-born you were born in the North-East in a family named Chen. You had three brothers and two sisters. When you were 46 years old you became a nun at a temple and never married. You became the head of that temple. On the 3rd of March you went South to beg money to rebuild your temple. On that afternoon you cross a bamboo bridge and fall off it into the river. You float to the South-East where you had previously been the lily flower. There you meet the Dragon King of the Thousand Seas (a god) and you tell the god that you worship Buddha and wish to build a temple for him. You tell him that you want to be-come a Buddha. The Dragon King says "you are not a lotus, you are only a lily. You cannot become a buddha." Now, you are reincarnated and the oldest child in your family and you still owe two lives and your life is just like a lily. You have married early. Your problem now is to split with your husband because you owe two lovers' lives. At mid-night you can have the shadow of your husband but you cannot touch his body. Don't worry about that. You have to do good. The Dragon King will then let you be a good lily in the South Sea."

Woman: "Can I still have my husband?"

Answer: "No. You can just have his shadow but not his body. When you lie on your bed and you close your eyes you will think of your hus-band."

Woman: "Is there any way to have my husband?"

Answer: "Impossible, because you owe two lovers' lives."

14) This woman has headaches.

Answer: "It is OK. You are not sick. It is because of hot weather, hard work. Use these charms (writes three) to drink and burn these five out-side your front gate."

Mr. Zhou stresses forgiveness and compassion. In the first instance above he tells the mother that it is her duty to forgive. He attempts to keep the mother-daughter relationship harmonious. He forecasts that the prob-lem will get better, which gives some hope to the mother and helps her through the problem. He also stresses using the appropriate channels to han-dle problems (1, 4, 7, 10), i.e., that some things are not his job. Yet after such admonishment he offers support. He doesn't stress rituals (2) or spending a lot of money on the dead, and so is quite the opposite of the Taoist priests. He always praises people for doing good and scolds them for not doing good. He reduces peoples' anxiety by reassuring them that he will help, or by giving them a charm to carry. As in (3), he helps people feel good about what has taken place, instead of dwelling on the negative aspect of the situation.

In dealing with serious physical problems, as in (4), he does send his clients to doctors and helps correct a problem most uneducated people have when using modern medicines, i.e., not using the medicine the way the doctor tells them (4, 6, 7, 8, 12). When he feels that the problem is mild he gives his own remedy (9, 14). On other occasions, he tells his clients to go to the doctor and gives them a charm or remedy of his own to help reduce anxiety.

In case five, he is very perceptive and effective in remedying the situation. In this case and in several others he puts the responsibility on the questioner to remedy the situation, even if it is not the client's own problem. He attempts to convince the person in this situation to stop creating the problem, by saying that the old ones need respect and that it is the daughter's duty to offer it. He promotes a reconciliation. That is the first step in rectifying a bad relationship.

Maintaining harmonious social relationships is the key to health (10). The virtues to strive for are (12) patience, kindliness, and friendliness. Where the relationship is irrevocably sundered (13: "Impossible!"), the explanation is made palatable by couching it in a comforting and unquestionable world of myth and legend.

The Psycho-social Significance   The above list and summary of the diagnoses vividly portray three prominent characteristics of shamans: The first is that the shaman is often ambiguous but optimistic in his advice. He warns about the use of courts, yet offers his support when the case is taken to court (1, 10). The young man (11) who wanted to know his fate was seemingly confused by the nebulous and even inappropriate answers. But this lack of precision is significant. It adds strength to the real purpose of the shaman. He is primarily concerned with conveying a message through intuitive and spiritual channels. The materialistic world and the requirements of specificity are unimportant in the limitless world of spiritual awareness. Whereas many of the questions above, and in general, deal with issues that are potentially tragic, the shaman's answers always provide reassurance and faith in a happy resolution. The contradictions and vagueness of the diagnosis engage the clients' imagination in an optimistic and accepting view of his or her own fate.

The second characteristic is that the shaman diagnoses an illness by observing an illness as a cultural-social problem. In some cases where the patient is absent or even dead, the *tang-ki* only hears the circumstances and is still able to discern the cause and to prescribe a treatment. In contrast to Western-trained medical doctors' concentration on specifics, shamans ignore symptoms.

> Treatment of symptoms, however sophisticated, focuses patients' attention on symptoms, thus reinforcing the anxiety and other negative feelings that helped produce the symptoms in the first place. An important

first step in correct treatment is to distract the patient from the sensible evidence of his negative condition. Witch doctors and medicine men . . . are very adept at this sort of distraction; whether they understand it or not, their elaborate dances and rituals, independent of their content, serve to get the attention of patients away from their symptoms, thus greatly increasing the likelihood that healing will occur.[6]

The Taiwanese patient is suspicious of the Western doctor who ignores the cultural and psychological milieu of the client. They feel that

. . . Ordinary doctors are forced to rely on other techniques besides just looking at the patient. [They neglect the patient by becoming involved in] feeling the pulse or listening through a stethoscope. Some . . . were quite scornful of doctors who used stethoscopes because their reliance on an instrument clearly indicated they had less native ability to diagnose the illness. Gods, however, need only look, and require no other technique.[7]

The third charactistic is that the shaman addresses all issues from medical problems, to social problems, to matters of fate as singular manifestations of the client's psycho-social imbalance. His status as an omniscient and omnipotent healer reinforces his effectiveness in the community [as a healer of individuals (explicit care of the physical and mental conditions) and as a guardian of society (implicit protection of the myths and archetypes)].

In summary, these are the three significant characteristics of shamans: their vague but optimistic acceptance of fate, their imagining of health as something larger than the elimination of a symptom in an individual, and their view of the patient as one who possesses whatever is necessary to restore health. The first characteristic is important because it expresses the values of integration and wholeness. Those are the familiar alter-egos reason and intuition. The second and third characteristics represent the complexity of analyzing the psycho-social significance of shamans, particularly from a vantage point outside the language and culture. Clearly, shamanism in Taiwan behaves as though the individual is within the society and the society is within the individual. Carl Jung believed that each individual is "a field of internal personal relationships, an interior commune, a body politic."[8] Jung personified internal forces. He called them Shadow, Anima, Ego, Self, and so on. He set about explaining mental health in terms of the psychodramatics of these personalities. These internalized personifications are concepts imported from the vocabularies of history, philosophy, and political science. The visions of integration and wholeness detailed in the previous accounts of shaman activity show how shamans are able to transcend ordinary perception of trouble or illness and unite, through ritual and tradition, the individual's internal cast and the individual with the external cast. As this unity is an attitude, a metaphysical, and a culturally-bound experience, it is the civilized territory of the healers and the believers. By its nature, it does not yield easily to exploration or explanation.

The shaman activity "works" for the believers and the healers, and that the numbers for whom it works are increasing, is significant. From that increase alone, in the face of the "miracles" of twentieth-century capitalist, secular, industrial development, one can infer that the basic human needs for health and security are not being met by the government on Taiwan.

The Warrior *Tang-ki*

The Healing Ritual Mr. Cun is a warrior (*wu*) shaman. He specializes in self-flagellation. Among his weapons are swords, nail-balls, swordfish blades, axes, a club with diamond-shaped blades, chairs covered with spikes, and different sized needles. Mr. Cun's fame stems from the fact that he has "the largest needle on the island." It measures over five feet in length, and is pushed through his cheeks and across his tongue. He can walk with it for several hours. Other *wu* shamans use needles to show the power they have over their god. They do this by pushing various-sized brass needles through soft fleshy parts of their body.

Mr. Cun is of average height, five feet seven inches, and thin. His two distinguishing features are a quick smile enhanced by an obvious silver-capped tooth, and extremely long fingernails on his little fingers. His first possession took place when he was twenty seven years old, in 1961. The possession occurred while he was worshipping in a temple. He had been in good health at the time.

After the initial possession he spent the traditional twenty one days of initiation rites in isolation, with only water. During this time he learned the rituals and obtained his power from his teacher. He has been at this temple for twelve years, and has become a master *tang-ki*. Twenty other *tang-ki* are associated with his temple. Three or four are female. (Several of his assistants are also female.) Mr. Cun travels around the island performing exorcisms.

Mr. Cun was recently elected to the head of his subward, but other than performing those duties he is a fulltime *tang-ki*. He does not charge a fee and makes no money from his services. Clients are expected to donate what they can to the temple for its upkeep. The only time he charges is when he has to travel to another city. Then he asks for travel and lodging expenses, food, and a small fee. The daily clients usually pay about $1 (U.S.). (Compare this with the $10 (U.S.) visit to a Western-style doctor.) Clients often bring food—usually rice and fruit—and an article of clothing. The latter is blessed and returned.

At the time of the interviews in 1978, he was forty four years old and was married with two children, a boy twelve and a girl seven. Both children were around during his daily ceremonies and sometimes acted as assistants. His son's first possession occurred when he was seven years old. The older shamans tell the story that the first time he put the needle through his cheeks he took soda and squirted it through the holes.

Mrs. Cun worked at the temple daily. She officiated at many of the services. Her main income was from selling the incense.

Like shaman Zhou's, Mr. Cun's temple is full of decorations and certificates. Banners of different colors cover most of the wall space, and each banner has a saying written on it. A letter from the president of the Taoist Temple Association hangs on the wall next to the certificate from the Association (each temple that is a member has a committee from the community that directs its operations). Also hanging on the wall are several pictures of *tang-ki* during festivals. Letters from many people who had been cured thanking the gods are also on display. Several ex-clients have become active supporters. One successful businessman, who was cured of ten years of insanity, contributes money generously.

There are many small statues of gods in the temple, set in a large glass case. A large statue, about one-fourth life-size, is of a god, *Tai-T'zu*, and a white horse. On the table in front of the entrance are flowers and *jian* (fortune telling) sticks. There is also a large glass case into which money is placed after a visit. Inside the temple, hanging on the wall, is a board with many pieces of paper hanging on hooks. These slips of paper are used along with *jian* sticks for fortune telling.

People who were given good business advice and are now successful also contribute. A temple committeeman who is a full-time journalist helps a lot during the day. He does this because his mother was cured by Mr. Cun after all the doctors had said that her case was hopeless. The god told him that his mother would be allowed to live for two more years and, according to him, she did. Since that time he has been very active in helping out at the temple.

The main *dou-tau* (assistant) is Mr. Hui, a sixty-year-old, retired elementary school teacher. He assists throughout the entire ritual. Other people lend a hand, but almost all transactions are through Mr. Hui. During trance induction he holds the stool Mr. Cun is sitting on, to keep it from flying across the room.

The induction, though violent, is very ritualized and almost exactly the same day-to-day. It concludes when Mr. Cun slaps his thighs twice and stands up. He then walks to the altar table and slaps it twice. He raises his arms and the other regular *dou-tau*, a female, removes his teeshirt, and ties a blue cloth around his waist, leaving a large knot on the backside. A sword or bladed-club is then handed to Mr. Cun. Usually he uses a sword and only leaves welts on his back, but some days he draws blood. When he is finished, he hands his weapon to his assistant and slaps the table again. A cry of "*tang-ki*" goes up from the people in attendance.

After the induction ceremony, Mr. Cun offers advice. He averages about thirty clients a day. Most are elderly women. Each client fills out a slip with her birthdate, name, address, and questions or problems. The problem could be someone else's and not necessarily the questioner's. Many of the questions are for men, but as the men usually are working, their wives come instead. Some clients are young mothers with children.

During a twenty-day period in the summer of 1978, Mr. Cun administered to 670 client problems. One client can have many complaints. The main reasons for seeking out the shaman are physical or medical. Out of the 670 problems, 322 were in this category. Questions regarding fate were second in number; there were 243. General advice on education, marriage, and social, business, or household anxieties ranked a distant third. Table 4.1 shows a breakdown of the queries. Note the break between problems #1 and #2 and the categories that follow. The first two categories deal with ten broad social and cultural issues, 80% of the shaman's labors, while the rest focus on the private life of the client.

During the initial contacts with clients, Mr. Cun would ask questions and many times seemed to be calculating using his fingers while silently contemplating his answer. After the diagnosis, he would prescribe certain behaviors, involving relationships with others, or rituals that a person must carry out on the spot, using incense, flag, and sword. He might also prescribe charms.

A Chinese character written on a charm or amulet commands the evil spirits to obey the *tang-ki's* orders. Some charms are written in the blood

TABLE 4.1
Classification of Client Problems

Problem	No.	%
1. Physical	322	43
2. Fate	243	36
3. Advice (Education, Marriage, Business, Household)	35	5
4. Birth	27	4
5. Calling Ancestors	13	2
6. Auspicious Dates	10	1.5
7. Protection or Blessing	8	1
8. Marriage Problems	6	.8
9. Miscellaneous	6	.8
TOTAL	670	

produced by the *tang-ki* during self-flagellation. The blood is considered to be the essence of the evil demon in liquid form. The blood on the *tang-ki's* body is evidence that the shaman is possessed and has control of the evil spirit. In religious terminology, the shaman is Yang: all that is sacred, light, good, and powerful. The blood is Yin: all that is death, dark, evil, and cold. The spirits reside in the Yin, or underworld. The gods reside in the Yang, or heaven. The shaman is the Yin, and the entering spirit is the Yang. The shaman has the ability to send the evil spirits back to the underworld through the cracks in the earthly firmament.

Other rituals of the *wu* include burning piles of spirit money. Mr. Cun, with flags and sword, would stand over the fire and chase away the evil spirits. One specialized ritual he performed involved a young child who was ill with an undetermined problem. Mr. Cun said that the child had been attacked by a ghost and it was very "heavy." "Heavy" means that the ghost was very powerful. Mr. Cun used an old scale, composed of a stick with hooks, spaced at varying intervals, and lifted the ghost out of the child. Once he separated the ghost from the body, Mr. Cun chased the bad spirit away, back into the Yin world of Hades. After that he wrote some charms and gave them to the mother. Descriptions of fate, power, and soul are given in terms of weight, hardness, and brightness. These are metaphors for strength, stamina, goodness.

The Public Exorcism   A public exorcism is a festive event, one which involves the whole community and sometimes even several communities. Mr. Cun began the day by sharpening his weapons. Two chartered buses transported Mr. Cun, six young shamans, two assistants, several members of the Temple Committee, and interested community members to a small town about sixty kilometers south of Taiczhong. The buses were met by a small pickup truck playing music through a loudspeaker system, and several thousand people milling in the streets. Mr. Cun's group joined another group of local *tang-ki* who had once been Mr. Cun's students and now have their own local temples. These *tang-ki* were the day's major performers.

Mrs. Cun acted as the coordinator for the two groups of *tang-ki*. She watched over the dozen or so young shamans who soon fell into trances. She directed the assistants to control the crowd and to hand weapons to the *tang-ki* and to carry out commands. The procession was led by select individuals, who carried poles with banners or characters, spiked chairs, or altars. The shamans began to flagellate themselves. Mr. Cun licked his tongue over a five foot nail and shoved it, with some difficulty, through his cheeks. His son fell into a trance and was hoisted onto the spiked chair. The other shamans soon began to flail themselves with swords and spiked clubs. The procession was broken up into several stages. They marched through town and back to the buses. Then they rode to a nearby temple, all the while burning incense to the gods. Finally, they took another short bus ride on the main road near the town of Waiyi, where the exorcism was scheduled to take place.

So many accidents had been happening in spots along this highway and so many people had been killed that the villagers felt the accidents had to be the work of malevolent spirits. The caravan of five or six buses, trucks and cars stopped in the middle of the road near the affected area. Mr. Cun, with a five-foot needle still sticking through his cheeks, led the way. His son was carried on a spike chair. Everyone else jumped out of the buses and about ten of the young shamans went into trances and blocked the highway. Traffic had to stop, and it backed up for miles. Eventually police directed traffic around the spot, but for about fifteen minutes absolutely no traffic got through.

The *tang-ki* were led by those who carried the lead pole, which bore the head-shaman's banner. They began searching for the evil spirits, running here and there and eventually finding them in the back shed of someone's home. The sedan chair carriers ran down an alley where the shed was located, and later to a tree where other spirits were found. Then they chased the ghosts away from those spots, and the *tang-ki* formed a large circle on the road, which no one could enter. Inside were the sedan chairs, carriers, the lead pole, and the local head *tang-ki*, who stood near a table where he carried out his work. The sedan chair carriers were literally thrown to the ground and stumbled around as the god fought the spirits. One of the carriers vomited and later, due to exhaustion, was replaced. The *tang-ki* flayed themselves, stood guard, or gave directions to the assistants. At the table, the head *tang-ki* wrote charms, burned spirit money in huge piles, and using the sword and flag chased the spirits back to the Yin world, or at least away from that place. He then ran into the town, to another place where spirits had been found. Throughout the entire episode he was blindfolded.

The local head *tang-ki* was totally responsible for carrying out the rituals, while the gods were responsible for finding the ghosts. The head *tang-ki* led the rest, throwing rice and writing charms. He counted the number of ghosts (five male and four female at one spot), and decided when they had gone.

This exorcism ritual represented a battle between the forces of good and the forces of darkness. The evil spirits were found and placated with food and money and then chased away. Each place was then purified.

Political Significance   The exorcism was an attempt to rid the local society of evil influences. These "influences" had been the cause of many deaths on the highway. The dangerous condition of the highway was the responsibility of the government, which had not taken steps to ameliorate the situation. The dangerous condition of the highway can be, and was also, attributed to evil spirits. The shamans, by means of the ritual exorcism, were able to relieve the high level of anxiety provoked by the numerous casualties and deaths on the road. By relieving this sort of anxiety, which was fueled by mass consciousness of the problem, the shamans acquired the confidence of a large group of people. Implicit in this shift in confidence is a downturn in the faith in, or tolerance for, Nationalist rule and protection.

Changes in group consciousness which have political roots or ramifications are rarely, if ever, publicly stated in Taiwan. The energy produced by the change, however, is tremendous. Often, fortified by this energy, shamans will experience visions, or ideologies, and recount them. Shamans traveling from village to village will tell versions of the stories of the millennium, the final day of judgment, paradise, and so on. These visions are familiar, and therefore powerful, archetypes of Taiwanese culture. As conceptual constructs offered to people whose living conditions are substandard and for whom social mobility is all but non-existent, they act as transformers. Inherently based on the ineffable and the seemingly impossible, the rhetoric of shamanism, the visions of restoration to order, justice, and salvation, offer the same promises to the Taiwanese as political rhetoric does to ordinary citizens of representative governments. In the latter form of government, the rhetoric has its own code, decipherable to the inhabitants. The rhetoric of the shamans, because it is so irrational, and because it describes the political climate of a population which cannot or will not speak directly or disclose the code, is a more powerful political tool. The visions, or ideologies, contained in the rhetoric carry more influence.

If politics is a combination of organizing principles and compelling sentiments, then shamans compose an atypical political force. They have a vision, and they can build the fever necessary to popularize the vision. They are not, however, clearly devoted to causes, and they do not have articulated position statements. Shamans defy political analysis because they operate sheerly on an internal referencing system. They cannot be adequately described by what they are for or against.

The Nationalist government recognizes that shamans are more than a highly-organized network of healers. They are aware that traditionally shamans have been a major force in providing information, stimulating and channeling resentment, and uniting different geographical communities against a common foe. Shamans have acted as "prime rural arbiters" of village and and inter-village disputes. Political alliances within and between villages have been made through the sacred legitimacy of the shaman.

> . . . divination through trance behavior may be responsible for a great deal more Chinese decision making than we normally imagine and might even be a factor of importance in understanding, for example, the galvanization of the countryside during revolutions or secret-society rebellions, or the patterns of alliances between and among villages throughout south China during periods of local raiding and warfare.[9]

THE POLITICS OF THE SACRED

The Medical-Political Connection

Shaman Zhou and Shaman Cun are above all public figures. Their work-places are at the hub of social activities. They are located on main streets, where they are easily accessible. Clients, friends, guests, or kibbitzers drop in at will to watch television, chat, drink tea, comment, or just hang out and smoke cigarettes. Letters, certificates, membership cards, name cards, and other memorabilia hang on walls or lay scattered on tea tables or trays. As a shaman becomes more prestigious, his or her quarters enlarge. Finally the construction of a temple becomes a necessity.* More people pack in, more incense is burned, and more cigarette smoke brings the walls and ceilings even closer together.

The shaman's healing practice involves him in all aspects of community life. He becomes not just a healer, but also a barometer of the physical and social diseases of the local society. He not only "cures" his patients, but must motivate them to want to be cured. And he can only do this if the environment is conducive to health.

The shaman's health-role and scope differ from those of a medical doctor. The western-trained medical doctor in Taiwan sees his patients privately in small rooms. He maintains a neat and closed schedule, with a few minutes for each patient. It has been observed that during the times when patients are not scheduled, the doctor will retire to his private room to nap or to do his research.[10] The design of his office space and his compartmentalized schedule support the allopathic orientation of his medicine. Each room and time have distinct functions. He would consider the congregation of patients and friends hanging out together in his office and clinic as unsanitary and possibly as beneath his social level. It is rare that a medical doctor in Taiwan (or in any Third World country) becomes deeply involved in local politics. When he does become involved, he usually abandons his medical duties and engages in politics at a national, not local, level.

Shamans, as non-allopathic practitioners, assume that all illnesses are essentially psychosomatic. By this they do not mean that disease is phony or unreal. To them illness is rooted in the unconscious mind. Diseases occur as a result of changes of consciousness. The martial arts of East Asia and the yoga practices of India have proven that one can control blood pressure, stop bleeding, and even self-induce a state of painlessness equal to that produced

---

*Government permission is required for temple status. This often becomes a legal hassle. Sometimes the shaman must conduct his activities unlicensed and surreptitiously. The government is very wary whenever a shaman becomes too powerful. There is always the fear that the shaman will rival officials for public favor and authority.

by ether or other anesthesias. Shamans believe that health derives from harmony among the great forces of the universe. Any disorder in the world will be reflected in the psyche of the individual. The rectification of one's inner balance can restore order to the world. In this light, the worst kind of attack on the individual is one which attempts to destroy the balance of the psyche.

A dramatic expression of this order of attack is contained in a set of two dozen propaganda posters published by the Nationalist government. They are designed to teach the Taiwanese how to behave. One poster depicts a Taiwanese family eating dinner. One half of the poster shows the wrong way for a person to eat bread dumplings—by shoving a whole fistful into his mouth at once. A second picture shows the proper way to eat—with small bites. The Nationalists engage in this campaign on the assumption that true Chinese civilization teaches propriety, dignity, respect, and tolerance. It is a part of the national mission to civilize the Taiwanese. But this mission is accomplished in a manner that promotes their humiliation. The values of the Chinese civilization are contradicted by the means used to promote them. Through caricatures of the fundamental activity of eating, deep psychological feelings of abuse and anger are engendered. Other topics utilized by the Nationalists include the proper way of disposing of garbage and waste water, warnings about eavesdropping on other's conversations, the respectful behavior of the children and wife of the head of the household while the latter is studying. These posters reveal more about the Nationalist's view of the native inhabitants than about the customs of the Taiwanese.

By means of such propaganda, the Nationalist government tries to compel the local Taiwanese to model themselves, "not with their own interests, intuitions, or modes of experience, but with the archetypes of behavior and systems of sentiment developed and maintained in the public domain."[11] The shaman represents a spiritual and cultural world that stands outside the domain of the KMT and its mythology. As a liaison between the Taiwanese and their archetypes, the shaman protects the standards for that world. This protection is not limited to medical healing: it inevitably becomes political.

Resistance

The Japanese Experience   The public and political role of the Taiwanese shaman was clear to both the Japanese (who outlawed it) and the Nationalist Chinese regime, which has recently outlawed some of the shamans' activities.

> Shamanism . . . is [not only] one of the important healing systems available in most of the rural areas in Taiwan but it is also a major vehicle for Taiwanese nationalism against the minority but dominant Mainlanders.[12]

It is important to note that almost no field work can be undertaken on this topic because of its sensitivity. Scholars are warned not to deal with it; some scholars deny it exists, and some scholars fear for the welfare of their informants and friends.

While Taiwan was still part of the Qing Empire it was no more than a frontier post of Chinese expansion. Until the reforms of Liu Mingquan (1887–93), the island was controlled by a group of local gentry, with religious factions providing or withholding support. Without the imprimatur of a local temple, a local notable had dubious authority.[13]

When the Japanese received Taiwan as a prize of war in 1895, they were quick to realize that they had to eradicate the hold of the religious leadership. The Japanese police investigated shamans and spirit cults. These investigations often concluded that the shamans gave rise to negative rumors: e.g., the gods of Taiwan hate the Japanese; they urge the natives to boycott Japanese goods; they call upon the Taiwanese to give up opium because a boycott will economically harm the Japanese who run the opium monopoly; the gods place blame for illness on the Japanese, who brought new diseases; etc.[14]

Inspired by the 1911 Revolution in China, the Taiwanese engaged in numerous revolts against Japanese rule. The leadership, in many cases, drew legitimacy from accompanying shamans who provided support from the gods. The Xilaian incident was one of the most widespread rebellions during the first generation of Japanese rule. The cult used a temple in Tainan as a base of operations. Relying upon traditional Chinese views of the powers of shaman-supported rebellions, a leader of this rebellion claimed: "If we follow the commands of the gods, then there is nothing that can happen to us. Even if our enemies number millions, still we are not afraid."[15]

The history of the acceptance of the spirit writing cult in the agricultural village of Holi in Central Taiwan reveals the close bond between political and religious commitments. In 1902, the Japanese government had taken control of the opium trade out of local, native hands and placed it under the jurisdiction of the government monopoly. Since the area of Holi was a rich source for the opium trade, the police were ordered to attack and arrest the natives. In one such incident, five people were killed and over eighty arrested. The economic consequences were grim. With trade cut off, a major source of income was lost. With local production controlled, the price of opium became staggeringly high. Transactions could only be made in cash. The cult claimed that it could cure the opium habit, and was invited into the village. Soon, however, the villagers were able to make their peace with, and profit from, the Japanese, and the activities of the cult diminished. Furthermore, the cult had no spirit medium (shaman) and had to rely on visiting mediums from other cults.

The Nationalist Experience   It was not until after reversion of Taiwan to the Nationalist Chinese government in 1945 that the cults and shamans, previously driven into hiding or forced to retire, began to flourish again. A middle-aged shaman named Jiu became very effective in predicting who among the villagers would return from the war with China. This period of revival was cut off by the revolt of February 28, 1947. Martial law was declared and all nocturnal assemblies were prohibited. Many of the shamans fled for fear of their lives. Some held seances and claimed that the gods would warn the congregation of army patrols or police dragnets. It was even believed that the sessions could be made invisible to the eyes of the police.

The government's attack on shamans was short lived. After land reform (1949-53) had reduced the landlord's power, the only local organizations which could garner support in Holi were the religious cults and their leadership. They basically provided the coordination and cooperation for building projects, transportation, and irrigation networks. The spirit writing cult, supported by shamans and literate religious leaders, provided a constituency for both inter- and intra-village activities.

Gary Seaman described a pattern of animosity between small holders and landlords or administrative representatives which broke out into major disputes.

> In 1949 this resentment was still very strong, and it provided the popular issue to mobilize support behind a coalition of men in Upper Pearl Mountain Village to establish a separate village government. The Nationalist officials agreed, and the people of Upper Pearl Mountain Village threw their support behind a coalition which elected Liang village head.[16]

Ex-shaman Jiu was one of the leaders of the coalition. The coalition had very little strength and soon was torn apart by feuding and factionalism. In fact, the fighting became so intense that a recall election, the first ever in Taiwan's history, was drawn up against Liang, the village headman. He negotiated a deal with the head of the spirit writing cult, Boss Ng. If the cult supported him, then he would support Boss Ng in the upcoming mayoral elections. The recall failed by four votes. Boss Ng soon became Mayor, and served for over 20 years.

> With Boss Ng's election as mayor of Upper Pearl Mountain Village, the political center of gravity of that part of the village naturally swung toward the groups which supported him most: the spirit writing cult, his own household, and his immediate neighbors. It is the custom of the members of the spirit writing cult to gather every evening at the cult headquarters. Since Boss Ng regularly attended at the cult, those from Upper Pearl Mountain Village who sought alliance and audience with him were also drawn to the cult. The converse was probably also true: those who were attracted to the cult for religious or personal reasons easily identified with its political leadership.[17]

Although Ng's leadership did not provide any specific ideology, it did promote values of human justice, honesty, and respect for the community, which at times transcended national goals and aims.

The Modernization Experience The successful economic development of Taiwan has created a burst of energy which has left many people with the feeling of having been abused. The low level of agricultural productivity and income has resulted in large migrations of rural residents to the city. The consequent social problems are evident: declining nutrition, inadequate housing, harmful working conditions, the rise of prostitution, the new phenomenon of juvenile delinquency, gangs, and drugs.

Nowhere is the damage more apparent than in ecological disasters. Nineteen out of the twenty-four rivers are severely polluted; the arsenic in the soil is at harmful levels; the noise and air pollution have either created new diseases or contributed to the spread of old ones.[17]

Shamanism has not been slow to respond to the new cultural and psychic crisis. The shaman has been called upon to process the casualties of modernization through rituals of spiritual counseling. The social dislocations created by modernization of the society have created a plethora of psychosomatic complaints and aberrant behavior.[18] In the following seance, the shaman is asked to deal with the problem of an untimely death. The dialogue with the spirit of the deceased exemplifies the shaman's legitimacy to chastise the youth's activities as harmful to Taiwanese society, and to offer an explanation for the death which promotes the traditional value of harmony and the innovative sanction against the excesses of modernization. The entire interpretation of events is couched in a universal mythological terminology which allows for optimism and comfort, and though encouraging stability, presents a strong and compelling critique.

> The criminal soul of a man who indiscriminately used agricultural insecticides on vegetables, thus harming other people. A case to instruct the world.
>
> At a temple in Taichung, 19th day of the 4th lunar month, 1971.
>
> The God of Ceremonies of the temple mounts the dais, saying, "The King of Hell Ch'u Chiang, Lord of the Second Court will tonight hold court at this temple, to pass judgement on a criminal soul, and to thus instruct the world. All of ye offer incense and receive him now; guard ye against loss of propriety."
> Now come the Horse Face General and Ox Face General of the Second Court, saying, "All ghostly wardens take your places, stand to attention!"
> Now come the Military and Civil Judicial Officers of the Second Court, saying, "Now comes the King of Hell, all of ye salute him!
> Ch'u Chiang, King of Hell, Lord of the Second Court arrives, singing,

"O how the world sinks lower with each passing day.
Virtue is engulfed and lost, Crime is everywhere.
If evil is not punished, forewarning of the way,
Then comes a rising tide, harming people's lives.

"Thus I come at evening to the spirit writing temple,
To judge the savage heart of this criminal soul,
A man who spread a poison on vegetables and fruit,
Spreading frequent afflictions, O how strange and foul.

"Tonight I have come to this temple here in Taichung, to judge the case of a criminal soul, so that the world may learn from it. I now command the Horse Face General and Ox Face General to take up their posts and mount a careful guard, that nothing happens to frighten the people here. The Earth God of this temple can take up pen on behalf of the defendant soul. I now command the Horse Face General to bring out the criminal soul."

The Horse Face General appears, saying, "And it please your grace, the defendant soul is here."

The King of Hell speaks, saying, "Oh you criminal soul, report faithfully your name and surname, your place of residence, your occupation, and your age."

The ghost says, "My name is Ho Ch'iu-chi, seventeen years old, and I live near Taipei. My occupation is that of farmer."

The King asks, "Do you know of what crime you are guilty?"

The ghost replies, "And it please your grace, I am guilty of no crime. I was out in the fields on a summer's day five years ago when I was struck dead by lightning. And it please your grace to forgive whatever I have done."

The King replies in anger, "You come before this court and still will not admit to the truth! In your lifetime you were unfilial to your parents and did not love virtue. You cheated for ill-gotten gains, you had no regard for human life. Everyday you used powerful insecticides on your vegetables and then put them up for sale. Thus the buyers after eating them would have these chemicals in their bodies, causing diseases like the gruesome symptoms of cancer. So you indirectly killed people, and yet you can still say that you have committed no crime. There is a saying: 'If you don't beat the drum, you get no sound; If you don't beat men, they won't confess!' I command the Ox Face General to give you 80 strokes of the great staff."

The Ox Face General answers, "At your command . . . . And it please your grace, the sentence has been carried out."

The King asks, "Criminal soul, do you confess or not?"

The soul answers, "Because my vegetables were infected with insects, if I didn't use insecticides, it would be impossible to grow them. It was not only me who used insecticides, and besides I didn't mean to hurt any one, so I don't understand why I am guilty of a crime."

The King, greatly angered, rails, "Criminal soul with the heart of a beast! Do you know why you were struck dead by lightning? It was because you only thought of ill-gotten gain, and did not give thought to the power of the insecticides, just using them willy-nilly. So when people ate your vegetables with so much poison on them, it would cause sickness in them. This is the reason that you are guilty in the eyes of heaven. Kuan Kung was greatly angered by your actions, and he thus commanded General Lightning to strike you dead, that you might bring no more trouble to others. How can you still not recognize your fault and repent of it? We are holding this court in a temple in Taichung. If you admit your guilt, this case can be a model to others in the world, thus you will have gained some merit. I will then reduce the charge against you. If you do not confess the truth, I will sentence you to severe punishment."

The soul replies, "I beg his grace to cease being angry, I confess it all."

The King says, "Relate then the details truthfully."

The soul says, "Because it is difficult to raise vegetables without using insecticides, I would get up every morning at dawn and go out to put insecticides on my vegetables. All I thought of was the money I could make. I would take them into Taipei in the early morning to sell. There are rules about the application and frequency of use of insecticides, as well as how long you have to wait before picking the vegetables after using them, but because business was so good and so profitable, I paid no attention to the rules, but just used insecticides willy-nilly. My father and mother would scold me for being of little virtue, so I would often argue with my parents, which was very unfilial. In the space of several years I hurt I don't know how many people, and thus incurred the wrath of heaven. When I was struck dead by lightning, I realized the magnitude of my sin. I beseech you farmers, don't be like I was and only think of profit, paying no attention to right conduct, not valuing human life, and using insecticides to indirectly harm others. If you do, you may be struck dead by lightning and have to appear in the courts of Hell to answer for your crimes. I beg your grace to treat me lightly!"

The King says, "Concerning your crimes of the careless use of insecticides and harming others, and being unfilial to your parents: You should be cast into the Lowest Hell, and should remain there eternally. But seeing that you have confessed your guilt and repent of your crime, appearing here in court to show others the right way, I will deal lightly with you. You shall be incarcerated in the 'Flying Pitchfork Hell' (*Fei-Ch'a Ti Yu*) and be tortured there for two hundred years. You will thereafter pass along to the Tenth Court of Hell, and be reborn on earth as an animal.

"I command the Civil Officer to record the deposition of the convicted soul, and carefully note all details of the sentence meted out to him. I exhort all of ye in the world of men—do not harbor avarice for ill-gotten gain, using insecticides to harm others. But act that ye may avoid the wrath of heaven, and the punishment in Hell that must surely follow. Herewith this case is ended. I command that all my cohorts and officials make ready to return to hell. I withdraw."[19]

The Current Political Struggle[20]

The government is aware of the politically disruptive potential of the shamans. In 1976, their activities were outlawed in Taibei. One *tang-ki* in Taibei complained that whenever he had a group of people at his temple, the police would show up and send everyone home. Nantou county hosts one of the largest and most beautiful Taoist temples in Taiwan. It was here in 1976 that two *tang-ki* initiates died, due to their religious activities. When questioned about this, the temple staff flatly denied that either was associated with the temple, or any nearby temple. Yet upon observation of the photographs within the temple, one can clearly identify several *tang-ki*. Outside the main temple, a small police office had recently been built. The police were not local but government police.

In addition to government surveillance, intimidation, and repression, the professional social scientists and the middle and upper-class Mainlanders actively deny the existence of *tang-ki*. Bernard Gallin often recounts his surprise at this self-induced ignorance.

> In 1965, . . . I live[d] in Taipei in a compound owned by the National Taiwan University. Next to the compound was a small village in which shamans (*tang-ki*) held ritualistic healing sessions almost every night. When I told some Chinese anthropologists and sociologists about these activities they refused to believe me, remarking that nothing of that sort was to be found in "sophisticated" Taipei. I finally was able to convince them only by leading them to some of the many places where they could observe shamans perform.[21]

Another serious factor which prevents observers from witnessing the obvious is the belief in the paradigm of modernization. This includes the faith that society, à la Max Weber's theories, will constantly rationalize and thus sweep away superstition and the irrational. In 1969, the anthropologist Frank Bessac proudly speculated that, owing to Taiwan's spectacular land reform and ensuing economic development, the pool of supernatural rituals and shamans was drying up. Bessac commented that,

> . . . partly because of the secularism introduced through scientific methods of farming, many villagers have turned to the philosophic agnosticism of educated Chinese although they are careful to maintain the ceremonial forms connected with customary worship because otherwise they fear that they will be criticized by their neighbors.[22]

It should be clear from the above examples that, contrary to expectations, the shaman and cult population of Taiwan's rural, and even urban, areas has grown and is not just a superficial desire to keep faith with one's next door neighbors.

The KMT government is extremely concerned about the politics of "superstition." In the November 1977 election in Gaoxiung, a reform candidate who opposed the incumbent used supernatural rites to attack the government's record. Shamans and priests declared that the KMT's ancestors were upset with KMT rule.

The government also realizes that this revival is occurring only among the Taiwanese. The political message is clear. Some Mainlanders consider that this manifestation of resistance is an example of a desire for Taiwanese independence. And it is true that the leadership of the current Democratic Movement (Dangwai) often visited temple fairs and religious festivals to present their views on the need for the Taiwanese to rule their own island. Ms. Lu Xiulian, now serving twelve years in prison on the charge of sedition, found temple audiences extremely sympathetic. When she recited the tragedies of Taiwan's sufferings at the hands of outsiders (read Mainlanders), members of the audience would break out in tears and in public displays of emotion. Whereas these gatherings do provide the opportunity to arouse the people emotionally, the cults and religious leaders merely stir up deep emotions of resentment, anger and rebellion, but have not provided any evidence that they call for independence.

In the fall of 1977, the government initiated a major propaganda campaign against the cult leaders. The assumption of the anti-shaman campaign is a very rationalistic western prejudice against superstition. The thrust of the government's propaganda is to stress the craziness of the shamans, their bad character, and their evil consequences. Case studies were employed to prove that superstition harmed the people. Examples included injury by a fire dance, pregnancy by immoral "religious" leaders, bodily harm by quack medicine, and so on. Not uncoincidentally, the group initially singled out for attack was the *Yiguan dao*, a Buddhist millennial sect which has a tradition of organizing shamans and instigating rebellion.

In addition to circulating free booklets detailing the harmful effects of native religion, the government is restricting the organization and freedom of these folk cults. By strict definitions of "religious activities" and through the use of licenses, the government hopes to tame and control these supernatural and politically dangerous activities and their leadership.

The pursuit of supernatural authority is a non-partisan undertaking. It is neither inherently for nor against a specific political party. Any secular institution would rightfully feel threatened by the development of this religiously inspired leadership. The error of the KMT is not so much in using legislation to control the danger in this situation as it is in refusing to confront the deep intellectual, cultural, and economic causes. The more the government restricts the spiritual activities of the Taiwanese, the more the shaman and other cultic leaders will be able to enhance their community identity as protectors of the native psyche. The real enemy of the state is the rural discontent fueled by unequal economic development and the disenfranchisement of large segments of the population. This discontent fuels religious activity and in so doing can re-kindle those passions which motivate political rebellion.

It is not at all startling to find religious irredentism and self-flagellant movements thriving in countries where an enormous breach exists between daily experience and political mythology—e.g., South Korea, Indonesia, Malaysia, the Philippines, and Iran. People turn to the irrational when the "rational" is too contradictory or painful to accept. Accounts of supernatural activity do not describe so much the world of spirits as they do the affairs of humans. The "way of seeing" of the shamans is probably the best way of analyzing shamanism in any of its contexts. Looking beyond the grotesquery of the nail balls and razored chairs of the Taiwanese shamans can bring in to focus the lack of harmony in the larger society. That imbalance in power is evident in the political struggle between the native Taiwanese and the KMT, and in the unequal political and economic development of the island.

NOTES

1. Kristoffer M. Schipper, "Neighborhood Cult Associations in Traditional Tainan," in *The City in Late Imperial China*, ed. William B. Skinner (Stanford: Stanford University Press, 1977), p. 651 ff. Although he does not specifically mention shamans, the politico-religious activities (p. 663) which the cults participated in were similar to the activities of the shaman. Shamans were quite active in Fujian and Guangdong. They came over with the earlier settlers. Many of these earlier rites are still preserved in Taiwan. But they have lost their historical paternity and are viewed as native.

2. James Hillman, *Re-Visioning Psychology* (New York: Harper and Row, 1975), p. xiii.

3. David K. Jordan, *Gods, Ghosts & Ancestors: Folk Religion in a Taiwanese Village* (Berkeley: University of California Press, 1972).

4. Interview with a Taiwanese graduate student at Stanford University.

5. A large part of the empirical observation is based on Jerry Schultz's manuscript, "Taiwanese Shamans: Traditional Healers in an Increasingly Industrialized Society," 1979.

6. Andrew Weil, *The Natural Mind: A New Way of Looking at Drugs and the Higher Consciousness* (Boston: Houghton Mifflin, 1972), pp. 170–71.

7. Emily Ahern, "Sacred and Secular Medicine in a Taiwan Village: A Study of Cosmological Disorders," in *Medicine in Chinese Cultures: Comparative Studies of Health Care in Chinese and Other Societies*, ed. A. Kleinman (Washington, DC: US Dept. of HEW, Publication NIH 75-653, 1975), p. 105.

8. Hillman, *Re-Visioning*, p. 11.

9. Jordan, *Gods*, p. 86.

10. Katherine Gould Martin, "Medical Systems in a Taiwan Village: *Ong-Ia-Kong*, The Plague God as Modern Physician,"in *Medicine in Chinese Cultures*, ed. A. Kleinman, pp. 131–32.

11. Joseph Campbell, *The Masks of God: Primitive Mythology* (New York: The Viking Press, Compass Edition, 1970), p. 240.

12. Wen-Shing Tseng, "Traditional and Modern Psychiatric Care in Taiwan," in *Medicine in Chinese Cultures*, ed. A. Kleinman, p. 178; Martin, "Medical Systems," p. 135.

13. Stephan Feuchtwang's work supports Seaman's study: "During the Ch'ing period, temples in Taiwan . . . functioned both as a proto-government and as rallying points in the communal divisions of society." "City Temples in Taiwan under Three Regimes" in *The Chinese City Between Two Worlds*, eds. Mark Elvin and William G. Skinner (Stanford: Stanford University Press, 1974), p. 262.

14. Gary Seaman, *Temple Organization in a Chinese Village*, in Asian Folklore and Social Life Monographs, Vol. 101, ed. Lou Tsu-k'uong (Taipei, Formosa, China: The Orient Cultural Service, 1978), p. 29. This work is the only study which attempts "to show a functional relationship between the form of religious organization and political activity" in the folk religion of Taiwan (p. 6). It provides historical background, but concentrates on a spirit writing cult from 1945 to 1973. Seaman includes shamans in his study, but claims they are different from the spirit writing cult leaders. In this paper I am not maintaining such tight boundaries.

15. Gary Seaman, *Temple Organization*, p. 129. See his Chapter 11, entitled "Religious Cults and Political Factions."

16. Gary Seaman, *Temple Organization*, p. 136. Gary Seaman has provided a major service in the study of the political aspects of shamanism and folk cults. He has gone beyond the usual catalogue of political "acts" to point out the economic and geographical nature of the religious inspiration. A study in American history which complements Seaman's work is by Paul Boyer and Stephen Nissenbaum, *Salem Possessed: The Social Origins of Witchcraft* (Cambridge, MA: Harvard University Press, 1974). They argue that part of the reason for the rise of witchcraft in Salem is the conflict between the old agrarian Salem and the new commercial Salem. In one of the most intriguing maps in their book they show that the attacks on witches came from one part of the township (the old) and that the witches who were brought to trial came from the other part (the new). The linkage of economic change to the rise of witchcraft and the justification of repression on the basis of prosecution of witches provide a fascinating account of the social relationship to spirit posssession. Without trying to summarize Seaman's work, I would only like to indicate that his division of upper and lower Pearl Mountain Village, and his account of the various factions corroborate Boyer and Nissenbaum's work. Perhaps other studies of villages in Taiwan will benefit from both of these works.

17. Robert Mark Selya, "Water and Air Pollution in Taiwan," *Journal of Developing Areas* (Jan. 1975):178, 192; "Taipei River Pollution at Serious Level," *China Post*, June 19, 1978, p. 12, July 4, 1978, p. 12. The major advocate of the ecological movement is Professor Lin Junyi of the Biology Department at Donghai University. He supplied the figures on DDT levels.

18. Colleen Leahy Johnson, "Psychoanalysis, Shamanism and Cultural Phenomena," *Journal of the American Academy of Psychoanalysis*, 9 (Spring, 1978):311–38.

19. Seaman, *Temple Organization*, pp. 102–05. Originally in Luan-You [Gifted Friend] #60 [Tai-Chung].

20. This section draws, in part, from Richard C. Kagan, "The Chinese Approach to Shamanism," in *Chinese Sociology and Anthropology*, 12 (Summer, 1980).

21. B. Gallin, "Comments," in *Medicine in Chinese Cultures*, ed. A. Kleinman, p. 278. Similar comments regarding research on the Chinese Revolution have been made by Edward Friedman. See *Backward Toward Revolution* (Berkeley: University of California Press, 1974), p. 84, fn. 61. "Chinese anthropologists, archaeologists, philosophers, etc., anxious to prove China's modernity to their significant others, their allegedly more advanced Western counterparts, have interpreted Chinese society so as to explain away its religious basis. Since their success leads to the conclusion that Chinese are protected and realistic, there has been little need felt to study the major continuing consequences of Chinese religion."

22. Frank Bessac, "The Effect of Industrialization upon the Allocation of Labor in a Taiwanese Village," *Journal of the China Society*, 6 (1969):13.

5 THE CHINESE JOINT FAMILY IN CHANGING RURAL TAIWAN

Bernard and Rita S. Gallin*

Modernization usually is described as inimical to complex family organization.[1] That is, the social counterpart of economic development is said to be the slow, but steady, dissolution of the joint family unit into its nuclear constituents. Within the context of a modernizing and industrializing society such as Taiwan is a society in which the viability of the large family apparently has not been undermined by the pressures of development.

The purpose of this paper is to describe the ways in which the joint family has continued as a vital unit in present-day Taiwan (although still as a minority family type) and to explore the factors that have contributed to its persistence. We will argue that the *raison d'être* of the joint family has not disappeared in this Chinese society and that, through conscious modification, it is maintained to aid in the achievement of socioeconomic goals.

First, we describe the research upon which the paper is based and give an ethnographic picture of the socioeconomic life of the village and area

*We wish to acknowledge the research assistance of Yeh Ch'uen-rong, a graduate student in Anthropology at Michigan State University, in the preparation of this paper, and of Anthony Lee, our field assistant during the 1978–79 work in Taiwan, in the collection of the data.

We also wish to acknowledge with thanks the organizations that provided financial assistance over the years and made our several field trips to Taiwan between 1956 and 1979 possible. Specifically, funding was provided by a Foreign Area Training Fellowship, a Fulbright-Hays Research Grant, the Asian Studies Center of Michigan State University, The Mid-Western Universities Consortium for International Activities (MUCIA), the Social Science Research Council, and the Pacific Cultural Foundation.

Finally, we wish to acknowledge the cooperation of the staff of the Institute of Ethnology, Academia Sinica, Taiwan for sponsoring us as Visiting Scholars and providing invaluable assistance that facilitated the research.

studied during the past several decades. Next, we discuss the traditional joint family and report the structure and operation of this large family type in rural Taiwan today. Then, in our discussion, we explore the reasons for its continued existence. Finally, we examine the implications that this traditional institution has for rural economic development in modern Taiwan.

THE RESEARCH

The research on which this paper is based spans a twenty year period of work with Hokkien Chinese whose ancestors (from Fujian Province) settled on the west-central coastal plain of Zhanghua County in Taiwan. The first field research, in 1957-58, involved a seventeen-month residence in a rural agricultural village, Xin Xing, and focused on socioeconomic life and change in the village and area.[2] This was followed by two separate studies, in 1965-66 and 1969-70, of migrants from the area to Taibei in which the influence of emigration on the social structure of the village community within the city, as well as within the home area, was investigated.[3] The most recent research, carried out during two months in 1977 and six months in 1978-79, involved a return to the village area and examined economic developments there and the way in which they have affected the lives of area residents. The research data, then, provide extensive documentation of the village and area over time. That is to say, they offer a diachronic view of the way in which these people have responded to modernization and how their lives are entwined with the economy of the larger system.

BACKGROUND

In 1957-58, Xin Xing village and the district of which it is a part were primarily agricultural. No significant industries or job opportunities existed locally to provide supplemental income or to absorb the excess labor produced by an increasing population on a finite land base. To augment family coffers, some villagers grew and marketed vegetables as a cash crop or hired out as farm laborers. But, for larger numbers of area residents, the solution to the lack of local economic opportunities was migration to urban centers.

This move to the city commonly was accompanied by the dissolution of the extant joint family as a result of geographic, economic, and ecological conditions.[4] We say extant because joint families were low in frequency of occurrence in the area as a result of internal family conflicts born of economically-based problems and general poverty. Yet, although joint families were least common in the area (as was true for most of rural China), prior to large-scale migration great theoretical importance had been attached to the large family, and this was reflected in villagers' behavior. For example, it had been quite common for families to attempt to disguise a split and to divide completely only after attempts had been made to mitigate the causes prompting it.

During the 1950s, however, local economic conditions, in combination with out-migration and the increasingly greater impingement by the government on the local area, created forces that furthered family division.[5] That is, new factors, added to the balance already weighed down by internal conflict, tipped the scale so that villagers saw insufficient possibilities for and limited advantages in the formation and maintenance of the joint family. Accordingly, as the stream of out-migration quickened, the dissolution of the joint family took place earlier and more openly than in prior decades.

For some families, this dissolution was complete. That is, rural-based and urban-based brothers (or two or more urban-based brothers) who previously had shared a common family residence and treasury formally divided and established financially independent and residentially separate conjugal units. For other families, the dissolution was functional only. That is, brothers did not formally divide but merely maintained themselves and their families as separate economic units. Notwithstanding the form the dissolution took, however, people's attitude toward the joint family began to change, and demands by the small family unit for independence from the restraints of the larger joint family were seen to increase.

This pattern began to change among area migrants to Taibei in the late sixties, however, and the emigrant population there included several nascent joint families, reflections of postponed family division by wealthier migrants with married sons. But, among the population in the rural area, the small family continued as the most significant unit in terms of actual behavior and values, that is, until the early and middle seventies.

During this period, non-farm-related industries and service-oriented enterprises burgeoned in the villages and towns of the rural area. These businesses all were labor-intensive, and most were small-scale and family-operated, carried on within the villages themselves in the homes of owners. Their introduction into the local area provided countless opportunities for non-farm employment and was accompanied by what might be called a "rebirth" of the joint family. That is, the inevitability of family division soon after the marriage of more than one son no longer was accepted as a given (nor considered beneficial), and the number of joint families in the area increased. For example, the data showed that the distribution of Xin Xing villagers by family type changed considerably over a twenty-year period, and there were almost three times as many joint families in the village in 1979 as there were in 1958–59 (13 and 5 respectively) (see Table 5.1).[6] In contrast, there were approximately one-half fewer conjugal families in the village in 1979 than there were in 1958–59 (33 and 65 respectively). To understand this increase in joint families, a review of the nature of the traditional Chinese joint family will be helpful.

TABLE 5.1
Population of Xin Xing Village by Family Type, 1958–59 and 1978–79.

Family Type	Period	
	1958-59	*1978-79*
Conjugal		
Number and percent of households	65 (66%)	33 (45%)
Number and percent of persons	337 (55%)	163 (30%)
Average number of persons per household	5.18	4.9
Stem		
Number and percent of households	29 (29%)	27 (37%)
Number and percent of persons	213 (35%)	194 (36%)
Average number of persons per household	7.3	7.2
Joint		
Number and percent of households	5 (5%)	13 (18%)
Number and percent of persons	59 (10%)	186 (34%)
Average number of persons per household	11.8	14.3
TOTALS – Number of households	99	73
Number of persons	609	543
Average number of persons per household	6.15	7.3

Sources: 1958-59, Household record book (*hukou*), Pu yan Xiang Public Office.
1978-79, Field interviews. (The figures represent all people considered to be members of Xin Xing households, regardless of whether they were registered and/or resident there.)

THE TRADITIONAL JOINT FAMILY

The joint family consists of several married brothers who, together with their parents, form one economic household that might be dispersed in residence. All the functions the conjugal units might have in other circumstances are almost completely subsumed within the structure of the larger family of which they are a part. This structure is hierarchical according to generation and age, and the oldest male serves as family head (*jiazhang*), or manager. Thus, in the joint family, while the authority within each of the several conjugal units lies with the husband and father of that unit, the ultimate authority for all members of the larger family theoretically lies with the *jiazhang*.

All the members of the joint family live under one roof, except for those who may work outside to supplement the family income and therefore reside, sometimes with other members of the conjugal unit, outside. The latter, however, are still part of the family that functions as a single cooperative unit in all of its activities—economic, social, and religious.

In theory, when each member of the joint family fulfills his or her role properly, this form of family structure has great advantages. For example, the large family makes it possible for people to work at a combination of occupations. That is to say, while most of the family lives in the village (or home) area and works (or supervises) the large landholdings that only a large family are thought able to accumulate, some of the members may work in the local area or outside it to diversify the family's economic base. Regardless of the diversified economic activities or dispersal of family members, however, all income becomes part of a joint treasury and is used to support the individual members of the larger unit.

There are clues in several strands of the literature, nevertheless, to suggest that variations existed in this traditional system. For example, Martin Yang writes that within the context of a large family in Shandong Province:

> No man can have any money of his own except what he has saved from his own allowance, since he is provided for out of the general funds. . . . [Nevertheless,] a young man may do some trading in off seasons. If he borrows money on his own credit and takes all responsibility for whatever risks are involved, the profit he makes will be his own and he will spend it as he wills.[7]

Furthermore, Yang notes that a wife ". . . may persuade her husband to accumulate personal property by hiding a part of his earnings, if he has any, or by grabbing from the family's income."[8] In short, possibilities existed for married sons within larger families to accumulate private money for use by their own family unit. But these were unusual occurrences.[9]

Still another source of private money within a joint family also was available, however; that is, the private, and usually secret, money brought by a bride to her new home. This money—called *sai-khia* in Hokkien, *sifang qian* in Mandarin, and *se-koi* in Hakka—reflected savings or personal gifts received upon marriage by a woman. Relatively little was recorded in the literature concerning such private money until the publication of Myron Cohen's work about the Hakka of Mei Nong in Taiwan.[10]

According to Cohen, the opportunity to accumulate *sai-khia*, both on mainland China and in Mei Nong, was controlled by the needs, and permitted at the discretion, of the joint family.[11] What this means is that although the daughter-in-law usually came into the family with *sai-khia*, the time permitted and methods allowed to add funds to her personal coffer were limited.

For example, she could work and earn private money only during times over which family control did not extend, such as the periods before breakfast or after supper when no family work had to be done. In addition, most daughters-in-law in Mei Nong joint households were permitted to sell produce from self-maintained vegetable plots, to retain the income so derived, and to use the money for any purpose they wished.

These purposes, according to Cohen, were varied and included personal support when the "financial manager is unwilling to supply funds requested . . . such as for special clothing, food, and refreshments for herself or her children."[12] Furthermore, they included investments in local money-lending clubs, and young wives rarely divulged to members of the joint family, or even to their husbands, the extent of their monetary involvement in such credit associations.

In a similar vein, Yang reports that in Shandong Province "the young wife could either invest this sum [*sai-khia*] in small home industries or lend it at interest to fellow villagers."[13] When her money was sufficient she might even use it to buy land, ". . . and this land would belong to the small family unit including herself, her husband, and children and not to the large family of her husband."[14]

In Xin Xing it was found that the practice of *sai-khia* was recognized in the "old days," but was not prevalent. (So rare, in fact, was the practice that no villager thought it important enough to relate spontaneously to us, and only after reading Cohen's work in the late seventies did we question the villagers about it.) The practice was atypical because of the poverty of the local people. Women had little opportunity to accumulate *sai-khia* before marriage, since any money earned was, by necessity, used to augment the family's meager income and to help pay for her dowry. If by chance a woman did manage to accumulate and to bring private money with her to her new home, it usually disappeared quickly, spent to provide for her own needs or those of her children.

In short, the accumulation and use of private money was, apparently, in large part, a function of a family's economic position. Moreover, although the practice by female, and male, members of the joint family was tacitly accepted, it was not encouraged "by the family at large."[15] This was so because the practice was seen to have worked to the family's disadvantage since when young husbands and ". . . young wives manage to make money, they become selfish, and, as a result, quarrels arise which threaten the unity of a large family."[16] Yet the practice might have been accepted because it worked to the large family's advantage; that is, it provided a channel via which individual family members could achieve a modicum of independence from its dictates and rules of submission and egalitarianism.

In the light of this observation, then, one might ask: what has happened to the joint family under the impact of modernization in Taiwan, an impact usually associated with demands for independence from the restraints of the larger family? How has the joint family responded to intrafamily strains generated by the development process? It is to these questions that we now turn.

THE MODIFIED JOINT FAMILY

The structural arrangement of the modern joint family among Xin Xing area residents and migrants to Taibei continues, in part, to resemble that of the traditional type described above. That is to say, the primary household in the village (or in Taibei) usually contains the majority of the members, although there may be individuals who work and live elsewhere. Furthermore, within the primary household each conjugal unit maintains its own apartment or rooms in a single large house. The members of these units, in addition, share the use of the kitchen, dining area, toilet and bathroom facilities, and the *gongting*, i.e., central room that houses the ancestral tablets and statues of the gods.

Daily meals continue to be eaten together and the costs of these, as well as medical and household expenses—e.g., utilities and taxes—are paid out of a single family treasury. In addition, gifts of money for weddings, funerals, house-openings, village rituals, and so on are withdrawn from a common coffer; in fact, assessments for village rituals are made on the basis of the number of people in the large family and the amount of land they jointly cultivate. Furthermore, all of the costs of a son's engagement and marriage and some of the costs of a daughter's dowry are covered by the family treasury. (We will return to this point shortly.)

Finally, much of the capital to begin businesses and all educational expenses—be they for grade school, high school, college, or apprenticeship training—are provided for by funds from the family coffer. This is so because the joint family, as in traditional times, strives for economic diversity. Thus, each son is encouraged to prepare himself for and to engage in a different trade, occupation, or profession on the basis of his abilities.

The disbursement of family money, for whatever purpose, also continues to be controlled by the senior couple in the family, although they may, if the amount required is large, consult with other adult members of the joint family about its use. The money they disburse is derived from any profits earned tilling the family's land and from wages and business income of family members, namely the father, sons, and unmarried daughters. The contributions of these individuals to the family treasury, however, are neither equal nor total, and it is this variability that first distinguishes the present-day arrangements of the joint family from those of the past.

For example, the father-*jiazhang* of the family continues to deposit all of his wages, if any, into the joint treasury. In contrast, daughters are asked to deposit only a part of their earnings into the common coffer; the remainder, minus a small amount of pocket money for the girls, is turned over to the mother, who usually invests it in a money-lending club until such time as it is needed to purchase the girls' dowries. This means that most of the daughters' wages are not used for the support of the larger family, but are saved for their own use at the time of marriage.

In a similar vein, sons also are asked to deposit only a portion of their wages or business income into the family treasury. The remainder is kept by them as savings for future economic ventures and/or investments, and, if they are married, as funds for the clothing and recreation of their own conjugal units. If the sons are unmarried, it sometimes is expected that a part of the money they retain will be saved for use at the time of their marriage.

The second change in the operation of the joint family that distinguishes present-day arrangements from those of the past concerns the contribution of daughters-in-law to the family. As observed above, daughters-in-law were expected to devote most of their time and energy to tasks that were required for family functioning, such as housework, care of the children, farming, and so on. Only during their spare time were they permitted to engage in activities that generated private money for use by themselves or by their own conjugal units. Now, in contrast, daughters-in-law not only are allowed, but indeed encouraged, to engage in economic activities during the time traditionally considered that of the larger family. Moreover, the money produced by these activities is considered to be their own, not the family's. In other words, daughters-in-law continue to be allowed to accumulate funds for their *sai-khia*, but at the expense of the larger family or, more accurately, at the expense of their mother-in-law.

For example, although daughters-in-law continue to share responsibility for many of the household chores—e.g., cooking, cleaning, washing, and so on—their mother-in-law, by necessity, also must assume part of this burden if her daughters-in-law are to engage in economically remunerative activities. Thus, much of her time, time previously spent supervising her daughters-in-law, now is spent supervising their children and performing part of their role responsibilities, such as preparing meals or working the family's land. Her daughters-in-law, accordingly, can work in local industries or in their own businesses.[17]

To summarize, then, over the past twenty years, some aspects of the joint family's structure have changed while others have remained the same. For example, traditional living patterns and certain financial arrangements persist. In contrast, other traditional financial arrangements as well as roles and role relationships have changed. The questions are, then: Under what conditions have these changes evolved? What effect have they had on relations within the family? And how can these changes be explained? It is to these questions that we now turn our attention.

DISCUSSION

The modification of the joint family has taken place during a period of rapid economic development and change. As the importance of business and industry has grown in rural Taiwan, the paramountcy of agriculture has declined. For example, Xin Xing villagers estimated that in 1958, 95 percent of the resident families' incomes were derived from farming and farm-related wage labor. By contrast, in 1979, 85 percent of the village families' incomes were derived from non-farm related activities. In a similar vein, in 1979, 61 percent of the resident population sixteen to sixty-five years of age considered non-farm business or labor their major economic activity (see Table 5.2). Moreover, one third of these people were working in thirty-six family businesses located within the village.

Many of these non-farm workers are returned migrants who learned skills, established business contacts, and accumulated capital while working in the city; not a few consciously went to the city to achieve these goals. The businesses, factories and service shops they operate in the rural area reflect a response to the intense competition and high costs of labor and locations in the city and, as might be expected, the obverse in the home area.

A large number of these people, however, are former agriculturists responding to the decrease in income obtainable from farming and to the increase in income attainable from non-farm activities. Agricultural profits simply cannot compare with the money to be earned as a entrepreneur or worker, and people attach higher importance to increasing their income than to farming. This is not to suggest that villagers have given up tilling the land. They have not. What it means is that farming is carried on almost exclusively by parents aged fifty-five and over and non-agricultural work by their sons, daughters, and daughters-in-law.

This arrangement is possible because the increasing modernization of agriculture has obviated the need for either a virile or a large labor force.[18] Moreover, this arrangement is possible because mothers-in-law now frequently perform part of the role responsibilities of their daughters-in-law, thereby enabling the younger women to engage in remunerative economic activities. That such role changes are common in Xin Xing can be seen from the fact that almost three quarters (70 percent) of the women who were under

TABLE 5.2
Non-farming Economic Activities of Resident Xin Xing Villagers 16 to 65 Years of Age, By Sex and Type of Employment, January–June, 1979

| | | | Type of Employment | | | | | | | |
| Sex | Family Business[1] | | Salaried or Wage Labor | | Part-time Piece-Work | | Totals | |
	Number	Percent	Number	Percent	Number	Percent	Number	Percent
Male (N = 100)	30	30.0	38	38.0	3	3.0	71	71.0
Female (N = 100)	14	12.8	40	36.7	4	3.7	58	53.2
TOTAL (N = 209)	44	21.0	78	37.3	7	3.4	129	61.7

Source: Field Interviews

1. The figures include the owners/managers of these businesses as well as family members who worked for them for indefinite wages.

forty years of age and members of joint families engaged in non-farm economic activities (see Table 5.3). By contrast, only one third (33 percent) of the women who were under forty years of age and members of conjugal families were able to work for salaries or wages.[19]

Such role changes among family members, however, have resulted in significant changes in intra-family relations. For example, the dominance and authority of the father has decreased considerably as his sons build an economic base independent of him through their own and their wives' earnings. In addition, the status differential between father and sons has narrowed as the economic value of sons has grown. Increasingly, the young men are brought into the decision-making process in recognition of their financial contribution to the family. Similarly, the dominance and authority of the mother has been undermined significantly by the economic independence of her daughters-in-law. Furthermore, the status differential between them has narrowed as their role relationships blur. Increasingly, mothers-in-law are heard to lament "she" is the superordinate, "I" am the subordinate.

Not surprisingly, as the authority of the elders weakens and the independence of their sons and daughters-in-law grows, the tie between the young husband and wife is strengthened. That is, their marital relationship tends to be more egalitarian, an egalitarianism manifested in a greater degree of joint financial control over money, a higher degree of mutual respect, and a larger number of shared recreational activities. For example, women, including daughters-in-law, frequently sit at the tables with men during festival dinners. Furthermore, as the independence and status of sons and daughters-in-law increase, their relationship with the wives' natal families deepens.

The latter is so for several reasons. First, since the daughter-in-law's relationship with her mother-in-law is less hierarchical, the young wife is relieved of her former fear of initiating more frequent visits to her natal home. Second, since the division of labor between the two women is less rigid, the young wife is more free to make the visits. Finally, and perhaps somewhat tangentially, transportation—for example, motorcycles, and taxis—is readily available. Yet, it must be noted that the cost of this transportation is financed by the young couple's earnings, not by that of the joint family.

The relationship of the elder couple with their unmarried children also has been affected by changing economic conditions in rural and urban Taiwan. For example, almost all children over age sixteen who are not attending high school are either training as apprentices or working in factories, locally or outside; almost none work on the land, and few from the area attend college. Most of these young people live at the workplace, and their relative freedom and economic emancipation tend to generate an attitude of greater independence in them. As a result, they are less willing to accede to their parents' dictates, or even advice. Increasingly, then, as parents realize the limits of their authority, one hears them perforce say, "The child has his own mind."

TABLE 5.3
Work Status of Xin Xing Married Women* By Age and Family Type, January-June, 1979

	Work Status					
	Working		Not Working		Totals	
Family Type/Age	Number	Percent	Number	Percent	Number	Percent
Conjugal						
20-39	4	33.3	8	66.6	12	100.0
40 and older	10	52.6	9	47.4	19	100.0
Stem						
20-39	7	50.0	7	50.0	14	100.0
40 and older	3	16.7	15	83.3	18	100.0
Joint						
20-39	7	70.0	3	30.0	10	100.0
40 and older	2	16.7	10	83.3	12	100.0

Source: Field Interviews

*Only women who engage in non-farm economic activities are included. All but two of these women identified work and housekeeping as their primary and secondary major activities, although not always in that order. The two exceptions indicated that they also engaged in part-time farming. One of these women was a member of a stem family and the other a member of a conjugal family.

In short, the authority of the senior couple has weakened as the independence of their children—married and unmarried—has strengthened. But, as observed above, parents tolerate this situation. There are two plausible explanations for this, both of which have a logical relation to the increase in joint families observed earlier. The first, is the parents' realization that the joint family is an excellent mechanism for socioeconomic success in a changing world. For example, economic diversification still is considered a requisite for achieving wealth and social status. Thus, a large family that consists of many potential workers, as well as other members who can perform tasks necessary for the functioning of the family (supervision of children, care of the land, etc.), stands a better chance of diversifying economically than does a family of small size.

Furthermore, extensive relationships with people outside the area also continue to be considered a requisite for achieving wealth and social status. This means that the importance of matrilateral and affinal relations has increased as the strength of lineage or kinship organization has decreased in the area.[19] Thus, a family that consists of several daughters-in-law and married-out daughters has more opportunity to establish and to cultivate such instrumental networks than does a family of small size. In short, the parents' realization that socioeconomic success can best be attained by a large family motivates them to try to form and to maintain such a family, even in the face of their diminished authority.

The second explanation for the parents' tolerance of their weakened authority is their realization that wealth and economic stability must be achieved prior to the inevitable division of the family if each new economic household is to have the resources necessary to develop into a joint family, thereby replicating the cycle and maintaining a successful family line over time. In other words, the parents want to postpone the division of the joint family until such time as all its smaller, constituent units are (1) self-sufficient and prepared to assume economic independence and (2) fully developed and equipped to grow and prosper on their own. As a consequence, they have modified the structural arrangements of the family to prevent conflictive and divisive situations from developing at too early a stage of its life cycle.

For example, we know that conflicts frequently developed in joint families over perceived economic inequities. That is, while each conjugal unit usually served as a pool of equivalent numbers of workers, the families of older sons (by virtue of their greater number of children) consumed more of the family resources. In addition, one or another daughter-in-law frequently demanded a greater share of the family purse for herself or her children or, on occasion, shirked her responsibilities to the family in order to earn private money.

These problems are mitigated by the arrangements of the modified joint family. For example, each son is asked to contribute only a portion of his income to the joint family treasury, and the amount requested usually is based on the economic circumstances of and number of people in his conjugal unit. In other words, each unit contributes an amount proportional to its income and to the share of family resources it consumes. Furthermore, daughters-in-law are allowed, indeed encouraged, to engage in economically remunerative activities and to retain their earnings as private money and for use by the members of their families. In this sense, then, the accumulation of *sai-khia* by a daughter-in-law—a practice traditionally considered destructive of family unity—now is considered facilitative, and even necessary, for family unity and continuity. Accordingly, the accumulation of *sai-khia* has become an important mechanism by which a daughter's-in-law personal economically remunerative activity is legitimized.

We also know that harsh treatment of a daughter-in-law by her mother-in-law could cause bad feeling between affines. Moreover, such treatment was a source of considerable stress for a young woman separated from a basic fount of emotional support and succor, i.e., her mother. These problems also are mitigated by the arrangements of the modified joint family. First, the diminished status differential between mother-in-law and daughter-in-law considerably decreases the likelihood that the elder woman will unjustly impose her authority on the younger woman. In other words, the daughter-in-law is left with less cause for complaint to report to her natal family. Second, the increased frequency with which the daughter-in-law visits her natal home provides her with more opportunities to vent her emotions and to satisfy any need she may have for reassurance or psychological support. Thus, she is better equipped to cope with strains engendered by the joint family situation.

Yet, the arrangements of the modified joint family also have advantages that are unrelated to the mitigation of conflict; these are recognized by family members and serve as additional reasons to maintain the large unit. For example, the joint family offers savings in money and time for its members. First, costs of daily living, gift giving, and taxes are less for the larger, single unit than they would be for several smaller, individual units. Second, costs of operating the land are less because crops can be harvested and marketed in one large, joint unit. And third, time spent performing daily chores is reduced because tasks are shared or rotated among family members.

In addition, the arrangements of the modified joint family greatly increase the economic potential and security of each conjugal unit within it. That is, the single economic base of the joint family serves both as a source of potential venture capital for member families as well as a source of protection when private capital is used to start a new enterprise. In other words, the profits of success belong primarily to the conjugal unit, but the losses of failure are shared by the joint family and its treasury.

In this sense, then, the modified joint family serves as a kind of holding company. Each conjugal unit, as well as the large family itself, benefits from the centralized banking services it offers, as well as from the protection it provides against financial loss. Thus, the failure of a new economic enterprise neither bankrupts the single conjugal unit nor the joint family itself.

In short, the many advantages of the modified joint family make it a valued institution in this changing society. As such, it is not surprising to find that conscious efforts are made to ensure its continuance. These efforts are not exerted by the senior couple alone, however. They also are undertaken by the young members of the conjugal units, including the daughters-in-law, as the following excerpt from an interview with a father-*jiazhang* illustrates:

> I want to divide the family now. Everyone is settled and I don't want the big responsibility anymore. But, the children won't let me. They say there's plenty of time yet.

SUMMARY AND CONCLUSIONS

The subject of this paper has been the Chinese joint family, an institution that has been maintained for millennia by well-to-do landlord and elite families, and by families able to diversify their economic base. A major advantage of this institution has been its ability to provide member conjugal units with the economic headstart required to grow and to develop the strength, wealth, and size necessary for their own security and continuity after family division.

Yet, the maintenance of the joint family always has been difficult and precarious, for internal strife born of economic insufficiency threatened its viability. Using the Xin Xing area as an example, we have shown the ways in which these conditions operated and precipitated the "premature" division of the family. For example, the response to problems of insufficient land-holdings and limited economic opportunities in the area during the 1950s and 1960s was out-migration. This high mobility, accompanied by a degree of social instability, was, we argue, a major etiological agent in the division of the joint family.

Beginning in the early and mid-1970s, however, economic conditions began to change in the area. First, agricultural conditions improved as a consequence of (1) a brief period of guaranteed rice prices in 1974-1975 and (2) an increase in farm mechanization. Second, industry began to burgeon in the area. Out-migration decreased and in-migration, or rather re-emigration, increased as people responded, in part, to these phenomena, and, in part, to the recession and inflation of 1974. Furthermore, within the context of these conditions, the number of joint families in the area began to grow.

We have argued that this growth, or more accurately the growth of the *modified* joint family, was a reflection of the institution's ability to further economic diversification. That is to say, the large family provides its members with the necessary economic base and security to begin new entrepreneurial activities. In other words, it serves as an important intra-family mechanism that allows its members to develop the venture capital necessary for economic diversity to take place. In this sense, then, the joint family might be viewed as a catalyst for, not an impediment to, rural industrialization and economic development.

NOTES

1. Scarlett Epstein, *Economic Development and Social Change in South India* (Manchester, England: Manchester University Press, 1962); Neil J. Smelser, "Mechanisms of Change and Adjustment to Change," in *Economic Development and Social Change*, ed. George Dalton (New York: The Natural History Press, 1971), pp. 352–74; Rodolfo Stavenhagen, *Social Classes in Agrarian Societies* (New York: Anchor Press/Doubleday, 1975).

2. Bernard Gallin, *Hsin Hsing, Taiwan: A Chinese Village in Change* (Berkeley: University of California Press, 1966).

3. Bernard Gallin, "Rural to Urban Migration in Taiwan: Its impact on Chinese Family and Kinship," in *Chinese Family Law and Social Change in Historical and Comparative Perspective*, ed. David C. Buxbaum (Seattle: University of Washington Press, 1978), pp. 261–82; Bernard Gallin and Rita S. Gallin, "The Integration of Village Migrants in Taipei," in *The Chinese City Between Two Worlds*, eds. Mark Elvin and G. William Skinner (Stanford, California: Stanford University Press, 1974), pp. 331–38; Bernard Gallin and Rita S. Gallin, "Sociopolitical Power and Sworn Brother Groups in Chinese Society: A Taiwanese Case," in *The Anthropology of Power*, eds. Raymond D. Fogelson and Richard N. Adams (New York: Academic Press, 1977), pp. 88–97.

4. Gallin, "Rural Urban Migration."

5. For example, the increased economic value of sons and daughters who migrated to cities to work tended to undermine the authority of parents and had an important bearing on family division. Moreover, the conscription of men, land reform, and taxation often made it beneficial for families to divide.

6. The sources of the data on family type contained in Table 5.1 are, as indicated, different. That is, the figures for 1958–59 are derived from *huKou* (family records) and those for 1979 from our own field survey. The accuracy and comparability of the two sets of data, however, were confirmed by correlation with other statistical materials. These materials included enumerations based on our own surveys and of field interviews with individual village family units cultivating land, maintaining livestock, and owning farm implements.

7. Martin Yang, *A Chinese Village: Taitou, Shantung Province* (New York: Columbia University Press, 1945) p.79.

8. Ibid., p. 80.

9. Ibid., p. 79.

10. Myron L. Cohen, *House United, House Divided: The Chinese Family in Taiwan* (New York: Columbia University Press, 1976), pp. 178–91, discusses the dearth of literature about married-in-women's private money.

11. Ibid., pp. 178–79.

12. Ibid., p. 181.

13. Yang, *A Chinese Village*, p. 79.

14. Ibid.

15. Ibid.

16. Ibid.

17. In fact, when a son reaches marriageable age he is encouraged to marry a girl who has had work experience in a factory or business. Moreover, after marriage, a room of the family house sometimes is turned over to an entrepreneurial daughter-in-law so that she may operate a business.

18. For example, the introduction of herbicides, power tillers, rice transplanters, harvesters, and irrigation wells operated by diesel engines or electric motors did away with many of the myriad tasks, as well as time constraints, involved in the cultivation of rice.

19. Furthermore, more of the women from joint families operated their own businesses than did their counterparts in stem and conjugal families (44, 0, and 7 percent respectively). In point of fact, members of joint families were more likely to operate enterprises in the village than were members of stem or conjugal families. For example, ten (77 percent) of the thirteen joint families in Xin Xing include members who own village-based businesses. By contrast, only four (15 percent) of the twenty-seven stem families and seventeen (51 percent) of the conjugal families include members who own local enterprises.

20. Bernard Gallin, "Matrilateral and Affinal Relationships of a Taiwanese Village," *American Anthropologist*, LXII (1960): 632–42.

6 MARRIAGE RELATIONSHIPS AS A RESOURCE: SINGAPORE CHINESE FAMILIES

Janet W. Salaff*

The study of sustained interaction between social actors is greatly enriched by research on the structure of social institutions under given economic conditions. By spotlighting the ways in which the quality of interpersonal interaction depends on socio-economic position it becomes clear that socio-economic forces give rise to distinctly different styles of personal relationships and conversely that modes of interaction between individuals help shape social class trajectories. My cross-sectional study of one hundred young Singapore Chinese couples demonstrates in a variety of ways (interaction between spouses, and between the family unit and wider kin groups) the close links between husband-wife interaction and the social standing of target families.

I seek through my stress on the interconnection of economic resources and family norms to show how working-class families in developing nations raise their living standards through a combination of their own efforts and utilization of state social betterment programs. By detailing the intimate re-

*This paper is part of a larger study on government-sponsored family policies in Singapore that reorganize popular resources to reward and sanction families better to adjust to the industrializing order. The results of the wider study are more fully reported on in Janet W. Salaff, "Structuring and Industrial Society: Class, Social Policy, and Family Plan in Singapore" (manuscript in preparation). I am indebted to the international development Research Centre (IDRC) (Ottawa) for the funding that enabled the collection of data on the topic and to Dr. Aline Wong, who collaborated with earlier stages of the study. The views expressed in this paper are my own and are not necessarily shared by IDRC or Dr. Wong.

lationships between social structure and national economic plans my research can assist programs to alleviate poverty and promote rational economic development and effective nation building in the Third World.[1]

In 1953, Marion Levy analyzed the role played by traditional family structure in the industrialization processes. Professor Levy hypothesized that the subordination of youth to the interests of their family group, demands and authority of the elder generation and ancestral traditions hindered all efforts to industrialize China. In contrast, the loyalty and obedience of Japanese youth and their families to the Meiji state was total, and this promoted the cause of modernization and development in post-Meiji Japan. Certainly Japanese youth were raised to follow the wishes of their elders, but two hundred years of Tokugawa rule led to a far greater degree of subordination to the central authority than was the case in China.[2] Scholars of economic and social development maintain that today's newly industrializing societies can only implement their ambitious economic programs by enhancing workforce and educational opportunities for young married couples. Such development measures are expected to liberate the energies of the young people who were formerly bound by traditional family regimes. My study of the impact of industrialization on social life shows how young Singapore Chinese families respond to and interact with state-initiated development programs.

The Chinese family is characterized by the weak marriage bond and strong filial tie, the lionization of male offspring, and the subordination of married daughters to their husbands' families.[3] The present study shows that the changes in the Singapore Chinese marriage bond are the key to understanding family structure in the Singapore industrialization process. My other works round out the picture by discussing the family roles of sons and daughters.[4]

Family functioning, norms and interaction among Singapore Chinese married couples are determined in the main by the social class background of the partners. In particular, marriages in the poor working class are segregated, and husbands and wives strictly distinguish their tasks by sex. On the other hand, tasks in the more affluent working and middle-class families are carried out jointly with a greater degree of sharing and interchangeability between the spouses. The modalities of this class-based marriage interaction are evident in the four principal domestic areas studied in this paper: bilateral division of labor; shared leisure and recreational activities; trust and the exchange of confidences between spouses; planning and mobilization of family resources to achieve advancement.

The evidence presented in this paper further suggests that a strong bond linking husbands and wives in these four main areas contributes to the forward economic momentum of the family and reproduces social class. In order to take advantage of state-initiated policies that integrate families into the process of rapid industrialization, Singapore young married couples must develop plans for the future, and the form of conjugal interaction consistent with such planning can contribute to the elevation of families out of poverty. On the other hand, the divided, segregated marital bond common in my working-class respondents impedes all efforts at future planning by the couple.

William Liu and others find that a segregated conjugal bond furthers the traditionally exercised control of the older generation on the marriage of the youth. These studies inquire whether this subordination to the patriliny intervenes in and hinders the couple from prospering in the socio-economy.[5] My empirical research shows that it is impossible for couples to be close to their spouses and to their elders at the same time. A Singapore husband cannot be close to his wife and mother simultaneously, and therefore must choose between them. The more affluent families generally manage this competition by assigning priority to the conjugal bond, whereas the poorer young couples are more frequently dominated by their elders. I conclude from my panel study that the lack of conjugal communication and sharing, and the subordination of the couples to the elder generation, seriously impede the formation and realization of effective family plans. My research considers that, in sum, social class shapes the planning strategies used by Singapore Chinese couples. In turn, these family relationships play their part alongside economic conditions in determining the economic future of my respondents.

RESPONDENTS

My study examines the factors contributing to the development of family plans for one hundred Chinese couples with at least one child, whose wives were aged twenty to thirty in 1974–76. Wives were contacted through factory rosters and district Maternal and Child Health Clinics. Each Singapore mother is registered in the clinic that serves her district, and we were able to use an ecological sampling frame and to draw respondents' names from clinic records in four settlements of substantially varied economic environments. Our study is not a random sample of families. The sample is comprised of a series of quotas for husband's occupation, to coincide roughly with the socio-economic structure of the populace as indicated in the 1971 census, and includes: couples whose husbands hold farm, menial, average, and above average working-class jobs; white-collar workers; and entrepreneurs. Working wives were oversampled to ensure adequate cases for analysis.

Couples were interviewed in considerable depth: the wives four times and husbands once, in five ninety-minute sessions. Usually interviews were held in the couples' homes, but respondents were also met at their work places, or on outings with myself and other interviewers.

A socio-economic measuring stick was developed from data generated by the interviews. The social class of each couple was determined from the occupations of the parents of the husband and wife, the combined income of the couple at the time of the interview, and their average educational attainment.[6] The one hundred couples are distributed by socio-economic level as follows:

Common working-class families, termed here "group 1" families

lower working class (group 1a families)	17
average working class (group 1b families)	41
	58 families

Better off families, termed here "group 2" families

upper working class (group 2a families)	19
middle class (group 2b families)	23
	42 families

BACKGROUND: SOCIAL CLASS AND POLICY IN SINGAPORE

Development of a family plan for the future enables Singapore working-class families to utilize new avenues toward a higher standard of living and better job skills that have been opened by the government in its program for transnational corporation-based industrialization. The governing People's Action Party (PAP, founded in 1954) is animated by the ideology of social democracy and affirms that the capitalist market system, modified by state economic regulation, can be reformed into socialism.[7] As part of this process of political-economic transformation, the state enforces economic and social policies aimed at ameliorating the many shortcomings inherited from British colonial rule: widespread poverty, massive unemployment, and a labor-intensive and service-dominated economy built upon Singapore's position as an entrepôt for the primary products of the hinterland, and a big British military base east of Suez.

The government has established statutory boards empowered to promote, with a minimum of interference from the legislature, infrastructural services that are central to economic growth. The government also invests wholly or partly in key industries such as shipyards, other charter industries, and Development Board Projects. Industries that are key to the new industrial order, frequently owned by foreign capital, are promoted by the government through substantial tax subsidies and economic incentives.[8] Numerous social services were financed with the stated aim of improving the quality of the new industrial labor force and at the same time providing economic benefits for individuals and families. These benefits include contributory pension programs; large blocks of working-class housing, and schemes to finance the purchase of these apartments through the pension plans; popular secondary education; technical training and post-secondary adult education costs; and hospital care and fertility limitation assistance.[9]

The government does not, however, promote income equalization or a comprehensive welfare state, since such policies would entail restrictions on the inflow of transnational capital, might also alarm indigenous capitalists, and are deemed too expensive for the state.[10] The government wishes not only to elevate the popular living standard by encouraging wage increases but also to break the cycle of poverty, by which "the rise in wages will not bring a better life to those families who increase their burdens by having more children to feed, clothe, and nurture." Statesmen fear "no amount of subsidies by the Government can remedy the lack of adequate food and care at home. . . . In fact, the greater the feather-bedding of large anti-social families, the greater will be the numbers of large families. . . . It is a vicious cycle which we must break."[11]

Mass educational efforts (rallies; posters; National Day celebration; popularly based institutions, such as community centers and the schools; government departments, such as the Ministry of Culture) are directed at the creation of a national identity and the formation of an elusive Singapore culture.[12] The stated goals of the Singapore education system are ethnic integration, equal opportunity for advancement, and promotion of the state economic strategies; hence, a standard core syllabus is taught to all Singapore primary and secondary students. The national identity promoted in this manner in the service of economic development stresses hard work and saving for the future as the path to family advancement.

Sociologists concerned with cultural reproduction have demonstrated that the behavioral norms inculcated in primary and secondary schools of the western world emphasize a "hidden curriculum," which legitimizes the mores of existing industrial society: obedience to authority, achievement orientation, the market place ethic, and the middle-class value system.[13] Although further research on this topic is needed, I believe that such an ideological syllabus is imbedded in Singapore instruction, and that the hidden curriculum further restricts nonconformity of Singapore youth, and enables the state-directed economic-centered ideology to take firm hold. Through the cultural institutions, therefore, citizens are encouraged to assume personal responsibility to avail themselves of the opportunities for work and education opened to all citizens by the state's industrial and social programs.

In addition to these positive measures socio-economic penalties are deployed in the cause of economic growth and political stabilization. For example, in order to reduce birth rates to lower the cost of national economic growth and to facilitate family social mobility a stringent set of negative sanctions were passed that penalize large families. Accouchement costs are raised after the first birth, and school enrollment choices are reduced for the fourth child.[14]

Taken together, in the absence of a welfare state or income equalization policies, the programmatic measures of the Singapore government directed to promote industrialization depend upon each family's efforts to upgrade its position. To do so, Singaporeans must develop farsighted economic plans if they wish to optimize their chance for a long-term economic improvement. These plans must also contain a certain content that takes into account policy measures, especially in the area of employment, upgrading through courses, purchase of public (HDB) housing for the family, and education for their children.

SOCIO-ECONOMIC INDICATORS

The four principal indicators of the ability of families to chart an upward course are: present economic standing; education; personal connections; and conjugal relationships. This paper will first briefly review the interrelationship of economic standing, education, and personal connnections, and then at greater length assess the marital resources of the couples interviewed.

(1) Family economic position   In the Singapore market economy, the work force is divided into discrete labor segments, the most prosperous of which is the sector of white-collar workers, trained craftsmen, and skilled employees in the highly capitalized and dynamic growth industries, represented by the large PAP unions. Secure employment is also provided for many skilled workers by those public services deemed important for economic growth and the civil service.[15] Shipyard worker, tractor mechanic, meter reader, and policeman are among the relatively more affluent working-class respondents (group 2a families) who are able to earn above-average wages and enjoy security of tenure. Lower-level managers, engineers, and civil servants are among the middle class (group 2b respondents). It will be shown that, on the whole, group 2 workers are the most fluent in family advancement planning.

The lowest income earners consist of a group outside the locus of high technology employment, hired by small and medium-sized firms, without a strong union, or located in less-profitable industries, considered unessential to economic growth. Examples of such low income earners are hawker, taxi driver, equipment operator for a contracting firm of fewer than five employees, and pineapple canner and tinsmith in small Chinese firms. This category of group 1 workers finds it difficult to develop family plans.

(2) Educational attainment and the transmission of cultural knowledge   English is joined by Malay, Mandarin, and Tamil as official languages in the Singapore school system.[16] English is the medium of international commerce and professional course instruction at the University of Singapore, and is the language of government affairs. Group 2 workers obtained English or Mandarin education as far as secondary or technical school, which paved the way to skilled labor and lower-rung supervisory positions. Those group 2b middle-class respondents who speak fluent English enjoy the widest employment opportunities and access to government social services in my sample.

Because of their roots in poverty, the ordinary workers, who generally terminated their education at primary school and acquired little English instruction, are effectively barred from all but unskilled or semiskilled positions. My poorer respondents found it difficult to secure promotions in the public sector and in occupations such as bus conductor or restaurant waiters. The chance of group 1 workers of attaining lower-level supervisory positions, such as forewoman of electronics assembly in a transnational capitalized factory, is also inhibited by lack of education.

Through their limited educational attainment and the hidden curriculum with its stress on obedience to authority and to existing rules, Singapore group 1 youth learn conformity to the wider socio-economy, but not mastery of their environment. This is one of the reasons my group 1 respondents accept their marital roles as inherited and unchanging, and invest little energy in altering the division of labor in the home and separate spheres of leisure activities that are sanctified by longstanding custom. Group 2 respondents, on the other hand, spent more years in school and learned to value planned cultural change, which they apply to the family relationships that they create in their marriages.

The jobs held by group 1 respondents require them to carry out standardized instructions and follow the commands of foremen and supervisors; they are positioned low on the hierarchy of power and influence. A narrow band of information and skills must be mastered on the job, a level of skills that is not readily generalized to other work settings.[17] This lack of transferability confines the working class to certain limited categories of jobs, including factory operative, craftsman, and laborer. The culture of conformity to orders taught in schools and on the job is reinforced in the home. It discourages young working-class parents from initiating change in their social environment, and appears to harden family role structure.[18]

In contrast, group 2 respondents are prepared for assumption of control over their employment milieu. Their longer schooling and work settings provide information which is pertinent to other jobs and industries and thereby broadens considerably the networks of job opportunity for these more affluent respondents. Better-faring families imparted confidence that their youth could exercise a measure of control over their work milieu. This confidence engendered by the group 2 home, school, and work settings carries over to the marriages of these better-situated respondents. Group 2 parents have been encouraged to mold their environment and master its difficulties, and a closer husband/wife relationship frequently results.

(3) Personal Relationships of the Respondents. The personal relationships that connect workers to a complex of opportunities and promote their aspirations originate in the family economic background. Group 1 couples generally matured in deprived households, headed by poorly paid and irregularly employed breadwinners. The fathers of many of my group 1 respondents had either perished or abandoned their families when the respondents were young teenagers. Many sons were therefore forced to quit, after only a few years of primary school, to take meagerly paid, minimally skilled positions with no economic future. Group 1 daughters helped care for the home and younger siblings or went out to work.

The kin and friendship networks of my group 1 respondents are comprised of workers in equally laborious, low paying positions, whose education is likewise rudimentary. These networks cannot provide suitable role models or ladders of advancement for the ascent from poverty. Group 1 respondents have few people in their personal circles to whom they can turn for information on social services, credit utilization, and effective assistance in career planning. Indeed, group 1 families are themselves the subject of demands for assistance by relatives and close friends, a situation which perpetuates their participation in this unpromising social network. The lack of resources makes it difficult for these working-class families to prepare workable plans for the medium and long-range future.

In the pre-industrial Singapore mercantile economy (pre-1957) families were able, through mutual benefit associations operated by clansmen and *hui guan (Landsmannschaften)*, to obtain introductions to jobs, short-term loans and credit, medical services, and even burial plots.[19] In contemporary industrializing Singapore, the dominating state bureaucracy has taken control over many social services previously offered by a wide variety of quasi-kinship groups. The status of the formerly powerful *hui-guan* and other kin associations has been greatly downgraded.[20] The modern family in industrial society links its members and social and governmental complex institutions.[21] Families now must obtain the bulk of their assistance from their immediate relatives and acquaintances and the state bureaucracy. In addition, large industrial firms may provide social services to their white-collar workers (such as insurance plans and educational scholarships for employees' children). However, group 1 workers are not employed by organizations with resources to offer, and they are connected in no other way with the wide circle of government apparatus and large private employers. Moreover, ordinary people cannot negotiate easily with well-educated, English speaking personnel with middle-class values in the government bureaucracy.

In contrast, group 2 families themselves emanate from an economically solid background. Their parents were alive and in the home while they were growing up and provided a stable domestic environment, secondary education, and targets for employment upgrading. Their network of fruitful personal and kin connections makes feasible the realization of the development of plans for their families by the upper working and middle-class parents of my sample.

These affluent families enjoy some control over the structures of their work setting, and they are likely to be employed by organizations with more social services for their employees (large industrial firms, government civil service, the educational system). Group 2 families are able to exploit the impersonal channels of the bureaucratic framework for jobs, education, insurance schemes, and other vital information necessary for the future of their families.

(4) Socio-Economic Background and Conjugal Relationships. The heritage of group 1 respondents consists of poverty and broken families. Constrained by this background, my blue-collar respondents suffer from personal illness, low wages and unsteady work, limited education and other misfortunes. Working-class deprivation gives rise to pessimism about future improvement and fosters resignation to the family lot. Common working-class folk attribute their poverty to their own shortcomings or to fate, and therefore regard major improvements as unlikely or at best governed by chance. Many of the ordinary working-class families live a week-to-week existence and seek diversion in petty gambling, without the guidance of a family plan. Lacking education and advancement prospects, they take the inherited family division of labor as a given, and they justify sex-linked roles with reference to biological imperatives.

Group 1 families are enmeshed in relations of reciprocal expectations with their kin. Husband and wife meet these social demands and requirements on different sexual planes, and, as we will see, their marriages appear to be weakened as a result.

Group 2 employees draw upon their secure environment for structure and strength, and since they are able to project positive economic experiences into the future, they can conceive of realistic long term family plans. The higher education of these couples enables them to transcend many traditional sexual scripts and roles, and they are more open to participatory domestic regimes.[22] Like the group 1 families, these group 2 couples avail themselves of family and kin support, but their kin have much more to offer. In addition, group 2 families, who can exploit the social services offered by work organizations and public agencies, are also better able to insulate themselves from many of the demands commonly articulated by grandparents and other relatives. They can therefore give pride of place to the marital bond in the family hierarchy. Group 2 families desire to stabilize and improve their socio-economic standing, a step that involves mutual cooperation and contributes to a stronger conjugal bond.

WOMAN'S WORLD, MAN'S WORLD: THE DIVISION OF LABOR IN THE HOME

The seventeen-group 1a family heads practice and uphold the tradition of distinguishing work and homemaking roles by sex, and none of the husbands provide much assistance to their wives in the home. Very few of the seventeen even occasionally aid their wives, and only when help is requested. This situation is illustrated by the responses of two wives to my query on their husbands' domestic responsibilities:

Lim Heng Chee, the wife of a rattan weaver in a small workshop, who lives in a one-room Tao Payoh HDB flat: "Actually men should not touch the work in the kitchen, but sometimes I ask my husband to care for the kids while I get the cooking done. My husband works all day, even on Sundays, and he has no time to help at home."

The wife of a daily-rated welder: "Homemaking is a woman's job. If a person is born a woman, she has to do it."

One source of segregated family roles is a difficult childhood upbringing. During their youth, many of my group 1 respondents experienced broken families in which their mothers toiled long hours at outside jobs to maintain the household. These men now desire their wives to care for their home, their children, and themselves in a solicitous way.[23] Many wives, for their part, vow not to see this experience repeated and attempt to stay at home with their families. (However, economic circumstances do not always permit them to limit themselves to household burdens, and over half of the group 1 wives labor for pay full or part time.) Women like the following would have preferred to make an independent economic contribution to the family, but are not permitted to do so by their husbands.

Tan Suan Ying, a housewife, was employed as a domestic servant (*amah*) before she married Eng Fong, a clerk in a British-owned soft drinks factory. Upon marriage, the couple decided that their poverty did not permit them to start a family immediately. They knew, however, that if all went well, Eng Fong would receive a twenty percent raise in two years, and they decided to wait until then before attempting to conceive a child. A son, Choo Swee, was born close to their third anniversary, and now in their fifth year of marriage Suan Ying is pregnant with her second, also a planned child. Soon after Eng Fong and Suan Ying married, Eng Fong's father and mother, whose relation was strained, decided to separate. Eng Fong's father lives apart with his first son and five grandchildren, while his mother resides with Suan Ying and Eng Fong in a one-room Housing Development Board (HDB) apartment. The family's single room is partitioned into two by a wooden screen. On the pallet on the floor of the one half sleep Grandmother and Choo Swee, while the couple sleeps in a bed in the other chamber. Grandmother cares for Choo Swee while Suan Ying does the daily marketing, and sometimes helps with the housework. Suan Ying feels that Grandmother is a strict disciplinarian, too quick with the bamboo rod when Choo Swee displeases her. "Either you beat them stupid or you push them into defiance. Both ways are wrong. I believe in explaining and persuading children, and my husband agrees. My mother-in-law tries to shock Choo Swee by pinching him and caning him. Despite all this Choo Swee is not afraid of her!" said Suan Ying.

In a separate interview, Grandmother Tan complained that Suan Ying pampers Choo Swee, who has been spoiled as a result. (Our interviewer in fact observed the child's petulance when asked to share sweets with an older cousin.) The two women apparently have several arguments a day over the discipline of Choo Swee, but each dispute is shortlived and the two have managed a *modus vivendi*. Eng Fong, while he notices that Suan Ying may be spoiling their child, would prefer a more modern solution than corporal punishment. While most families in my sample administer corporal punishment to the young, this punishment is usually administered by the parents and not the grandparents. Eng Fong limits his opinions of child rearing to his private views and does not take an active role in Choo Swee's upbringing. He is prepared only to moderate Suan Ying's presentation of her case against the mother-in-law. "The old ones don't have long on this earth. They've worked all this time and gave us an opportunity to get an education. Even if there are arguments and quarrels, we must forget a little and let them have their way," he counsels. Suan Ying carries the burden of the dispute over childrearing techniques on her own.

Suan Ying left her position as an *amah* when she married, and Eng Fong has consistently opposed Suan Ying's return to work. "My husband says a family must be together at home. We had a lot of quarrels over this, but he won. He said women are made to stay at home. But I say it's because he's jealous. Before I had my son I was very bored, and for the first two years of marriage I slept a lot and whiled away my spare time visiting friends and my husband's sister's family. Now I'm used to being at home." In my opinion, Eng Fong's concern over Suan Ying's work is due in part to his upset over the separation of his parents and to his determination that his family remain unified and that his wife conform to his expectations; and in part, too, he desires his wife to raise their children in a modern, achievement-oriented manner.

Many group 1 Singapore husbands toil a long work week, which includes either extensive overtime or moonlighting on a second job. These men often sacrifice Sundays and holidays, or whatever free time their regular employer allots them, in order to supplement their pay check. They invariably return home from work each day thoroughly exhausted, and are excused from family work. The wife of a daily-rated ship demolisher at the Tai Chung Company in Jurong does the housework and sews garments for a local factory at home for extra pay; she excuses her husband from performing tasks in the home. "I can tell you that his work is really very heavy. That's enough for him." The couple considers the husband's long hours and arduous buffalo labor a sufficient family contribution.

Many of these men also seek to escape their workday burdens and frustrations by socializing with their co-workers before journeying home, which leaves them little time to spend at homemaking chores.[24] A tailor, whose trade is based on the erratic custom of visiting British, American, and other navymen in the Sembawang harbor, regularly gambles at dice and cards in his workshop with his workmates long after working hours. His wife sighed, "I don't expect my husband to help. In fact, I'd be really happy if he just came home."

Husbands of higher rank in my sample (determined by parental economic background, couple's earnings, education, and occupational status) are far more willing to share tasks in the home. Such men may accompany their children on grandparental visits and to public school or day care in the morning. They may also perform marketing chores and occasional cooking and housecleaning duties. Twenty-three husbands in my sample carry out at least one such household-childcare task on a regular basis, twenty-five occasionally perform such tasks, whereas the remaining fifty-two males rarely or never share in the maintenance of the home and the rearing of their children. Most of the regular cooperators come from group 2 backgrounds, while the remainder stem from group 1b families. None of the seventeen lowest ranking (group 1a) men regularly share household tasks.

Two white-collar group 1b men, a store clerk and postman, both English-educated, exemplify the finding of this study that relatively secure white-collar careers are associated with greater household task sharing. Soo Chih Tung, a clerk, English-educated through the fourth form, is the major breadwinner for the family unit of thirteen which includes his wife, Hing Lee, their two children, his parents, and his six younger siblings, four of them school-aged children. Grandmother arises at five o'clock each morning to prepare a breakfast of rice porridge for the family group, while Mother awakens at six with her toddlers, bathes and dresses them, and begins housecleaning. Grandmother markets and returns at eight with the groceries, which Mother uses to prepare lunch for the eight of those who will be at the table. In the early afternoon, Hing Lee continues housecleaning and naps with her youngsters, and at three begins preparation for dinner aided by Grandmother. The dinner hour is at six.

Although the grandparents indicated their preferences to Mother that Chih Tung be exempted from all domestic chores, he nevertheless assists with sweeping and mopping the bedroom floor and dusting the bedroom cupboards. Chih Tung also clears the dinner table at night. Hing Lee told the interviewer, "My husband closes the bedroom door when he's doing the mopping and cleaning for me, so his parents don't see it. I don't have the energy to stand on a stool to clean the top of the cupboards, and he helps me with this chore once a month." It is difficult for Chinese sons to side with their wives and resist their parents' traditional views, and yet in this family Mr. Soo appreciates the dimensions of his wife's tasks and persists in supporting her in the home. His white-collar job and high school education bolster his commitment to a relatively egalitarian family form, and he takes his wife's part in countering pressures on her from the elders.[25]

When asked whether husbands should help in the house after their daily work shift and on weekends, Choo Kin Kiah, a postman's wife, affirmed: "It's better that we don't spoil our husbands!" Kin Kiah explained that her husband already cares for the children after he returns from his job. "I would like to go back to work in a couple of years when my youngest child is in primary school, and I'm counting on increased help from him at that stage." Women like these benefit from their husbands' awareness that men bear some responsibilities for managing the household. The rather well-considered views of these couples on home tasks translate into long-term norms of family cooperation and betterment.

Since the better-situated wives have come to expect and rely upon substantial assistance from their husbands in the home, these wives may feel embittered and even betrayed when this aid is not forthcoming. Thus a group 2 electronics factory section head, pregnant with her second child, complained about her mate, an accountant in a European trading firm: "He used to help me with the housework, but then he was injured in a car accident and ever since has complained of backache. Now, instead of helping me, he buries his head in a book or newspaper. I fought a long battle to educate him, but now I've given up on him." In contrast, ordinary working-class wives, who never expected that their husbands would assist them in home affairs, do not voice such disappointment at their spouses' nonparticipation.

In sum, improvement of the quality of life in the domestic arena is an important consideration in the world view of men who are secure in their jobs and have received schooling in the English language stream or through secondary level. While husbands and wives rarely put in equal time in the home chores, a minimum thirty-minute daily stint at a prescribed chore suffices at least to demonstrate the typical group 2 husband's commitment to redefine his position in the home away from an inherited, ascribed role. Most group 1 men, in contrast, grew up in broken homes where they received little parental nurturant care, have low educational attainment, and hold insecure, arduous jobs at which they toil long hours in the company of men. These environmental factors are associated with minimal sharing of household tasks.

LEISURE: TOGETHER AND APART

My interviewing experience and overall assessment of the functioning of these families led me to conclude that families which share not only domestic tasks but also leisure activities strengthen their marriage relationship. The pursuit of ordinary recreation and entertainment outside the home in each other's company is associated with the ability of husbands and wives to plan for the future.

Some husbands and wives infrequently partake in joint social outings, have no common friends, and seldom deliberate family matters. Other couples may share leisure-time activities, hold friends in common, and conduct lengthy discussions of family issues. A third, intermediate form of husband-wife interaction is discernible, in which the partners converse often about family matters, but rarely seek recreation and entertainment together or in the company of mutual friends. Each of these three styles of communication is found in my sample (Table 6.1). The distinct and segregated form of social life prevails in my group 1a families, while the pattern of shared activities and discussion about children and home predominates in group 2 couples. Group 1b families practice the intermediate form of interaction.

Extra long hours of toil by the poorly-remunerated group 1 wage earners leave the couples little time together. Independent entrepreneurs pass a twelve-hour day at petty commerce. After working hours, the camaraderie of friends is sought and enjoyed separately by each marital partner, and even on weekends, family excursions and outings are seldom planned. Since lower working-class women accept their husbands' absence from the home as the male's prerogative, their marriage tie is rarely enriched by relaxed hours during which the couple's relationship can be developed in new directions.

Group 1 women have been trained to consider themselves primarily as rearers of children and keepers of the hearth, to take greatest pleasure in raising children, and their maternal role is the core of their being. The care and welfare of their children in many cases takes precedence over the marital bond as such, as is found in working-class families elsewhere.[26] Women with

TABLE 6.1

Leisure and Communication Patterns, Young Married Singapore Chinese Couples, Number of Cases

	Segregated[a]	Mixed[b]	Joint[c]	NI[d]	Total
Group 1					
1a Lower Working Class	13	3	1		17
1b Average Working Class	11	18	11	1	41
Group 2					
2a Upper Working Class	3	5	11		19
2b Middle Class	5	7	10	1	23
TOTAL	32	33	33	2	100

[a] Segregated: Husband and wife have separate leisure activities and friends.
[b] Mixed: Couples either discuss family problems or share leisure activities or friends, but do not share both leisure and communication.
[c] Joint: Friends, leisure outings and discussions are shared.
[d] NI: No information.

young children gain moral and material support from other child-centered female relatives and neighbors, and they frequently visit their own mothers or mothers-in-law for advice (for example, on the best western or herbal medicines for an ailing child). Mothers may care for a daughter's or daughter-in-law's child during the day or for an entire week while the child's mother is employed or if she is unable to cope with her infant. Neighbors rotate shopping chores and will mind a sleeping child while its mother is marketing. Women must look beyond the marital bond to obtain these vital services, and the network of relations between women that is crucial to the work of housewifery is central to their daily activities, and enables young mothers to cope with the strains and dfficulties of homemaking in poor families.[27]

When they go out to work, group 1 women command the lowest wages of all the female respondents in my sample, and their lack of economic opportunities and potential intensifies their root attachment to home and children. Group 1 women who prefer not to adopt the nurturant role must locate female relatives to rear their offspring for them at low cost, since poverty precludes formal or semi-formal institutional childcare arrangements. There is no free daycare in Singapore, and all women without money must draw on their relatives' services or perform all nurturant duties themselves. Thus, involvement in the network of supports between women reinforces the total commitment of group 1 women to their children as their main duty, and is at the base of sex segregated, male- or female-centered leisure activities.

Lim Heng Chee, the wife of the rattan furniture maker introduced earlier, is entirely dedicated to her children. Heng Chee told our interviewer that prior to the birth of her first child, she and her husband, Lee Keong, attended a Mandarin cinema once each month. After the baby was born, however, the couple terminated their cinema-going, and no other form of shared entertainment took its place. At home in her tiny flat with two pre-school children, Heng Chee has now become adjusted to her domestic duties and responsibilities, and has not yet become restless. Heng Chee is pleased that she has found two good friends in the same apartment block, and she takes her children along when she joins these housewives in marketing expeditions. Lim Lee Keong, who rarely sees Heng Chee in her weekday home setting, scarcely knows her friends and instead maintains a set of work-centered acquaintances whom she never meets. Heng Chee explained in resignation, "It's impossible for us to visit friends and relatives together because my husband works until after sunset seven days a week."

The extended employment hours of lower working-class men and women frequently preclude a common evening meal, which deprives them of the occasion for family togetherness and sharing of experience. Aw Boon Eng is a public school caretaker, who works a twelve-hour shift and is married to Swan Tzu, a homemaker. The couple has two toddlers. Swan Tzu and Boon Eng live in a one-room, first floor rented apartment in the poorest

Housing Development Board estate. Swan Tzu commented in a listless voice, "My husband says it's too hot and stuffy to bring his friends into our one-room flat, and so he goes out frequently with them on his day off. Sometimes they go to the movies together. Since my husband often works through the dinner hour and never lets me know when he will return, the kids and I don't wait for him to eat. There's always something left over for him if he wants dinner." Swan Tzu provides for her husband's needs, but his chronic absence from home has stunted her marriage relationship.

The Tai family resides with the parents of Tai Chun Kim, a smith in an iron works. One year after the birth of her daughter, Tai Kwan Yan resumed factory work, this time as a seamstress in a garment factory. Kwan Yan's job limits her opportunity to arrange outings with her husband. "We seldom have time to go to the movies, but I have asked Chun Kim many times to join me at the market, or at least for gatherings on my side of the family. There's an outdoor bazaar at Milestone Eleven down the road from us, but Chun Kim won't come along in the evening, and my sisters or sisters-in-law join me instead. Before I went back to work, my husband and I occasionally strolled in the lane at night, but that's no longer possible because I have to do my housework after dinner, and when I've finished it's about time to go to bed. So Chun Kim just sits and reads the paper and watches television in the evening. Last Sunday my brother came here to drive me and my daughter to Mother's place for an overnight visit. Chun Kim didn't want to come. Unfortunately he's not as close to my family members as I am to his."

Young Singapore Chinese mothers find it important to make frequent calls with their new offspring to the home of their family of origin, and they usually desire their husbands to accompany them on these filial visits.

Sim Man Wah sells pop music cassettes from his tiny stall in an outdoor market in the Golden Mile Shopping Centre. Sim Soo Kee is a seamstress in a small garment workshop. Each Saturday evening, the Sims and their three and five-year-old children attend a film show. Once in a while, Mr. Sim closes his shop early on a Monday or Tuesday at dusk and comes home to take the family for a neighborhood stroll. Their walk leads the Sims to an outdoor dinner in a hawker's stall in one of the neighborhood market bazaars. Soo Kee and the children would enjoy more of these weeknight excursions, but Man Wah's normal workday extends until 9:00 P.M. Soo Kee is dismayed by her husband's late hours and the consequent limitation on family life. "I eat dinner at my mother's while Man Wah eats at his stall. By the time he comes back home, the children are already sound asleep, and the next morning when I bring them to their babysitter on my way to work, Man Wah is still in bed. Except for Sunday mornings, he has no chance to spend time with our children. What sort of family is it when the father doesn't play with the kids? I can't help showing my anger to him when he comes home late every night!"

Soo Kee and Man Wah maintain different circles of friends, and the couple makes no effort to bring members of these groups together. Soo Kee, in addition, spends much time with her mother, sister, brother, and aunt who reside in nearby housing estates, where she eats dinner and where her eldest child goes after school. Man Wah's chronic absence from their home and that of her parents is more troubling to Soo Kee than their separate circles of friends. Soo Kee's desire that her husband become a closer companion to the children is shared by the other working-class wives who are busy with their relatives and friends.

Nearly half of the families in my panel reside in extended households, and since Singapore is small in area, relatives in any case are never far away. It is usual for women to build relationships with their mothers, sisters, or mothers-in-law that center around children and the home. In addition, most husbands and members of the older generation permit wives and daughters-in-law to develop ties of mutual support with neighbors. However, group 1 women are generally expected by their husbands and parents-in-law to attenuate friendships, hobbies, and relationships formed at work and school prior to marriage, in favor of home-based family roles.

Mr. Song Kok Liang, a crane operator at a construction site and his wife, Yoon Mei, who assembles electronics systems in a foreign-owned factory, are parents of two children. The Songs have never travelled out of Singapore, but Yoon Mei wishes to pay a social visit to a group of former co-workers who have returned to their homes and birth places in Malaysia. "My husband would not let me go. He even scolds me when I return home at ten after visiting mother one mile away, saying, 'Women shouldn't stay out so late.' He would only let me visit across the border if he accompanies me, but there's little chance of that."

Mr. Song answers (somewhat accusingly), "It's true. You do return home very late!"

His wife makes no response.

We asked Hong Suan Bee, a production line worker in an electronics firm and mother of one, who is married to an office messenger, "Do you go out with your friends after work or visit them at their homes?"

"No. However, some of the Malay girls at work have a freer attitude and go out to enjoy themselves, even though their husbands are unhappy about it. But some of their marriages end in divorce. Before marriage I played the drums in a rock band. We entertained at parties and social events, but I can't accept such work anymore. People would ask, 'Why does a married woman go around doing things like that?' "

"But don't you think you should enjoy yourself after marriage?"

"How can I enjoy myself when I have to spend all my free time caring for my husband and child?"

Most women in my sample are compelled to dedicate themselves to the rearing of their infants. Generally, this is a sought-for role in which there is comfort. However, two or three of my interviewees clearly prefer alternatives to domestic duties. Chen Soo Ying, wife of a van driver, is a mother of two children, aged four and one. She belonged to her husband's circle of friends even after the birth of her first child because her mother took in the child to foster. Soo Ying recalled their happy times together, "He likes partying and drinking, and he encouraged me to dress up and carry a nice handbag and accompany him to nightclubs. We always stayed out until two or three in the morning." The care of two children, however, was more than Soo Ying's mother could manage, and so Soo Ying has to care for the new baby alone. Wai Fung then excluded his wife from his circle of friends.

Wai Fung joined our conversation: "Four of us go to the races every Sunday and bet on the horses. I used to take Soo Ying with me to the track and to the nightclubs, but she has to stay home now with our infant. So occasionally when I visit the night spots we book some of the girls to dance with us. Recently, however, our luck ran dry, so we go out much less frequently. But I still regularly have dinner with my friends because I do not care for Soo Ying's cooking."

Married group 1 women thus must withdraw from many social activities they might have enjoyed prior to marriage. Mau Lai Teng is a seamstress and Hau Soon, her husband of three years, works in the Sembawang shipyard. The couple lives with their young child at the home of Hau Soon's parents. They belong to the affluent working class (group 2a respondents), because of their high joint earnings and above-average parental occupations. However, due to their relatively low educational attainment and sex-segregated work environments, the couple can be found in the minority of the three affluent (group 2) workers with segregated leisure time activities (Table 6.1).[28] Lai Teng confided that her mother-in-law frowns upon her visits to friends. "It's not often that I go out with my girlfriends, because Mother-in-law is so suspicious of the people I see. She wants me to go out only if Hau Soon comes along. I was invited to attend the birthday party of a former co-worker. I asked my husband about it, and he felt I should not go. He said what use could a married woman have in socializing at a party? I saw his point of view and decided not to attend."

Group 1 men, however, do continue their hobbies and social activities after fatherhood, although wives attempt to curtail such pursuits if they feel the menfolk are not taking proper care of themselves or the family. Toh Kee Huat, married to Sam Chen, a mechanic with the Singapore Bus Service, is the mother of two. Sam Chen gambles regularly outside of working hours. Sometimes he also takes a day off to join his friends at cards and dice. Sam Chen is sometimes required to go underground for several days to evade his creditors. "Sam Chen often puts in overtime, and how do I really know whether he stays at work or goes out with his chums to gamble? On occasion Sam Chen stays away two nights in a row and worries the hell out of me. At such times I tell myself that it must have something to do with his gambling. Sometimes I trail him and I find him at the home of a buddy. I make a fuss in front of all the card players there. I take him home with me, but he goes back again a day later."

"Do you know your husband's friends well?" the interviewer asked Chen Sieow Wah, a housewife and mother of two, married for five years to a crane operator for a small Chinese subcontracting firm. "No, Ah You seldom invites his friends home. They used to phone him, and Ah You would rush out to meet them at a coffee shop. He would only leave them after midnight, and I scolded him each time he returned. It's not that I objected to his nights out, that was his affair. But he should limit his late evenings to Saturdays or before a holiday. As he is a crane driver, I want him to have enough sleep. His job is too dangerous for a tired man."

Blue-collar women are thus tied into a network of females that excludes their husbands due to their dependence on kinswomen and neighbors for daily necessities and services, enforced withdrawal from activities that might bring them into contact with men, and their husbands' participation in their own separate work-related circles of male contacts and friends. The women's sphere is exemplified by Heng Lai Neo, married for ten years to Heng Choo Soo, a well-paid crane operator at the Jurong Shipyard, and the mother of five children. Lai Neo found it difficult to raise her children, and three of them were taken in by relatives of Choo Soo. Lai Neo now has little housework to do, and she spends much of her day playing mahjong with the neighbors on her housing estate floor. Her eldest daughter, who went to live with Choo Soo's grandmother Heng and a spinster sister soon after her birth, remains there now. Choo Soo developed the habit of visiting his sister's home after work. "Choo Soo always eats dinner at his sister's place on the way home from work. He says that my cooking is poor. He started dining at his sister's during the first year of our marriage, and this has been going on ever since. I don't complain about it, because I feel he's not a bad husband, though one cannot say that our marriage is ideal. I am the type who feels there is no need for a husband to be with me all the time. Although I do like company, I can always visit the neighbors and my girlfriends who live nearby." When our interviewer called at Lai Neo's flat she always found several neighbors visiting. The neighbors buy breakfast for each other at the nearby market, play mahjong, and participate in excursions to worship the deities of the Taoist and Buddhist pantheon on the gods' birthdays.

Couples with education and secure, white-collar jobs are likely to share leisure time activities, as seen in the following group 1 cases. Soo Chih Tung, a store clerk with form four English education, makes a point of taking his wife to the cinema or to a hawkers' bazaar every weekend. He understands that Hing Lee, who manages an extended household of thirteen people, is virtually housebound. (Chih Tung's assistance to Hing Lee at home was mentioned above.)

Tan Suan Ying shares confidences and leisure-time outings with her husband, Eng Fong (see the Tan family above). Eng Fong attended English secondary school for four years, and I gathered that because of his education and his office work setting he obtained his position independently, without the assistance of family and friends, and can maintain it in the same manner.

"Eng Fong always informs me when he plans to go out after work, even if I do not ask him," recounted Suan Ying. "But his job is quite exhausting, and he even has to work on Sundays, and so he stays home most evenings and watches television before falling asleep. Once in a while he asks me to go somewhere with him, but I'm also tired at night. Eng Fong is very considerate, and sometimes when friends invite him for dinner, he declines because he prefers to have meals with us at home. However, there was one problem. In the past Eng Fong used to be very jealous. But now that I have a child, I'm allowed to go out anywhere I like without him. When I went marketing before I had my son, my husband even asked my neighbor or his mother to accompany me. That's how trustful he was!"

Suan Ying smiled brightly when she told our interviewer that, just the day before, Eng Fong had taken the day off from work to take her and the children to the zoo (an hour's journey by bus), in celebration of Choo Swee's second birthday. On the way home the family stopped off at a hawker stall in an outdoor market for supper. Suan Ying contrasted her own close, marital bond to the more segregated relation of her parents-in-law. "While they were together, they seldom discussed anything, and now they have separated. My husband and I always plan our activities together," she stressed.

Suan Ying did not hesitate to talk about her personal life to the twenty-two-year-old, newly-married woman who interviewed her for this study. "I'll tell you frankly, woman to woman: men like sex. If you don't submit to them, they will find other, younger women, and you will lose their heart. That's one of the reasons why they marry. One is to have children, the other is for sex. We must understand them. However, if you agree to sex without enjoying it, men can detect it and will not be happy. Fortunately, I enjoy sex with my husband." But Mother-in-law Tan sleeps on the other side of the wood partition in the family's single room apartment, and Suan Ying is reluctant to have intercourse with her husband when Mother-in-law is home. "I only agree to it when my mother-in-law goes out for a while in the evening. Eng Fong often gets annoyed with me over this. But I worry about what will happen if Mother-in-law should get up in the middle of the night to use the lavatory, or to get a drink of water. She might hear us, and I'd be so embarrassed!"

The higher earnings, education, and secure white-collar status are resources that provide the support for the group 2 pattern of joint leisure-time activities and discussion by husband and wife (Table 6.1). Goh Min Ti is an inspector in a medium-sized garment factory who counts and approves the pieces produced by each worker on her floor. Her husband, Chee Boon, is employed by the Singapore Utilities Commission as a door-to-door reader of electric meters. The couple have two children, six months and three and one-half years old. The Gohs reside with Chee Boon's parents and eight of his brothers and sisters in a one-bedroom, rented HDB apartment, which contains a former kitchen now converted to another bedroom, a living room where family members sleep, a dark kitchenette and bath. Min Ti and Chee Boon are given the bedroom to themselves. The couple enjoys shopping together on the weekends. In the street markets the couple chooses bright red satin cloth for Min Ti's frocks and clothing for their toddlers. They stroll through the outdoor market place looking for bargains and unusual market stall displays, and then stop at a hawker's restaurant for a bowl of noodles. In the past, the couple would cap the late afternoon excursions with a visit to a Mandarin or English Cinema. However, Min Ti became annoyed with her mother-in-law's insistence on joining them at the cinema.

After Min Ti and our interviewers had met informally on six or seven occasions, she unburdened herself to us about her mother-in-law. "That old woman is not a bad person, but she doesn't understand that I want to be alone with my husband. I didn't like the idea of mother-in-law interrupting our time together when she came along to join us at the movies." Many a paternal grandmother who lives with the family of a son desires to be part of the leisure-time outings he plans with his wife. The grandmother's claim to this role is reinforced by the tradition that she shares household leadership with her husband. Chee Boon does not wish to hurt his mother's feelings by excluding her from cinema-going, but he is also sensitive to Min Ti's discomfort at her presence. Therefore, the couple substitutes evenings at ten-pin bowling and walks along the waterfront. They also come home earlier and spend more time watching television. Like many other young, salaried husbands in my panel, Chee Boon is torn between filial loyalty to his mother and demands of his parents, and the need of his spouse for loving attention. This dilemma is typically solved when group 2 couples like the Gohs placate the older generation and give primacy of place to the marital relationship, while stopping short of a formal break with their elders.

Another example is Yeo Seok Hong, a primary school teacher, and his wife Kim Lui, a semi-skilled worker in a pottery factory. The couple has a two-year-old daughter, Barbara, who since her birth has lived with Kim Lui's mother. They chose this arrangement because there are no crèches for infants of working parents, and they believed that Kim Lui would be unable simultaneously to raise Barbara and to carry on her work in the pottery factory. As a teacher, Seok Hong is pleased that Maternal Grandmother has a set of moral standards which she imparts to Barbara and is gentle but firm in her unbringing. The Yeo family owns a two-bedroom apartment in the Tao Payoh district, a ten-minute walk from Maternal Grandmother, and visits Barbara three times a week. The couple shares their apartment with Seok Hong's mother and younger brother and sister, aged twenty and twenty-two, and both unmarried. Paternal Grandmother provides day care for Li Li and Li San, the two children of her married daughter (Seok Hong's older sister), who lives elsewhere and also works full time.

Paternal Grandmother expresses the wish that Seok Hong and Kim Lui spend more of their leisure time in the home, but the couple prefers to be alone together. Seok Hong said, "When we first marrried I occasionally took my wife out to eat in a restaurant, and we also tried bowling once or twice. Now because of our expenses with Barbara, and since prices have gone up so much, we seldom eat in restaurants. Only movie tickets are cheap, so we go to the cinema at least once a week. With one dollar's ticket you can enjoy air conditioning for two hours. Quite worth it!"

Yap Sian Ho, a homemaker, has been married for five years to Wai Hon, who is a lower-level supervisor with a firm in the Jurong industrial zone. Wai Hon holds a degree in mechanical engineering from the HMS Dockyard Technical College. The Yaps have two children, aged two and five, and reside in a small, detached house located in Sembawang. The fathers of both Wai Hon and Sian Ho are deceased, and their mothers reside together with the Yaps. Maternal Grandmother assists Sian Ho in her homemaking chores and helps with childcare when Sian Ho markets or visits her friends, or when the couple goes out in the evening. Paternal Grandmother, however, does not share in day-to-day home maintenance or child care, and generally keeps to herself. Sian Ho said, in an exasperated tone of voice, "My mother-in-law is a funny case. She can talk intelligently, but her behavior is very peculiar sometimes. Wai Hon has no love for his mother. When he was small, she never took care of him, never prepared good meals, and never worried when he came back late from play or school. Whenever Wai Hon was ill, he had to wait until his father came home to take him to the doctor. His mother just didn't care. She stays in her own part of the house now.

"Mother-in-law tried to control me when I first married. If I didn't wash the day's clothes by that day, she would have something to say. But I put her in her place. First, she's not the one who's washing the clothes, so it has nothing to do with her. If she were intelligent and logical, I would respect her, but she's such a simpleton, I don't listen to her. She's not a bad person, just strange. I sure wish that my sister-in-law would see more of her mother, so she would know what I have to put up with."

Wai Hon was questioned later about his mother's relationship with Sian Ho, and he concurred with his wife. "Well, it's not proper to say much about the old folks; they've lived a hard life. But Mother and Sian Ho are from two different generations, and it's perhaps natural that they don't see eye to eye. We're thinking of sending Mother to my sister's home for a while. Mother and daughter always get along well."

Sian Ho is acquainted with most of Wai Hon's friends and office mates, and she frequently entertains them. During an interview, Sian Ho was preparing jello and sandwiches, while Wai Hon helped in the kitchen. Sian Ho explained that she was cooking a light meal for some of Wai Hon's friends. Wai Hon remarked, "At times my friends invite me to join them for a drink to meet some salesmen, and I call my wife to tell her I won't be back directly after work. If time allows, I like to come home first for a change of clothes." Sian Ho added, "The only complaint I have about Wai Hon is the late hours he keeps at some of the drinking parties."

Among my sample, there are a number of families who bring their children along when attending ceremonial occasions, such as weddings or birthday celebrations, or when attending the cinema. When the Yaps are invited to a wedding banquet, however, they do not take their children. "How embarrassing it would be!" Sian Ho exclaimed. "My friends don't do such things these days. My mother looks after our children for us."

On other types of socializing, Sian Ho added: "Wai Hon accompanies me when I drop in on my girlfriends and their families, unless it's an obvious hen thing. When one of our children is ill, we both accompany the child to the doctor, and we both go for appointments at the family planning clinic. We try to do everything together." The Yaps were close together in their day-to-day interaction and approach to life, and in this regard they are representative of my group 2b families.

SHARING CONFIDENCES

The majority of the group 1a couples report that they rarely conducted extended conversations on deeply personal subjects. For these seventeen poor parents, the most frequent topic of discussion seems to be coping with poverty. Despite their sustained efforts, these couples have found no practical way out of their impoverished circumstances.

Aw Swan Tzu, the wife of a caretaker in an elementary school, was adopted at an early age by a poor domestic servant. The foster mother consented to an arranged marriage for Swan Tzu, when she was only fifteen, to a man of twenty-eight. (Aw Boon Eng's discomforts at home with Swan Tzu and their children were discussed earlier.) Swan Tzu reported that she calls Boon Eng her "old man." "We don't say more than a few words to each other. If we talk more than that we'll end up quarreling. Usually we dispute about money or the children, and we stop talking to each other for one or two days. Aw Boon naturally prefers to spend time with our daughters to spending time with me. Anyway, I'm used to keeping things to myself. My husband doesn't get along with his mother, and he has no money to give her. She works as a cook for a well-to-do family, and lives with them. When I have a problem I phone her. A week ago I suddenly found I was bleeding profusely, and so she called my sister-in-law to look after the children when I went to the hospital." (Swan Tzu was referring to a menstrual complication.) "I came back the same day. I never told my husband where I had been. I don't tell him things like that. But I have to return to the hospital for another checkup, and then I'll tell him because he will have to look after the children."

Chen Sieow Wah is married to a heavy equipment operator for a small construction subcontractor: "I only tell my husband some of the important things about the house and the children which I feel he needs to know. Such occasions are when I need his help around the place. Otherwise it's unwise to tell your husband too many of your real problems and predicaments. If we really show our feelings in a quarrel, then we'd have had it, wouldn't we? You know what men are like. Men only tell you what they want you to know. I keep a bank account of my own without Ah You's knowledge. Ah You would not give me enough housekeeping money, especially when he is running short, if he knew I had funds of my own."

Working-class wives turn to their mothers as confidantes when they cannot share grievances or resolve problems with their husbands. Soo Kee, married to Man Wah, who operates a small kiosk in a shopping center, remarks, "There must be someone with whom you can talk when you're upset, right? Mother lives in the adjacent housing block and my married brother lives close by, too. It's fortunate that I'm surrounded by my people." Although Soo Kee feels that she and Man Wah discuss most matters and are generally communicative, she does not disclose everything, nor does she expect that her husband would listen to her if she did.

Tai Chun Kim, a smith in an iron works, and Tai Kwan Yan live with Chun Kim's family. The Tais, like most other group 1 couples, feel that they do not need to discuss their working lives with each other. Two months before she was interviewed for this study, Kwan Yan went to work as a seamstress in a medium-size garment factory. Kwan Yan was soon unhappy with her inability to sew rapidly and well enough to earn a decent wage, and during the three-week period of our interviews with her, she was considering changing her line of work. Just before our last interview, she transferred to a plywood factory. When Chun Kim was asked by the interviewer, "Did your wife discuss with you her desire to change jobs?" he replied, "Why should she discuss it with me? It's her own work. She saw the ad for the new job in the papers and went there to apply. When she came home from her first day of work, she told me where she had been. That's all. If I switch jobs, that's my own business, too." Group 1 employees like the Tais follow the directives of supervisors and foremen on their jobs, which seldom accommodate their imagination or creative talents. Such couples believe that there is little they can do to enrich their working lives, and that it is useless to discuss work-related issues at home.

The Tais also find that long hours at work hinder their ease of discussion and communication. Kwan Yan explains, "There's so much work to be done that by the time housework is completed, my husband is fast asleep. I can't say that this is something to be regretted, however, because after being married for some time, there's really nothing to talk about." The absence of conversation and evaluation of their lives outside the home limits their understanding of each other's insights and abilities, and makes difficult or impossible their charting of an effective course for family betterment.

Group 1 men who reside patrilocally with their families of origin rarely sever their close bond with their mothers. The wives of these men are sometimes dismayed to find that the confidences they share with their husbands become known to their parents-in-law. Tai Kwan Yan informed us, "It's not always wise to tell men everything. Money is always a problem. You see, when men know that you've got a bank account, or some money of your own, they will give you less of their pay checks. Once when I entrusted part of my pay check to Chun Kim for deposit in our bank account, he told his mother how much I was earning, and Mother-in-law then expected a higher contribution from us after that. I was very angry at him for that.

"It's sometimes hard for me to talk to Chun Kim because of his mother. Mother-in-law is unhappy about my return to low-paid factory work, and instead she wants me to stay at home, help her with the housework, and present Chun Kim with a baby boy. A while ago I told Chun Kim how upset I was about Mother-in-law's attitude. But even though he was sympathetic to me, he asked that I put up with her complaints for the sake of family harmony. When I quarrel with Mother-in-law, Chun Kim usually holds his tongue, so I've stopped expressing myself to Chun Kim also.

"When I return to my own family home for a visit, I tell my sister and mother a little about my problems here with Mother-in-law, but I keep most of my household difficulties to myself when there's no way for them to help." When Chinese women like Tai Kwan Yan marry and reside patrilocally, they are expected to bear whatever burdens their parents-in-law place upon them. The wife's differences with her in-laws often create friction in the marital relationship itself, unless the husband unequivocally reassures his wife that he sides with her. But such is not the case for group 1 couples.

Group 2 families, with higher earnings and middle schooling, generally share confidences and deliberate jointly in family decision making (Table 6.1). Low Ah Mui is an instructor in a textile company in Jurong industrial township, married to Low Jee Kwan, welding supervisor in a Jurong company. Jee Kwan helps his parents by giving them $120 each month. Ah Mui told the interviewer, "My arguments with my mother-in-law are longstanding, but luckily Jee Kwan takes my side. Jee Kwan is the eldest son, and so his mother wanted us to have a large wedding banquet, but she was unwilling to pay for it. She postponed the marriage, too, because she is a superstitious woman and couldn't ever decide on a suitable date. So we went ahead and we registered our marriage and lived together in the apartment we had already rented. My parents-in-law wanted us to live with them after our marriage, but I felt that their one-bedroom flat was too crowded, not well kept up, and far from Jurong where I work, so I told Jee Kwan that I preferred to get my own flat. These things must be talked over first. Mother-in-law then must have been a little resentful.

"Mother-in-law wanted Jee Kwan to borrow money from his brother to pay for the wedding banquet. But we went to see her and said if she wanted a big dinner, she would have to give it herself, because we were not going to sink ourselves in debt at the start of our marriage! Jee Kwan was a a little bit afraid to tell his mother this, but I didn't care. I said it to her straight, face-to-face. Mother-in-law seems to think that just because Jee Kwan and I lived together as man and wife before the wedding ceremony, I would be under his thumb, and I would either be required to do his bidding or be cast aside. But of course that's not how it is with modern couples like us.

"Well, Mother-in-law insisted that if there were no formal dinner, I would not be allowed to step inside her house. I was quite upset, and I answered that if I were not allowed to serve her tea like any other daughter-in-law on that day in my wedding dress, I would never go and see her again. For a long time afterwards I did not have contact with Mother-in-law, although I used to visit my father-in-law at his tailor shop.

"Eventually, Father-in-law and Jee Kwan persuaded me to give Mother-in-law face by choosing an auspicious date to serve tea to her. She gave me an *ang pow* (red paper-wrapped gift), which I opened when I returned home. Jee Kwan told me that I would receive some nice jewelry, but the *ang pow* contained only $4. What a shock for us! Jee Kwan was horrified at how shabbily Mother-in-law treated me, expecially because he is supporting his parents.

"Whenever I came across a wedding, I used to cry because it reminded me of my troubles. But Jee Kwan told me, 'So long as I treat you well, everything is all right.' "

Group 2 wives like Ah Mui invariably value the support of their husbands. Mee Hok Beng is married to Lok Kwan, a photographer who owns his studio. Lok Kwan is a widower with four children, and he and Hok Beng have an infant of their own. Hok Beng's mother came to live with the couple after they married to mind their five children while Hok Beng assists her husband in the studio. Hok Beng's father lives with Hok Beng's eldest brother. From time to time Hok Beng's mother returns to her eldest son's apartment to care for her husband.

Hok Beng said, "Lok Kwan originally did not want Mother to live with us. He felt strongly that a married couple should have privacy and intimacy. But what else could I do? I needed my mother's help in looking after the children." Hok Beng continued, "A woman should marry. Otherwise who would she have to talk with? Your mother may love you, but after you become mature and have your own family and your relationship with your husband, she understands less of your innermost thoughts. There are many things which you can discuss only with your husband. A husband like mine is good company."

Couples who confide in each other and deliberate vital family mattters are committed to their marriage and willing to invest energy to improve the quality of their lives and those of their children. Shared sentiments mean that the couple invest the marital relationship with the full weight of their personal beings. Further, the sharing of confidences reflects the assumption of these partners that the future of the marriage bond is theirs alone to decide. Consequently, couples who discuss family matters take more effective steps for their own and their offspring's future, and there is a close association between marital communication and future planning.

PLANNING TOGETHER

Singapore families must themselves set aside funds in order to advance their socio-economic position through the main channels provided by the government, such as the purchase of an HDB apartment and upgrading jobs through special adult education and technical courses. Individual families are also expected to fund fully their children's education. In my sample sixty-two couples were able to one degree or another to advance their status by deliberately organizing family resources and personal energy to prepare for the future. The remaining thirty-eight families, mostly from group 1, could do no more than cope with the legacy of poverty and existing difficulties (Table 6.2).

Group 1 families can rarely save funds for the future, and these families find it difficult to discuss at home ways to free themselves from the poverty cycle. The jobs of group 1 men provide few promotions or ladders of advancement, and consequently these men regard family improvement discussions as essentially pointless. Group 1 men are insulated from the concerns of their wives and their families by their workday environments. Their mates on the job, and in all-male, leisure-time company, and the male family members who have assisted them in attaining and retaining their positions reinforce a masculine environment. Consequently, many group 1 men are unfamiliar with the techniques of joint husband-wife forecasting and planning.

TABLE 6.2
Couples that Plan Together for the Betterment of their Families: Job, Housing, and Educational Plans (number of couples)

	No Plans[a]	Some Plans[b]	Numerous Plans[c]	No information	Total
Group 1					
1a Lower Working Class	13	3	1		17
1b Average Working Class	17	16	7	1	41
Group 2					
2a Upper Working Class	4	9	6		19
2b Middle Class	3	4	16	—	23
TOTAL	37	32	30	1	100

[a] No plans = couple cannot save money for children's education or purchase of HDB public housing; no effort on part of either spouse to upgrade occupation.
[b] Some plans = couple is able to make a plan either to attain job or housing improvement or to bank money for the children's education.
[c] Numerous plans = couple makes plans to better the family future in two or more areas of occupation, housing, or education.

Thriftiness is valued, but most of the lower working-class and many ordinary working-class are unable to save more than a few dollars monthly. Chen Sieow Wah, the wife of a crane driver for a small firm, was asked, "Do you discuss family finances with Ah You?" "No, we don't." She gestured with her left hand, "Ah You earns so much," and then she extended her right hand an equal distance, "and we spend so much. There's no use asking him for more, because he can't produce it, anyway. But Ah You does try to look after the needs of our family, and every month brings home another toy for our small children. He leaves the shopping to me. I buy what I think we need and he seldom complains. With husbands, the less one says about these things the better."

The Lims, a rattan chair weaver and his homemaker wife, have established a division of labor, but beyond that they do not discuss their purchases of food, clothing, or furniture for their one-room flat. Lim Heng Chee: "I seldom buy clothes. As long as the ones I have are clean and still in good shape, I don't mind wearing them. But the bad thing about living here is the gossip behind your back about your clothes and your family life. These kinds of neighbors are just as poor as we, but they always put on airs. With the door closed no one can see what we eat, but we do have to be careful about what we wear.

"Usually Lim Lee Keong doesn't comment on the things I've bought, but he becomes critical when he thinks that I've spent more than an item should cost. Lee Keong is the one who usually does the shopping for the children's clothing because there are shops which sell children's clothing at very reasonable prices in the area where he works."

Group 1 families have considerable difficulties budgeting their slim resources, and purchases are a source of contention. Low Hoy Hoi keeps house for Low Fuk Leong, who drives a heavy goods vehicle for his uncle's company. Hoy Hoi makes most of the daily purchases of food, clothing, furniture. Hoy Hoi explained to the interviewer how difficult it was for the family to reduce expenditures to a level in keeping with their budget.

"I have always been very careful in spending money since I was a young girl. When I went to the movies, I always bought 50¢ or $1 tickets. But when we were dating, my husband would buy $2 or even $3 seats. What a showoff! I used to get angry with him because of his extravagance. Once, when he insisted on paying top prices for the best seats, I refused to see the film and returned home alone. Since we married, I have managed our budget. I made the choice of the bedroom set, and I am going to decide how to fix up our new apartment." The interviewer asked Hoy Hoi, "Does your husband have any opinions about your choices?" "He does! But I won't let him decide. You see, we haven't got much money, and he still wants luxury furniture for our new flat. He even wants to buy a color T.V. Not practical at all. What we really need is a fridge, a cheap set of sofa chairs, and an extra cupboard. Color T.V. has to wait at least several years."

However, Low Hoy Hoi could not dissuade Fuk Leong from one final extravagance: "Two years ago Fuk Leong bought a second-hand car. He likes to drive and fix cars. He didn't tell me beforehand because he knew that I long objected to a car. The car itself cost only a few hundred dollars, but maintaining a car, gas, and parking fees are very expensive. I grumbled and, but what's the use!"

In the large, tightly knit family of the poor, the small checks of the income earners must be stretched to the limit to provide food, clothing, and shelter. This resource scarcity engenders chronic husband/wife disputes over limited family saving potential. Tai Kwan Yan and Tai Chun Kim live with Chun Kim's mother. Kwan Yan recently resumed employment and was then in a position to contribute occasional small sums of cash to help her needy father, a retired fisherman, and her homemaker mother. Kwan Yan does not discuss this financial outlay with Chun Kim. Quietly, Kwan Yan also sets aside small sums from her paycheck for her child's future and as a modest form of family insurance. "I don't believe in combining my wages with those of my husband. If I did that, he would give more of our surplus to his mother, without thinking of saving for the rest of us. I can't understand why we aren't as important to him as his mother."

"What can the future hold for your children?" the respondents were asked. The responses of the poor families differed markedly from those of the affluent. The poorest couples do not deliberate at length on plans for their children's future. Lee Lai Wok, a vendor of homemade cakes, was asked, "What kind of education would you like your children to have?"

"I don't know. It depends on their abilities."

"Have you thought about some jobs they might qualify for?"

"I don't know. It all depends on them. When I come home at night I have to get my goods and cart ready for tomorrow. I haven't got the time and energy to think of the future."

Chen Sieow Wah never attended school, and her crane-driver husband, Ah You, obtained only two years of primary education. The couple lived with Ah You's family until 1974, and in 1975 moved into their own rented one-room HDB flat. Sieow Wah appears unable to decide upon her children's education.

"What language stream will you choose for your children's education?" Sieow Wah was asked.

"I have not decided. I don't think that far ahead. If a child attends an English school, he will have a better chance of finding employment. On the other hand, a son who is English-educated may be less filial than one who is Chinese-educated. Let the children decide when they have gone to kindergarten."

"Do you really think such a young child can make that kind of decision?"

"Well, if my children prefer Chinese, that's fine. And if they choose English, that's all right too."

"What are your husband's views?"

"Ah You has not made up his mind yet. Anyway, there's no point my saying 'English' or 'Chinese' because my mother-in-law is influential in our family, and she may have her own ideas."

"Would you really allow your mother-in-law to control your children's education?"

"If she wants to take that responsibility, let her go ahead."

Close husband-wife collaboration on budgeting, education of the young, and job upgrading is alien to the life history and experience of group 1 Singapore Chinese families. Group 2 couples, inspired by the prospects of advancement held out by their more solid and secure economic positions, in which their talents are in demand, build closer conjugal relationships and are more practiced in formulating and implementing family plans. These more comfortably situated couples have obtained some measure of control over their work lives and are generally able to anticipate continued improvement in their futures.

Possession of the economic resources for family betterment encourages, and indeed requires, couples to discuss together the best deployment of their labor power and income. Decisions made within the family by means of discussion are considered binding and are then jointly carried out. This pattern of husband-wife interdependence and initiative in planning for family futures further strengthens the couples' ability to deploy their resources more effectively for advancement. A minority of group 1 couples and a majority of group 2 couples engage in joint communication (as seen in Table 6.2) which widens the gap between the more-affluent couples and their poorer brethren.

Only eight group 1 couples develop numerous family plans. White-collar workers predominate among them. Choo Tzu Pheng is a postman who nets $300 salary monthly. He is the sixth of seven children of a civil servant who passed away when Tzu Pheng was an early teenager. Tzu Pheng was consequently only able to obtain primary 6 English stream schooling, but he was prepared for brighter prospects by his father, and his English schooling that qualified him for a postman's position. Now secure in a good civil service post, Tzu Pheng is a planner. He and his wife have two sons. The couple continually revises its educational program for the children. Tzu Pheng told our interviewer, "It is quite expensive now to educate the children. I have deposited $20 a month in the post office savings bank for the children since their births in order to save for their education in the future."

The interviewer questioned Tzu Pheng, "The world is changing rapidly. How can you tell what kind of education is best for your children?"

"I know the world is changing rapidly, so we cannot rely on a single plan. We must revise our goals from time to time depending on the prospects in Singapore and the world."

Group 2 husbands and wives share their views while outlining and implementing their family plans, but their contributions frequently carry unequal weights. Often one spouse is clearly the leader, who makes final decisions after mutual consultation. The wife of a skilled carpenter said, "My husband is brilliant, and sometimes I think he knows everything. He tells me a lot of things about people and the world. He's teaching me. He works hard on the job, and I've never heard him complain about the effort. My husband even keeps a mental record of my menstrual periods so I don't become pregnant."

A typical group 2a respondent, Yeo Seok Hong, a primary school teacher, is married to Kim Lui, an assembly worker in a pottery factory. The couple's desire to share their leisure-time activities was mentioned above. Kim Lui told the interviewer, "My husband tells me about his work, and I also confide in him, especially when I have a problem. We talk about the child, improvements to our house, and other things. Once you become an adult and raise a family, you especially have to think about their interests. You must plan every action carefully and think through all the possible consequences beforehand."

Seok Hong commented, "When I was still in high school, I came to believe that a person should stay single if his income is not sufficient for two people, and a couple should not have any children until its income is sufficient. Then when children come along, you have to think about their proper upbringing. I often tell my wife that actually one child is enough, but I think we will probably have a second child."

The interviewer asked Seok Hong, "Suppose you were earning $2,000 a month. How many children would you like to have?"

"I would still want two."

"Why not more than two?"

"With more income, but not more children, I would be able to give my children better quality care and upbringing. Besides, people should think about the conditions and situation of Singapore as well as their own family."

Group 2b middle-class couples have access to even greater financial resources, which spurs on their ability to plan for the future. Tok Kim San operates a one-man driving instruction business, and his wife, Sor Ngee, stays at home with their two children. The Tok family purchased a two-bedroom HDB flat in 1974 for $6,700 in cash and accumulated an additional bill for about $2,000 for renovations. Sor Ngee told the interviewer, "We are not very rich, and we try to save every penny we can. We don't skimp on the children's food and education, of course, but we do try to cut down on luxuries, otherwise we never could have saved up enough money. Three years ago we paid $3,000 in cash for my husband's car. I hate buying things on installment-purchase.

"I am a hard-working woman, and I am good at economizing. I handle all of our household finances, I make sure that food and clothing for the children comes first, and that we save a little each month. As a result of the planning I've done, we were able to pay cash for this flat and the driver-training car as well!" Sor Ngee continued matter of factly, "My husband calls me his 'Minister of Finance' and his friends call him a 'model husband' because he has relinquished all of his financial power to me. I'm not trying to dominate him, but he is poor in handling money, while I am a much better planner."

CONCLUSION

Sex specialization of domestic tasks and leisure-time activities is deeply rooted in group 1 working-class Singapore families. Wives care for the children, do all of the housework, socialize with their neighbors, and visit relatives on their side of the family, while husbands work to fill the family rice bowl, fraternize with their mates, and call upon their blood relatives. Joint husband-wife social activities are infrequent, and friends and acquaintances are not usually shared by both spouses. Just as important, there are few conjugal discussions on upward paths for the family. Indeed, bereft families cannot tell how their employment prospects will be influenced by such factors as market supply and demand and government policies, and they are effectively powerless as individual units to bridge the chasm separating them from higher class standing. The weak conjugal planning bond of poor families, their lack of an economic surplus, and their inability to utilize institutional facilities for improving their jobs, housing, and education of their youngsters are all components of a baneful cycle of poverty. The poor possess no channels for routine career advancement or even income upgrading. Restricted by their limited opportunities, the deprived are necessarily consumed with day-to-day concerns and crises, which they feel powerless to alter; similarly they are unable to modify the inherited tradition of sex-segregated roles.

If a solidary conjugal relationship could be achieved, such a liaison could stiffen family resolve to plan successfully for a brighter future and to exploit existing opportunities for Singapore's social programs. Even if impoverished families conceptualize the goal of husband/wife planning for the family's future and seek to attain such a conjugal bond, they find it difficult to spare the necessary time, energy, or funds to achieve such a relationship. Moreover, these couples find themselves enmeshed in a set of kin and peer relationships that makes difficult the realization of closer conjugal planning. Impoverishment thus encompasses both the realms of economy and social structure, and the Singapore poor are trapped in a cycle of poverty that leads from unsteady and poorly paying work to little time, information, or funds to plan for the children's education to a future of ill-paid jobs for the children.

The resources and structures that encourage foresight are available to group 2 families, who harbor and seek to realize much greater expectations than the working-class poor. The more-affluent families are better able to assess and realize their economic potential. They have more resources to invest in family betterment and are generally able to raise their sights beyond the near horizon. Husbands are more likely to accept responsibility for domestic matters and nurture of children.

In group 2 families, husbands prove willing to side with their wives in conflicts with their mothers. The husbands' willingness to support their wives deepens the confidence of the wives in them and strengthens mutual trust. In contrast, the inability of group 1 men to take their wives' part creates mistrust and hinders communication. The subordination of group 1 families to the wider patriliny is a structural feature that impoverishes the couples' ability to plan effectively the deployment of whatever resources they have, whereas the saliency of the conjugal relationship in group 2 families strengthens even further these well-endowed couples' future prospects.

The joint husband-wife decision making that marks the group 2 families is rooted in their social-class position. In turn, the ability of these couples to draw upon their joint energies to formulate family plans aids them in maintaining or improving their position in the class order in the future. Sociologists would state that family structure in the Singapore working class reproduces the class order. This means that family structure contributes to the perpetuation of the social class system in a variety of ways, and here I have stressed that families situated in occupations without money or power cannot organize their family lives to elevate their economic position. Families in occupations with superior resources and backgrounds are encouraged by their work environment and peers to strive to improve children's opportunities.

NOTES

1. Magdalena Sokolowska, "Poland," in *Family Policy: Government and Families in Fourteen Countries*, eds. Sheila B. Kamerman and Alfred J. Kahn (New York: Columbia University Press, 1969), pp. 239–69.

2. Marion Levy, "Contrasting Factors in the Modernization of China and Japan," *Economic Development and Cultural Change*, 2 (1953): 161–96.

3. See for example Francis L. K. Hsü, *Under the Ancestors' Shadow* (New York: Doubleday, 1967); Marjorie Wolf, *House of Lim* (New York: Appleton-Century-Crofts, 1968); Marjorie Wolf, *Women and the Family in Rural Taiwan* (Stanford: Stanford University Press, 1972). Useful works on the family in People's Republic of China include William L. Parish and Martin K. Whyte, *Village and Family in Contemporary China* (Chicago: University of Chicago Press, 1978), and Norma Diamond, "Collectivization, Kinship, and the Status of Women in Rural China," *Bulletin of Concerned Asian Scholars*, 7 (1975: 25–32; Kay Johnson, "The Politics of Women's Rights and Family Reform in China," (Diss. University of Wisconsin, 1976).

4. Janet W. Salaff, *Working Daughters of Hong Kong: Filial Piety or Power in the Family?* (Cambridge: Cambridge University Press, 1981); Janet W. Salaff, "Structuring an Industrial Society: Class, Social Policy, and Family Plan in Singapore" (manuscript in preparation); Janet W. Salaff, "Support for Chinese Women at Work: Social Class and the Extended

Family," in *Modernizing Women: Studies in Social Policy and Social Change*, eds. Ann Cottrell and Naomi Black (Beverly Hills: Sage, 1981).

    5. William T. Liu, "The Myths of the Nuclear Family and Fertility in Central Philippines," in *Beyond the Nuclear Family Model: Cross-Cultural Perspectives*, ed. L. Lenero-Otero (Beverly Hills: Sage, 1977), pp. 974–96.

    6. A socio-economic status scale (SES) was constructed:

      1. For each of the following variables a couple received a score, which was the average of the wife and husband's individual score on that variable. The sum of the scores on variables (a) to (d) is the couple's SES score.

        a) SES of couple's parents:

lower working-class (marginal occupation, unemployed)	1
average working-class (blue collar, white collar, lower supervisory and self-employed petty capitalists)	2
middle class (professional, lower managerial and private entrepreneur)	3

        b) Educational level of wife and husband:

illiterate	1
primary education	2
secondary education	3
post-secondary education	4

        c) Occupation of wife and husband

marginal and unemployed	1
blue-collar, lower supervisory and technical	2
white collar, self-employed, upper supervisory and technical	3
professional, administrative, executive and private entrepreneur	4

        d) Combined monthly income of wife and husband (Singapore dollars)*

less than $300	1
$301–600	2
$601–900	3
$901–1,200	4
over $1,201	5

      2. Range of SES scores possible: 4.0-16.0

SES	Scores	Number of Couples
Group 1: ordinary working class	4.0–8.5	58
1a: lower working class	4.0–7.0	17
1b: average working class	7.5–8.5	41
Group 2: affluent workers	9.0–16.0	42
2a: upper working class	9.0–9.5	19
2b: middle class	10.0–16.0	23
		100

    7. The Singapore government's ideology of political economy is discussed in *Socialism that Works: The Singapore Way*, ed. C. V. Devan Nair (Singapore: Federal Publications, 1976).

    8. Lee Soo Ann, "The Role of the Government in the Economy," in *The Singapore Economy*, eds. You Poh Seng and Lim Chong Yan (Singapore: Eastern University Press, 1971), pp. 91–3; Kunio Yoshihara, *Foreign Investment and Domestic Response* (Singapore: Eastern University Press, 1976).

---

*The exchange rate at the time of the study was roughly $2.45 = $1.00 US

9. Stephen H. K. Yeh, ed., *Public Housing in Singapore: A Multi-Disciplinary Study* (Singapore: University of Singapore Press, 1975); Peter S. J. Chen and James T. Fawcett, eds., *Public Policy and Population Change in Singapore* (New York: The Population Council, 1979).

10. Toh Chin Chye, Health Minister, "Free health services could mean bankruptcy," *Straits Times* (Singapore), December 10, 1976; "Objective of Social Welfare," in *Singapore Bulletin*, 8 (May 1980): 9, quotes the acting Minister for Social Affairs as having said, "The objective of social welfare aid is to provide relief but not to cover the entire subsistence."

11. Chua Sian Chin, Health Minister, in *Parliamentary Debates* 32, 150–1 (Singapore).

12. Seah Chee Meow, *Commmunity Centres in Singapore: Their Political Involvement* (Singapore: University of Singapore Press, 1973).

13. Michael A. Apple, *Ideology and Curriculum* (London: Routledge and Kegan Paul, 1979); Pierre Bourdieu and Jean-Claude Passeron, *Reproduction in Education, Society and Culture* (Beverly Hills: Sage, 1977); Jules Henry, *Culture Against Man* (New York: Random House, 1963); Raymond Williams, *The Long Revolution* (London: Chatto and Windus, 1961).

14. Chen and Fawcett, eds., *Public Policy and Population Change in Singapore*.

15. An important discussion of economic dualism for the U.S. is found in Robert T. Averitt, *The Dual Economy: The Dynamics of American Industry Structure* (New York: Horton, 1973). An analysis of the implications of a dualistic economy for labor is contained in Peter Doeringer and Michael Piore, *Internal Labor Markets and Manpower Analysis* (Lexington: Lexington Press, 1971); Seymour Spilerman, "Careers, Labor Market Structure, and Socioeconomic Achievement," *American Journal of Sociology*, 83 (1977): 551–93. The concept of segmented labor in the Singapore labor market is found in Pang Eng Fong and Liu Pak Wai, *Education, Socioeconomic Status and Labor Market Success: A Case Study of Manufacturing Workers in Singapore* (Geneva: International Labour Office, World Employment Programme Working Paper, October, 1975), WEP 2–18/WP 7. See also Frederic C. Deyo, *Dependent Development and Industrial Order: An Asian Case Study* (New York: Praeger, in press).

16. Christine Inglis, "Chinese Education in Southeast Asia," *The Development Studies Monograph No. 10* (The Australian National University) 1977, 110–35.

17. Spilerman, "Careers, Labor Market Structure, and Socioeconomic Achievement," *American Journal of Sociology*, 83 (1977): 551–93.

18. Melvin L. Kohn, *Class and Conformity: A Study of Values* (Homewood, Ill.: Dorsey Press, 1969).

19. Ho Ping-ti, *Chung-kuo hui-guan shih* (History of the Chinese *Landsmannschaften*) (Taipei: Hsüeh-sheng Shu-Chu, 1966).

20. Chan Heng Chee, *The Dynamics of One Party Dominance: the PAP at the Grass-roots* (Singapore: Singapore University Press, 1976).

21. Marvin B. Sussman, "Family, Kinship and Bureaucracy," in Angus Campbell and Philip E. Converse, eds., *The Human Meaning of Social Change* (New York: Russell Sage, 1972).

22. Shostack distinguishes between "modern" and "traditional" working class marriages. Modern blue-collar families are most often led by well-paid, mobile, and young manual workers and are marked by a high degree of integration and closeness between husbands and wives. Traditional families are most often headed by the poorest-paid, least well-educated, least mobile blue-collar husbands and fathers. Striking in such families are the separateness and isolation of the marriage partners, a clear delineation of tasks, and a considerable number of separate interests and activities. Arthur B. Shostack, *Blue-Collar Life* (New York: Random House, 1969), 126–41. John Scanzoni, "Occupation and family differentiation," *The Sociological Quarterly*, 8 (Spring 1967): 187–98.

23. Lillian Rubin, *Worlds of Pain* (New York: Basic Books, 1977). Rubin studied blue-collar workers and urban North American communities, and found many men from broken homes were determined that their own families conform to a stereotypic home-based domestic scene.

24. Michael Young and Peter Willmot, *Family and Kinship in East London* (London: Penguin Books, 1957), describe the after-hours leisure patterns for British traditional working-class men.

25. For North American examples, see Shostack, *Blue-Collar Life;* Mirra Komarovsky, *Blue-Collar Marriage* (New York: Random House, 1964), pp. 119, 171, 180, 196, 201; Herbert J. Gans, *The Levittowners: How People Live and Politic in Suburbia* (New York: Pantheon, 1967).

26. Cf. Shostack, *Blue-Collar Life*.

27. See Carol Stack, *All Our Kin* (New York: Harper and Row, 1974). Stack describes female-centered networks of exchanges of goods and services in a poor working-class urban Illinois setting.

28. E. E. LeMasters, *Blue-Collar Aristocrats* (Madison: University of Wisconsin Press, 1975), points out that blue-collar males in all-male work environments have more stereotyped treatment of women than do white-collar men who regularly interact with women at their workplace.

7 ACHIEVEMENT MOTIVATION AND SMALL-BUSINESS RELATIONSHIP PATTERNS IN CHINESE SOCIETY

Richard W. Wilson and Anne Wang Pusey

INTRODUCTION

In this paper we will discuss relationship patterns that are the target for reform by Chinese modernizers, but which, paradoxically, are also the source for the achievement motivation that is critical for modernization. We shall do this by first analyzing a pattern of achievement motivation that is grounded in a social and psychological environment that is quite different from the context of achievement motivation in American society. In the middle part of the paper we will examine a specific case study, that of a Chinese restaurant in the United States, the findings from which elucidate the more general achievement motivation problem. Lastly, we will point out how Chinese attempts to construct new relationship patterns can build upon the unique foundation that achievement motivation has in Chinese culture.

MOTIVATION TO ACHIEVEMENT IN CHINESE SOCIETY

In a study of achievement motivation of Chinese and Americans, Pusey analyzed forty Chinese college students and fifty-eight American college students with a wide number and variety of testing instruments. The object of the study was to determine and compare the relative degrees of achievement motivation of the two groups and, if possible, the sources of this motivation.[1] Achievement, in accordance with McClelland, was defined as a motivation, or desire, "to do better in competition and to reach a standard of excellence."[2] The achieving individual is characterized by a willingness to be different from others, by a desire to take the initiative and be innovative, and by hard work and curiosity concerning whether goals (usually defined as profits) can be maximized.[3]

Using propositions largely generated from studies of western subjects, Pusey began her analysis with a discussion of the relevance of existing theories of achievement motivation. In essence, these state that the development of achievement motivation is critically dependent on independence training in early childhood.[4] In this regard she noted that comparative studies of Chinese and American child-rearing practices have generally found that Chinese mothers allow their children less independence and freedom of exploration than is true for American children.[5] Based on this finding, many scholarly reports have predicted lower achievement motivation for Chinese than for Americans.[6]

Two decades ago, Morris found that in interpersonal relationships Chinese are more receptive and sympathetically concerned than Americans, and that the inspiration for their concern tends to come from outside the self, leading to responsiveness to these outside sources.[7] Americans, on the other hand, were found to be more self-indulgent. In a similar vein, Francis Hsu described Americans as "individual-centered," and postulated that Chinese desires for success are inspired by a concern for the family and a wish not to let the family down.[8] Pusey noted how Chinese sensitivities toward "face" and the need to live up to the expectations of other people contrast with the American form of fear of failure, which is more self-concerned and which describes a person alone in a hostile world.[9]

With these ideas as a basis, Pusey then devised and administered tests to determine the relative degrees of achievement motivation of Chinese and Americans and whether this motivation is related to attitudes regarding independence or conformism. In addition, tests were also given to determine whether achievement motivation is related to "face consciousness" and "group orientedness," a possibility not noted in western literature on this subject. Lastly, suspecting that fear of failure might underlie strivings for success, a study was made of the degree to which individuals in both groups can be characterized by such a fear.

Table 7.1 sets forth a test of means between Chinese and Americans (regardless of sex) for achievement motivation as such (Ach), achievement motivation as the result of independence training (AI), achievement motivation as the result of conformity training (AC), face consciousness (F), and group orientation (GO).[10] As can be noted from Table 7.1, no statistically significant difference was found between the two groups in overall achieve-

TABLE 7.1
T-test of Means Between Chinese and Americans Regardless of Sex

Scale	Means for Chinese n = 40	Means for Americans n = 58	t (df = 96)	P
Age	20.4	19.0	3.77	.002
Ach	52.0	51.1	0.62	
AI	119.6	128.2	− 4.13	.002
AC	149.1	159.6	− 3.66	.002
F	82.5	67.0	6.98	.002
GO	48.0	39.1	6.00	.002

ment motivation. In terms of achievement motivation as the result of independence training, Chinese subjects, as predicted by the literature, scored significantly lower. Surprisingly, the same subjects also scored significantly lower on achievement via conformity. In terms of face consciousness and group orientedness, the Chinese subjects scored significantly higher than their American counterparts, confirming the hypothesis that Chinese are more sensitive to face and are more group oriented than Americans. In separate tests of fear of failure no statistically significant difference between the two groups was found, lending support to a conclusion that Chinese do not develop more fear of failure than Americans.[11]

These results are given greater meaning when a further examination is made of correlations between the scales for achievement as such, achievement motivation as the result of independence training, achievement motivation as a result of conformity training, face consciousness, and group orientedness. The correlations for Chinese and Americans are shown in Table 7.2, while those correlations which are significantly different between Chinese and Americans are indicated in Table 7.3.[12]

TABLE 7.2
Correlations Between Achievement Scales for Chinese and Americans

Ch n = 40

		Ach	AI	AC	F	GO
Am n = 58	Ach		− 0.2	.391*	.350*	.314*
	AI	− .171		− .064	.066	.044
	AC	.286*	.106		.355*	.426**
	F	− .020	− .409**	− .124		.747**
	GO	.221	− .436**	.216	.467**	

* P < .05
** P < .01

TABLE 7.3

Correlations Significantly Different Between Chinese and Americans

	Chinese Correlation	American Correlation	P<
AI × F	.066	− .409	.02
AI × G	.044	− .436	.02
AC × F	.355	− .124	.02
F × G	.747	.467	.05

For Chinese, the test results indicate that achievement motivation correlates significantly with face consciousness (P < .05) and group orientation (P < .05). As a sub-category achievement motivation as the result of conformity training is correlated with face consciousness and with group orientation (both at P < .01), and face consciousness and group orientation are also very highly correlated (P < .01). As a result of these findings, the hypothesis that Chinese who are more group oriented and who have greater sensitivity concerning losing face will be more achievement-motivated is supported.

The hypothesis that Americans who are sensitve concerning face, or who are more group-oriented, will be less individually-oriented achievers is also confirmed by the test results. As expected, achievement motivation as the result of independence training and face consciousness are both negatively correlated within the American group (P < .01); and achievement motivation as the result of independence training and group orientation are also negatively correlated (P < .01). Unlike the Chinese, achievement for Americans does not correlate significantly with face consciousness or group orientation, and the lack of significant correlation here also holds true with regard to achievement motivation as the result of conformity training. Therefore, contrary to the findings that characterize Chinese, we observe that Americans who are more group-oriented and who are more sensitive to face tend not to be achievers, either in settings where independence is valued or in settings where conformity is valued.[13]

Face consciousness and group orientation are significantly and highly correlated within both the American and Chinese groups (P < .01 and P < .01) but, as Table 7.3 indicates, the actual correlation for Chinese is significantly higher than the correlation for Americans. As a consequence, we can conclude that face consciousness and group orientation are two attitudinal dispositions that are more closely related for Chinese than they are for Americans.[14]

Chinese are as achievement-motivated as Americans, but this motivation appears to derive neither from independence training nor from conformity training. Rather, the findings indicate that Chinese who are more face-conscious and group-oriented have higher achievement motivation than Chinese who are not. In effect, then, Chinese have a basis for achievement motivation that is unrelated to those hypotheses regarding achievement motivation that have been generated using western subjects. Achievement for Chinese is not self-oriented but is rather self-other oriented. The attainment of individual achievement does not result from learning to be independent or learning to be conformist but rather is an aspect of group achievement. As Pusey says:

> . . . both the individual and the group share the result of . . . success. If an individual's achievement can bring good to the group or be shared by the group, his being different from the rest of the group is accepted and his initiative is appreciated.
>
> This early encouragement [of] individual achievement and group achievement, plus the training [in] identifying one's self with [the] group and the pressure on conforming to the group's values should make the Chinese highly achievement motivated but they tend to explain their motive for achievement in group terms and attribute their success to their groups, teachers and parents.[15]

These findings, couched as they are in somewhat technical language, suggest that in work environments Chinese motivations for success are unrelated to the criteria that have been advanced to date as explanations for western achievement oriented behavior. Success for Chinese tends to be a group enterprise rather than a striking out on an individual path of discovery. The group for whom Chinese achieve, however, is the one toward whom they have the greatest sensitivities concerning loss of face. Traditionally this group was the family, and for it individual Chinese would work incredibly long and hard hours. The warmth and security of family, however, were never perceived as duplicated in the larger environment, which had to be approached with caution and reserve.

THE CHINESE RESTAURANT BUSINESS

Before beginning this analysis, the reasons for choosing the case study in question and its relevance will be discussed. A few words also need to be said concerning the method of analysis that has been used. To begin with, a Chinese restaurant, while not nearly so glamourous an organization as the military or communes, is a ubiquitous organizational type found throughout the world. It is the form of Chinese work enterprise that non-Chinese are most familiar with, and with which they have the most contact, although few give any thought to the patterns of interaction that take place there. Whatever the locale, a Chinese restaurant outside of the People's Republic of China is also the example, par excellence, of small-scale Chinese entrepreneurial activity that produces a uniquely Chinese product in terms of distinctly traditional Chinese relationship patterns.

It can be reasonably asked, however, whether business organizations in Hong Kong and Taibei, or those that are similarly organized in the United States, truly depict traditional Chinese relationship patterns. We assume that small-scale businesses in these three locations have been modified to some degree by their particular environments; we also believe that the patterns of relationships in these organizations give a clearer indication of traditional attitudes than would be the case for large-scale modern industry or for organizations where the nature of work relationships has been permeated and modified by the rhetoric of a modernizing ideology. Paradoxically, we believe this assertion holds especially true in the United States, where traditional Chinese work patterns may be self-consciously reinforced as a response to the intrusiveness of "alien" work relationship patterns. By this we do not imply that there is not considerable similarity in the operation of a Chinese business and its American counterpart. Many of the tasks that are performed are highly, if not completely, similar, and the objective of maximizing profit is clearly the same. Beyond these similarities, however, are differences in work style, in business outlook, and in work relationships which are significant in nature.

The case study that is analyzed here is a Chinese restaurant of which this author, Richard Wilson, was co-owner for two years. This restaurant, which could seat approximately one hundred people (i.e., a middle-sized restaurant), was located in central New Jersey, in what had formerly been a hotel. Although the number of employees fluctuated depending on business conditions, the average number was ten, including cashier, waiters, dishwashers, kitchen help and cooks. Wilson himself was not involved in the daily management of the business, which was the responsibility of his Chinese partner. He did, however, spend sufficient time at the restaurant to be able to observe carefully the relationship patterns among those who worked there. It should be pointed out that the business was not staffed by the members of a single family. This is an important point, for many traditional Chinese businesses were family organizations. The results presented here, however, reveal clearly the importance of family ties and, more importantly, the ways that non-kin have traditionally dealt with each other in work relationships.

During the time that observations were made at the restaurant, and subsequently, we have attempted to corroborate the findings from other sources and, therefore, to the best of our ability no statements will be made that we do not believe are generally true for this type of organization. In attempting to describe the relationship patterns that were observed, some overlap among the categories of analysis proved to be inevitable. This is to be expected, however, since the analysis does not deal with the organization in terms of its formal procedures or output, but primarily in terms of the pattern of interpersonal relationships that were observed among those who worked at the restaurant, and of the values and attitudes that were thus manifested by these behavior patterns.

The Network of Relationships

All men are equal, all claim the same privilege of preying on their fellows. The idea of responsibility to the State . . . is not yet envisaged; it hardly enters at all into the consideration of modern Chinese . . . *for the reason that the old spirit of family enrichment at the expense of other families is the paramount motive.*[16]

Workers in a Chinese restaurant can be divided in terms of who is an insider and who an outsider on a horizontal level of analysis, and of who is a leader and who a follower on a vertical framework of analysis. Looking first at the horizontal network of relationships, in terms of the dimension of "insider/ outsider," one notes a set of concentric rings where the inner ring, which encloses insiders, is the area of greatest social obligation while those beyond the outside ring occupy the area of least social obligation. The "insider/ outsider" dimension, then, refers to concrete groups or specific individuals and is attitudinally mirrored in terms of a dimension of "obligation/no obligation."

On Taiwan it is rumored that businessmen keep three sets of books, one for the government, one for their business associates, and one for themselves and their family. Whether or not this is really true, it is clear that for the traditional owner-manager the greatest sense of obligation is not to the business organization and its members as such, but rather to the family. In order of decreasing magnitude, this feeling of obligation declines from the family to the associates, next to the employees, and finally to society at large. Actually, however, having a primary obligation to other family members is true regardless of the formal position that one occupies in the business; from the lowest dishwasher to the highest manager this feeling is manifested, and no doubt this strong sense of primary obligation to family members rather than fellow workers is one reason why Chinese restaurants are frequently staffed by members of the same family.

Since each member of the business has a primary obligation to his family, the solidarity necessary to attain these goals will be maintained against those who are outside the organization. From the standpoint of the outsider, be that outsider a customer, a supplier, or a creditor, it may appear as if the employees have a high degree of internal group unity, indeed, that they are almost like one large family group. Patterns of speech among employees, and particularly between the employees and the *laoban*, or manager, are replete with in-group terms and with deference patterns that are similar to those used in primary groups such as the family. In addressing others, the prefix *xiao*, meaning little or young, or *lao*, meaning old, may be affixed as appropriate before the last name, giving the superficial impression of intimacy and concern. This appearance is extremely misleading. In reality the obligations that are fixed between employer and employee are only those which are dictated by custom, contract, or the law. It is assumed that employees will receive their meals and, in some cases, will also receive free room. There is also, of course, a commitment on the part of the owner-manager to pay whatever wages have been agreed upon. There is no necessary feeling, however, that the employer has an obligation for cases of disability or sickness, help toward retirement, or general payments for welfare. These obligations, which are clearly understood with regard to family members, are ignored whenever possible for others including close work associates.

When one examines vertical hierarchical relationships between leaders and followers, the attitudinal category of "obligation/no obligation" has a counterpart in the category of "loyalty/disloyalty." In large American bureaucracies, explicit stress is often placed on developing leadership qualities in those who occupy supervisory positions. Ideally speaking, this means to care about subordinates, to foresee their needs, to help in solving work-related as well as personal problems, and to make opportunities for advancement available. Good followership, on the other hand, involves committing oneself to the organization's goals, producing high-quality work, giving loyalty to one's supervisors, and obeying directives as required. These relationship patterns among individuals at different hierarchical levels are, of course, ideals that are frequently violated in practice. They stand, however, in sharp contrast to the actual patterns observed in the much smaller-scale Chinese restaurant business in America.

Of course, Chinese employers and employees place some emphasis on mutual loyalty, for the organization could not survive without it. As Wilson's business partner responded when asked whether workers should feel loyalty toward the boss,

> Of course, an employee must have loyalty; if you work you have to have this. Every employee has to be loyal. No boss will hire someone who is not. If there is a money situation, then there must be an additional way or feeling with someone.

The "additional feeling," however, is largely directed toward keeping just sufficient peace within the organization, so that everyone's primary obligations toward self and family can be realized. Otherwise, as a Chinese waiter said of the restaurant where he worked in New York City, "restaurants here are like in Hong Kong and Taipei. The boss is king, the workers are slaves."[17]

The dishwashers, at the lowest end of the restaurant hierarchy, receive the least desirable work and are looked down upon by the other employees. At the other, and upper, end of the spectrum is the Head Chef, who occupies the position of "pit boss." Workers fear the Chef who, traditionally, has the authority to discharge anyone below him who he feels has insulted him or who has not properly carried out his responsibilities. Virtually at his whim, he can prevail upon the Manager to dismiss employees, sometimes to make way for relatives who may be seeking employment.[18] Job tenure and security for workers is generally viewed in a callous, even casual, way by the employer. Workers who have performed as ably as possible, but who have earned the displeasure of the Manager, may be told to depart without notice. In one case Wilson was told that an old man without family, employed at the restaurant and living in one of the upstairs rooms, had been summarily discharged for his presumed slowness in the kitchen, despite his apparent willingness to do most of the least desirable jobs. In another case, an alternate Chef, supporting a son in college, was dismissed without notice because business for several weeks had taken a slight downturn. (Several weeks later there was a business upturn, but by then, of course, this able and well-trained individual was not available.) In both cases immediate considerations determined the job tenure of the worker; there were no additional criteria of a personal nature, or even legal restraints, that impinged upon these personnel decisions. Alternatively, Wilson was often told how disgruntled employees, sometimes as a group, will wait until the busiest moment on a weekend night and then walk off the job, hoping to cause as much difficulty and embarrassment as possible for the Chef and/or the Manager.

Attitudes Concerning the Dimensions of Exploitation/Sharing and Cooperation/Conflict

In analyzing the attitudes of owner-managers, the first subjective dimension to be used is that of "exploitation/sharing." As should be clear from the previous discussion concerning the dimensions of obligation and loyalty, the attitude of managers in the business organization is geared toward obtaining the maximum amount of work from those who are employed, in order thereby to obtain as much profit as possible. Waiters and busboys frequently work a twelve-hour day and the remuneration may be less than $1.00 an hour in wages, plus tips.[19] This, of course, may still give a waiter an income in the neighborhood of $12,000–$14,000 a year. In order to obtain this salary, however, waiters may spend hours helping to prepare food and doing general carrying and cleaning-up work around the restaurant. Normally they will work six days a week and, in many restaurants, they must pay the employer to replace them if they become sick. No pay is given for vacation nor for overtime. However, with regard to working hours, the same number of hours of labor that are expected of workers generally also hold true for the Chef and the Manager. As Wilson's business partner put it,

> No overtime! In this regard, there is no difference between worker and boss. If they become friends, the worker will be happy to work more. If the boss is stingy, the worker won't stay there—if you work in a Chinese restaurant, you have to work that long. You don't have a choice.

In many Chinese restaurants the lot of the illegal worker is an especially bitter one, for such individuals are in the United States without the authorization of a visa and without permanent residence. These workers, by the nature of their illegal status, cannot be covered by any government-sponsored disability or welfare program and frequently work for the lowest possible wage; they are the workers who are most vulnerable to the whims of the employer. The low cost of their labor and the lack of any need to provide benefits for them make them an attractive source of additional profit for many restaurant owners.

In analysis of employees, an important initial attitudinal dimension is that of "cooperation/conflict." Only recently has there been any effort to unionize workers in Chinese restaurants. Relationships among workers and between workers and managers is one based primarily on custom and personal relationship, and is not generally subject to the restrictions of a formal contract or to inputs arising from worker membership in an alternate organization such as a union. Perhaps for this reason it is difficult for employees to express grievances; their fear of unemployment or of being blacklisted with other potential employers is usually sufficient to maintain organizational peace. If disagreements arise which cannot be speedily resolved, the resulting tension will often be resolved, not by resort to a formal grievance procedure nor by adjudication by a union-management group, but by the abrupt dismissal of the employee or by the employee leaving the job. Cooperation, then, is not a formalized objective of work relationships, and few buffers, beyond those built into traditional politeness patterns, exist to resolve frictions when they occur. As a consequence, both employers and employees perceive the possibility of conflict as a distinct likelihood in their relationship, and they are alert for subtle signs that may indicate that tension has arisen. Only by being alert can they hope to have sufficient time to take whatever steps may be necessary to protect their own interests and objectives.

Attitudes Toward the General Social Environment

The attitude of the Chinese restaurant owner-manager toward the general social environment can be noted on a dimension of "trust/suspicion." In colloquial language, we might sum up the generally suspicious and negative feelings that are manifested as "dog-eat-dog." For instance, when asked what he disliked about American society, Wilson's partner replied,

> I don't like American Insurance Companies and the biggest company is the one that is government controlled. You always feel that they are not honest. Even if you can read English, you still cannot understand. They almost always cheat you. But if you don't have insurance, then you're dead.

The basic attitude is that one lives in a hostile world where one must always be on guard against being cheated by another. For this reason it is vitally important in the restaurant that the person at the cash register be a family member if at all possible. This desire, of course, is partly indicative of a lack of trust of other employees, but in a more fundamental sense it reveals the feeling that one must tightly control all knowledge about money matters, since revelation of financial data will only make one vulnerable to outside auditing and intervention. In the end, of course, business relationships among members of different families founder on this very point, for if the outside, non-familial world is perceived as hostile and obstructive, then the potential for deception pervades all financial dealings between non-kin.

Degrees of trust in the general environment are reflected on an attitudinal-behavioral dimension of "risk-taking/risk-avoiding," which, expressed more lengthily, means to give something that one owns in the present in order to reap more benefit in the future versus taking all that one can get at the moment, in the hope that one will eventually obtain a sufficient amount to establish a firm basis for obtaining more in the future. As an example, putting money into advertising or into larger portions of food, in the hope of attracting greater numbers of customers in the future seemed, to Wilson's partner a poor way to do business; rather, one labored long hours for little return and made the portions as small as the customer would accept in order to obtain the maximum possible profit in the present, with the hope that, with this profit, one could then risk expanding the business later. This, of course, is the same attitude that partially underlay the firing of the alternate Chef which was noted earlier. In that case, a business downturn called for an immediate reduction in personnel without heed to the thought that, if business conditions improved, the lack of a trained Chef familiar with the restaurant's dishes would be severely felt.

Wilson's partner, who was keenly aware of how hard Chinese work, often expressed an admiration tinged with bewilderment and amazement for the way that Japanese seem to organize, cooperate, and succeed in business operations. Yet even though he could put forth many reasons for Japanese entrepreneurial success (which never, significantly, included the concept of an organization's members having loyalty and sense of obligation first and foremost to the organization itself), and was willing, in addition, to listen to suggestions, it was at the point of actual practice that deep-seated attitudes manifested themselves in business operations.

CONCLUSION

A number of dimensions have been noted which outline attitudinal aspects of traditional relationship patterns among non-kin in small-scale Chinese business organizations. These attitudes and the behavior patterns that are associated with them can be summarized as follows: there is a limited sense of obligation toward non-kinship-related fellow employees, concomitant with limited mutual loyalty between non-kinship-related leaders and followers; cooperation in work relationships is conditional on the maintenance of work conditions which promote personal or family-related objectives; exploitation by owner-managers of workers who are not related by family ties is expected; toward outsiders there exists suspicion and a feeling that one must get what one can in the present, for one never knows what the future will bring.

The nature and intensity of individual relationship patterns appear to be strongly related to the success or failure of a traditional Chinese organization. Certain relationship patterns release energy, while others tend to block organizational effectiveness. Clearly, many traditional Chinese organizations were highly successful. With the exception of imperial institutions, however, such organizations tended to be dominated by single families or were characterized by pseudo-family style relationship patterns (e.g., secret societies). When strong blood-related group loyalties underlay identification with work organizations, the attendant cohesion and harmony reinforced the probability of organizational success. When the members of organizations had competing family claims, fragmentation and conflict were always potentially possible, due to the perception (and mistrust) that work associates might subordinate organizational objectives to their own family's goals at the expense of others.

Achievement motivation for Chinese is related to being face-conscious and group-oriented. In examining traditional Chinese relationship patterns, therefore, it is critical to be aware of the particular groups toward whom Chinese are oriented, and with whom their "face" is most vulnerable. We believe that for the workers in a traditional Chinese business organization the family is preeminently important as the group which motivates achievement and that this focus dominates and influences patterns of behavior and attitudes within a business and toward the business environment. Obligations and loyalties are primarily directed toward the family, and this fact, understood by all, is both the source of motivation and the goal of one's endeavors. High degrees of achievement-oriented behavior are manifested, but lead to the most successful results when the partners in enterprise are related by family connections. Among those not related by kinship, the condition of obligation and loyalty to family interests first and foremost, implicitly recognized, creates a relationship environment that is dominated by suspicion regarding motives and by an incentive for exploitation among unequals.

Modern Chinese nationalists have sought to destroy the pattern of primary loyalty to the family and to replace it with a loyalty to the society as a whole. By so doing, they hope to establish a firm basis for political loyalty to the nation-state and work loyalty toward large commercial, industrial, or agricultural enterprises. Only by doing so, they believe, can the restraints on development posed by "feudal mentality" be destroyed and energy released for the tasks of modernization. It is no accident, or so it seems to us, that as a result heavy emphasis in education, propaganda, and national campaigns has been placed on changing the focus and pattern of social loyalties in Chinese society. Yet, paradoxically, such efforts appear to minimize the very source of cohesiveness and effectiveness in traditional Chinese organizations.

Our findings indicate that achievement motivation for Chinese is group-oriented and that rewards for achievement are frequently couched in group terms. There is, however, no theoretical reason for an a priori designation of a particular group toward which individuals need be oriented nor for a particular form of reward. The transition to larger group loyalties may not be smooth, but we can predict that as Chinese come to identify with, and have primary loyalty to, larger and larger groups in the social system, these groups will become the focus for achievement motivation and that group's particular success (in terms of whatever objectives it sets) a source of reward for the achievement-oriented individual. Unlike westerners, whose pattern of achievement motivation requires tangible individual reward, modern Chinese may well be able to work long, hard hours for benefits that largely accrue to a particular social unit, or even to society as a whole.

NOTES

1. Anne Wang Pusey, "A Comparative Study on Achievement Motivation Between Chinese and Americans," M.A. Thesis, Bucknell University, 1977, pp. 1, 14.

2. Ibid., p. 1 (based on D. C. McClelland, *The Achieving Society* (New York: The Free Press, 1961).

3. Ibid., p. 1.

4. D. C. McClelland, J. W. Atkinson, A. Clark, and E. L. Lowell, *The Achievement Motive* (New York: Appleton-Century-Crofts, Inc., 1953), pp. 297–304.

5. S. F. Kriger and W. H. Kroes, "Child-rearing Attitudes of Chinese, Jewish and Protestant Mothers," *The Journal of Social Psychology*, 86 (1972): 205–10.

6. Ibid., R. W. Scofield and C. W. Sun, "A Comparative Study of the Differential Effect Upon Personality of Chinese and American Child Training Practices," *The Journal of So-*

cial Psychology, 52 (1960); and D. C. McClelland, "Motivational Patterns in Southeast Asia With Special Reference to the Chinese Case," *Journal of Social Issues*, 19 (1963).

7. C. Morris, *Varieties of Human Value* (Chicago: The University of Chicago Press, 1956), pp. 33-34.

8. Francis L. K. Hsu, *Americans and Chinese* (New York: Doubleday Natural History Press, 1972).

9. Pusey, "Comparative Study," pp. 9-10.

10. Ibid., p. 25.

11. Ibid., pp. 24-29, 45.

12. Ibid., pp. 30, 34.

13. Ibid., pp. 31-32 (The material from this and the preceding paragraph are based on this source.)

14. Ibid., p. 35.

15. Ibid., p. 13.

16. J. O. P. Bland, "China: And Yet Again," *The Atlantic Monthly*, July 1927, p. 104. (Italics in original—quoting Walter H. Mallory from a work published by the American Geographical Society. No citation.)

17. Donald G. McNeil, Jr., "Unionization of Chinese Restaurant Breaks a Grim Tradition," *The New York Times*, 8 July 1978, pp. 21, 24.

18. Ibid., p. 24.

19.-Ibid., p. 21.

8 THE CONCEPT OF *GUANXI* AND LOCAL POLITICS IN A RURAL CHINESE CULTURAL SETTING

J. Bruce Jacobs*

The "How" of Lasswell's pithy definition of politics—"Who Gets What, When, How"—actually embodies two questions.[1] First, how do people organize themselves in order to attain their political objectives? Second, once organized, how do they proceed to use this organization to reach their goals? This essay seeks to answer the first question: "On what bases do Mazu Township citizens organize themselves in order to attain their political objectives?"

People organize political alliances on a number of bases including personal interests, ideological commitments, interest in particular policy issues and particularistic ties. In Mazu, because most policy decisions are made at higher levels and because material resources available in the township are few, political alliances are formed only on the basis of a "close" particularistic tie called a *guanxi (kuan-hsi*; Hokkien: *kuan-he*. This study presents a model describing and analyzing the concept of *guanxi*. It begins with an outline of the model.

*Reprinted from Chapter III. "The Concept of *GUANXI*," in J. Bruce Jacobs, *Local Politics in A Rural Chinese Cultural Setting: A Field Study of Mazu Township, Taiwan* (Canberra, Australia: Contemporary China Centre, Research School of Pacific Studies, Australian National University, 1980), with the author's permission.

AN OUTLINE OF THE *GUANXI* MODEL

Three variables determine the "closeness" of a *guanxi*.* The first variable, the existence or absence of a *guanxi* base, need not present too many difficulties to the political participant. A person seeking allies will first turn to persons with whom he knows he has a *guanxi* base, but should he desire to ally with another person, he may approach him directly, or through an intermediary, and attempt to discover a *guanxi* base on which to develop a closer *guanxi*. If they discover a common *guanxi* base, then the alliance may develop; if they cannot discover such a base, they may need to rely on intermediaries.

The existence, or non-existence, of a *guanxi* base determines the existence or non-existence of a *guanxi*. However, a *guanxi* may vary according to "closeness" or "distance," and this variation depends in turn upon a third variable, affect or *ganqing (kan-ch'ing*; Hokkien: *kam-cieng*). The relationship between these three variables is outlined in Table 8.1.

The closer the *guanxi*, the more likely a political alliance will be formed and maintained. Yet, it must be emphasized that participants in the politics of Mazu have considerable leeway in setting the values of their *guanxi* and that the values of *guanxi* may vary over time. These processes are described and analyzed below in the discussion of the dynamics of *guanxi*. We begin, however, with an analysis of *guanxi* bases.

AN ANALYSIS OF *GUANXI* BASES

The existence of a close *guanxi* depends, in the first instance, on the existence of a base for the *guanxi*. What constitutes a base for particularistic ties prob-

Table 8.1
A Schematic Outline of *Guanxi* Model

Guanxi Base (Independent Variable)	Affect (*Ganqing*) (Intervening Variable)	Value of *Guanxi* (Dependent Variable)
Present	Good	Close
Present	Absent	Distant
Absent	Absent	Non-existent

---

*I have used the Chinese term *guanxi* for three reasons. First, I wish to emphasize the analysis pertains to Chinese particularistic ties and not to particularistic ties in general. Secondly, the most accurate translation, "Chinese particularistic ties," is quite awkward. Thirdly, non-speakers of Chinese have indicated that such simpler English translations as "relationship" and "connection" confuse more than they enlighten owing to a lack of equivalency between languages.

ably varies from culture to culture. In Chinese culture (and perhaps cross-culturally), a base for *guanxi* depends on two or more persons having a commonality of shared identification. That is, each of the persons having a *guanxi* base shares an aspect of personal identification which is important to them as individuals, such as identification with family, hometown, school or place of work. Such identification may be ascribed, e.g., native-place or lineage, or it may involve shared experience. For example, the teacher and student in a teacher-student *guanxi* share identification with an experience important to them, the education of the student, while those tied by classmate *guanxi* share identification as graduates of the same school as well as a shared educational experience. The Chinese terminology for many *guanxi* explicitly recognizes this commonality: the word *tong* (Hokkien: *tong*) meaning "same," or "shared," is followed by a word describing the commonality such as "native-place," "education," or "place of work".

The ultimate importance of any particular *guanxi* base to any individual varies with the importance of that base to the identity of the person concerned. The process of acculturation assures, however, that patterns of identification do emerge. Four factors affect these patterns of identification; thus a typology of *guanxi* bases. First, the *level* in the political system helps determine which particular *guanxi* bases play important roles. At the central level, university classmate *guanxi* may loom large, while in a township the paucity of university graduates may make this *guanxi* irrelevant. Likewise, kinship *guanxi* tend to be more important at the village and township levels than at the province or center. Second, even within the township, we must consider *whom* the *guanxi* tie. In Mazu Township the co-worker *guanxi* is an important link between township leaders, but unimportant between leaders and voters. Third, the type of political *arena* affects the importance of *guanxi* types. *Guanxi* relevant to a territorial system with universal suffrage may be unimportant in a bureaucratic arena. Last, the relative importance of *guanxi* bases may vary over *time*. For example, co-worker (bureaucratic colleague) *guanxi* appear more important than classmate *guanxi* during the Song Dynasty while the reverse is true during the Ming and Qing dynasties. Quite possibly changes have occurred on the Chinese mainland since the founding of the People's Republic.

The following typology analyzes the importance of *guanxi* bases within Mazu Township. While hypotheses are offered about *guanxi* bases at higher levels, the reader should note the data for these hypotheses are not so established as the data for Mazu.

Locality People tied by locality *guanxi* share identification with a native-place. The importance of locality as a *guanxi* base at higher levels in Chinese society has been discussed by many authors, including Nathan, Folsom, Fried, Ho, Skinner, and Jacobs.[2] The locality *guanxi*, however, also proved to be the single most important politically relevant *guanxi* in Mazu Township. The importance of the locality *guanxi* at this very low level in the political and social systems suggests a previously unsuspected pervasiveness and importance for the locality *guanxi* at all levels of the various Chinese polities.*

In addition to the strong Chinese identification with native-place, two attributes help account for the importance and pervasiveness of the locality *guanxi* at all levels of Chinese politics. First, the concept of "locality" or "native-place" is *flexible*. Locality can range from a natural village to a regional grouping of provinces, depending upon the scope of the political arena. Persons who identify native-place as a village or portion of a township in township politics will identify with an entire county at the provincial level. Chinese sometimes indicate this flexibility by distinguishing between a broader concept of native-place (*datongxiang*) such as the whole of Fujian Province and a narrower concept (*xiaotongxiang*) such as Southern Fujian. The *extensive* nature of the locality *guanxi* derives from this flexibility. One can always organize more political allies on the basis of locality than on the basis of kinship, classmates, or co-workers.**

Election data, backed by interviews and observation of elections, confirm the importance of locality in Mazu Township. In the multi-village Township Assembly electoral districts used since 1961, candidates almost invariably have received the bulk of their votes from their native village, while candidates in the multi-township County Assembly electoral districts have depended upon their own township or sub-township section for their principal support.[3] These candidates seek votes and the voters cast their ballots on the basis of a commonality of shared identification with native-place between candidate and voter.

One example showing the importance of the locality *guanxi* occurred during the March 17, 1973 County Assembly election. The maternal uncle (mother's brother [*jiujiu*; Hokkien: *a-ku*], an important Chinese kinship relation) of Township Assemblyman Shen Daiming of Village P was none other than Su Donggang of Village QR. Naturally, Assemblyman Shen belonged to the South Faction. During the County Assembly election, however, Township Assemblyman Shen supported his fellow-villager Liang Yingdi

---

*Generally, at higher levels, the locality *guanxi* ties persons who are residing in an administrative centre away from their native-place. The general Chinese term for the locality *guanxi*, *tongxiang* (Hokkien: *tong-hiong*), can be literally translated as the "same native-place" *guanxi*. (*Xiang*, the same character as "rural township," here means the less specific "native-place"). Within Mazu, almost all political leaders and voters continue to live in their native-place and the term "locality" is used (*diyu*; Hokkien: *te-hng* for which the Mandarin is *difang*). Regardless of residence or terminology, however, the *guanxi* remains the same, a commonality of shared identification with native-place.

**Skinner suggests two further explanations for the importance of locality *guanxi*: (i) many other *guanxi* "were subsumed by and reinforced *t'ung-hsiang* ties" and (ii) "*t'ung-hsiang* . . . cut across class and other vertical . . . *kuan-hsi* which tended to be class-specific".[5]

against Su Jiuping, the candidate of his maternal uncle, despite the fact Shen and Liang had been leaders of opposing Village P factions for several years. Assemblyman Shen explained, "the same-village *guanxi* [an aspect of the locality *guanxi*] has priority".[4]

Kinship In Mazu Township *guanxi* based on kinship ties are second only to the locality *guanxi* in political importance. Gradations and complexities abound in the Chinese kinship system, but two general categories of Chinese kinship *guanxi* suffice for our analysis: agnatic and affinal.*

The attributes of the patrilineal, patrilocal Chinese kinship system differentiate the political utility of the agnatic and affinal kinship *guanxi*. Mazu Township political leaders say a candidate's most reliable support is his *agnatic* kin. But agnatic kin are limited both in number and in geographic scope (generally to one natural village).** The agnatic kinship *guanxi* can prove crucial in village affairs, but its numerical and geographical limitations mean that those desiring political success at higher levels must combine the agnatic *guanxi* with other types of *guanxi*.

While agnatic kin do generally provide one's most reliable support, exceptions to this rule do occur. The "brittle relationship between adult brothers" reported by Margery Wolf and also observed in Mazu by Fang-chih Huang Jacobs and me can severely damage this core of support.[6] An extreme example of fraternal conflict occurred in West Township. Brother A decided to run for County Assembly and Brother B, in an effort to defeat his hated sibling, ran for the same office. Both won. At the victory celebrations a rope reportedly divided the ancestral hall so that neither side would trespass on the other's property. Such hate consumed these brothers that they were unable to agree on funeral arrangements when their father died. Some informants claim that they desired to cut their father's corpse in two, before wiser men mediated a solution preventing such an unfilial defilement.

While less reliable than agnatic kinship *guanxi*, *affinal* kinship *guanxi* offer more opportunities for political use by being more numerous and more geographically widespread. Figure 8.1 illustrates why affinal kin are so much more numerous than agnatic kin. In the simple family outlined in the figure, the first generation consists of a married father and his sister who has mar-

---

*This division follows Mazu practice, where most people clearly distinguish agnatic kin (*qintang*; Hokkien: *chin-tong*) from affinal kin (*qinqi*; Hokkien: *chin-chiek*). On occasion one can hear Mazu residents use the term *qinqi* to include both agnates and affines and a few people say this usage is correct. Most Mazu informants, however, insist the term *qinqi* does not include agnates.

**Patrilocality assures limitation to one natural village. Ethnographers have reported lineage branches in neighbouring villages, but this atypical pattern did not occur in Mazu Township with one possible exception: the Jin of Village G1 had the same origin as the Jin who dominated adjacent, single-surname Village H, but no kinship, political, social, or religious consequences flowed from this fact.

ried out. The father and his wife have one married son and a daugher, who has also married out. The agnatic kin consist only of the father and son and their wives. (The married-out sisters, although technically agnates, have become part of their husband's families). The affinal kin, by contrast, consist of (1) the father's sister's husband's family (agnates and affines), (2) the father's wife's family, (3) the son's wife's family, and (4) the daughter's husband's family.

The multi-village distribution of affinal kinship *guanxi* is not accidental. Mazu's residents, like those in Xin Xing, deliberately attempt to develop a widespread network of dependable *guanxi*, and affinal kinship provides the best channel.[7] In the course of the first field study, I carried out an affinal kinship survey, recording the origin and destination of the bride (or uxorilocal groom) in 2759 marriages. The affinal kinship patterns for Mazu Township, as well as a number of tentative findings dealing with spatial aspects of Chinese marriage, are dealt with more fully in Jacobs.[8]

Kinship *guanxi*, then, play an important role in Mazu politics. Agnatic kinship *guanxi* are important on the village level, especially in villages where one or a few lineages predominate. Affinal kinship *guanxi* play an important role at the multi-village level as well as within villages. One can, of course, establish affinal kinship alliances at higher levels. For example, in Peacock County each of three very important political families has affinal *guanxi* with the other two. These families have each produced a prominent county-level political leader: (1) County Assembly Speaker (1954–1958) Xie Canlan of Mazu Township, (2) a County Assembly Speaker (1961–1968) who later became County Executive (1968–1973) and (3) a County Executive

Figure 8.1

Affinal Kinship *Guanxi*

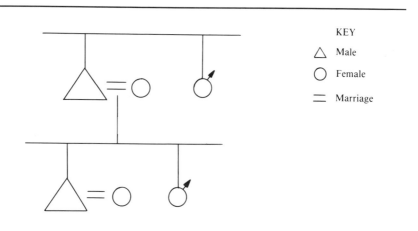

(1973–1976). However, biological limits on the number of one's kin require that other *guanxi* also be utilized at higher levels in the political system, where a successful political career cannot be based solely on the insufficiently extensive affinal and agnatic kinship *guanxi*.

Co-Worker The co-worker (*tongshi*; Hokkien: *tong-su*) *guanxi* proved to be of importance among Mazu Township political leaders who came to know each other during employment at the Township Public Office, the Farmers' Association, or in Sugar Company work. Work occupies a major part of a person's waking hours and co-workers, while working together and attempting to accomplish similar goals, often find they come to share an identification with work-place and each other. The co-worker *guanxi* developed during work with the Sugar Company played a crucial role in the founding of Mazu Township's North Faction.

In governmental organs co-worker *guanxi* are most apt to develop within a unit such as a Public Office Section or among supervisory personnel such as the group of Section Chiefs in the Public Office. The close *guanxi* between Township Executive Huang and Construction Section Chief Lai began when the Huang worked in Lai's section.

Although important among Mazu leaders, the co-worker *guanxi* has little importance in tying Mazu's leaders and voters. The limited number of staff positions in Mazu Township organs necessarily limits the extensiveness of the co-worker *guanxi*. We would expect co-worker *guanxi* to be very important in politics at the central level, however, where substantial bureaucracies exist and compete for material and policy objectives.

Classmate The important classmate *guanxi* has strong historical antecedents. Students who studied and passed the imperial examinations together developed a type of *guanxi* with widespread implications for the imperial Chinese polities in which degree holders wielded so much power. One of the first (and yet finest) ethnographers of China, Matteo Ricci, described the classmate *guanxi* which he observed almost four hundred years ago:

> In this acquiring of degrees there really is something worthy of admiration in the relationship that grows up between candidates of the same year. Those whom fortune has brought together in attaining a higher degree look upon one another as brothers for the rest of their lives. There is mutual agreement and sympathy among them, and they help each other and one another's relatives as well, in every possible way.[9]

With the elimination of the imperial examinations in 1905 and the development of numerous universities in China (as well as widespread study abroad by Chinese), the single imperial degree-granting institution as a source of important classmate *guanxi* diffracted into a much more scattered series of degree-granting institutions, with a consequent diffusion of the classmate *guanxi* and its impact on Chinese politics.

The classmate (*tongxue*; Hokkien: *tong-hak*) *guanxi* in Taiwan today must be differentiated into two types: the literal classmate *guanxi* and the alumni *guanxi*. Alumni associations often play key roles in the campaigns of their members for public office. In the December 23, 1972 Provincial Assembly election (in which the county served as the electoral district), Mr Chen, the party nominee from the Mountains, received strong support throughout the county from agricultural school alumni including Mazu Township Farmers' Association General Manager Sun Doubi and Mazu Township Public Office Secretary Xu Baize. Naturally, the literal classmate *guanxi* (in which students actually sit in class together) is closer, but less extensive, than the alumni *guanxi*.

The greater importance of education to the identity of a person with higher education than to a person with little or no education means the classmate *guanxi* is of more importance between two former university classmates than between two former primary school classmates. Since in the imperial Chinese polities and in Taiwan's present political system, personnel at higher governmental levels have higher educational backgrounds, the classmate *guanxi* seems to have a more important role at higher levels of the political system in comparison to lower levels. The classmate *guanxi* also loses some of its effectiveness if one classmate gains higher education. Thus two primary school classmates generally feel a closer classmate *guanxi* with each other than with a third classmate who has gone to university.

The greater importance of classmate *guanxi* at higher levels does not mean classmate *guanxi* play no role in Mazu Township, but they clearly are less important politically than locality, kinship, or co-worker *guanxi*. The Japanese severely limited educational opportunities for Taiwanese, and most Mazu leaders educated during the Japanese period (before 1945) received only six or eight years of education. Many younger leaders under forty, who completed their education after Restoration to Chinese rule in 1945, finished junior or even senior high school, but very few of the university graduates from Mazu have returned home to live.

Within a village the classmate *guanxi* has helped some younger Village Heads gain a few votes, but this source of votes has been minor in comparison to the votes gained through other *guanxi*. Some Township Assemblymen also noted the classmate *guanxi* has helped them gain a few votes outside their native village in the multi-village Township Assembly electoral districts. Thus, the classmate *guanxi* does play a role in Mazu politics, but this role appears much less important than the role played by classmate *guanxi* at higher levels of the polity.

Sworn Brotherhood   Many Mazu citizens, including political leaders, have sworn brothers (*jiebai xiongdi*; Hokkien: *kiat-pai hia:-ti*). The sworn brother *guanxi*, however, seems unimportant in the establishment of political alliances in Mazu. Sworn brotherhood, rather than being an important *guanxi* in itself, seems only to symbolize an extant *guanxi* which the parties wish to make closer. Informants only mentioned the sworn brotherhood *guanxi* when discussing its betrayal (or when I directly inquired about it) suggesting that, for political purposes, the closeness of the sworn brotherhood *guanxi* does not exceed the closeness of the underlying *guanxi* upon which the sworn brotherhood is based.

Surname   The same surname (*tongxing*; Hokkien: *tong-se*:) *guanxi* also proved to be unimportant in Mazu Township politics. Strongest indications came from South Mazu, where the surname Su accounts for substantial majorities of the populations in Villages N1, N2, P and QR. These Su, however, are divided into at least six non-consanguineous lineages, each of different Mainland origin: one each in Villages N1, N2, and P and three in Village QR. Village QR also has a fourth important lineage surnamed Liu.

In Village QR the four lineages cooperate closely on the basis of the locality *guanxi*. Relations between each of the Su lineages and the Liu lineage are as close as between the various Su lineages. No special *guanxi* besides the locality *guanxi* binds the non-consanguineous Su in Village QR. Likewise, no special *guanxi* binds the various Su lineages in the different villages. Political alliances between these South Mazu villages are based primarily on the locality *guanxi* and secondarily on the affinal kinship, co-worker, and classmate *guanxi*.

This finding surprised me, but the explanation is not difficult. In most of Taiwan (including Mazu Township) more than half of the population shares the ten most common surnames.[10] This great extensiveness of surname commonality results in a lack of special feeling between two otherwise unrelated persons of the same surname. In Mazu, therefore, people do not organize for political (or other purposes) on the bases of the same surname *guanxi*. (If a surname is rare, two otherwise unrelated persons sometimes feel a special *guanxi* with each other; but, since the surname is rare, the utility of the same surname *guanxi* for obtaining political support is quite limited in this case).

We can hypothesize, however, that same surname might be important in urban areas and/or at higher levels of the political system. Fried distinguishes lineages and clans by focusing on descent: "Unilineal descent groups based on demonstrated descent I call lineages; those based on stipulated descent I call clans".[11] If, as the data for Taiwan and Imperial China suggest, clans are primarily an urban phenomenon while lineages exist primarily in rural areas, I would hypothesize the same surname *guanxi* would have political utility primarily in urban areas.[12] Fried's study of a clan in Taibei gives some indications of the validity of this hypothesis, but Taibei's large refugee population may make Fried's findings atypical.[13] In his social history of Lugang, a much smaller urban centre (yet also the destination of a large migration), DeGlopper tells of the organization of non-consanguineous surname groups primarily for semi-ritualized battles during the nineteenth century.[14] Yet surname in modern Lugang has little importance.[15] Testing the hypothesis that the same-surname *guanxi* has relevance primarily in urban settings must await further research.

Same surname may also play a role at higher levels, and between lower and higher levels in the absence of more useful *guanxi* bases. One township leader suggested he would use a same-surname association to reach a high official with whom he had no *guanxi*, and some voters suggested they *might* vote for a candidate of the same surname in a high-level election if none of the candidates had any other *guanxi* with people in the locality. An extension of the same surname *guanxi*, the phratry, also played a role in the November 19, 1977 election, when a Mazu Township leader supported a Provincial Assembly candidate because his brother and the candidate's paternal uncle were both directors of the same phratry association.*

Teacher-Student   The teacher-student *guanxi* had no political importance in Mazu Township. The strongest teacher-student *guanxi* naturally develop when a student has close and intimate contact with his teacher over an extended period of time. Since no senior high schools, universities, or graduate schools exist in Mazu Township, very few such academic *guanxi* can develop. Those teacher-student *guanxi* which do develop in the Township pertain mainly to skills such as cooking and the martial arts. In such a case the Taiwanese call a teacher *shifu* (Hokkien: *sai-hu*), literally "father in learning". One's fellow students are called *shixiongdi* (Hokkien: *sai hia:-ti*), or "brothers in learning". The quasi-kinship terminology indicates the importance of these *guanxi* to those tied by them, but in Mazu I learned of no such teacher-student *guanxi* having political importance. Likewise, when the Nationalist Party nominated a teacher, Mrs Chen Xijing, for County Assembly in the March 17, 1973 election, her attempt to utilize her teacher-student *guanxi* for political purposes failed completely since many of the older students had migrated to urban areas while the younger, more recent students—being young—could not influence their parents.

We have now discussed seven bases of *guanxi* (locality, kinship, co-worker, classmate, sworn brotherhood, surname and teacher-student). While I have indicated some do not have too much relevance to Mazu Township, each clearly belongs in a typology of *guanxi* bases. The field studies suggested two further bases of *guanxi*: economic and "public". Whether or

---

*A phratry (*zongqinhui* or *lianzong*) joins together two or more surnames which trace their origins back to a common ancestor. Thus, Chinese marriage is supposed to be phratry-exogamous as well as surname-exogamous. A list of clans and phratries registered in Taiwan can be found in Li.[16]

not these are true *guanxi* bases will require further research, but we introduce them here.

Economic   *Guanxi* are often used for economic purposes. In discussing the dynamics of *guanxi*, for example, Mazu political leaders often use examples from the world of business. Yet, for the most part, these examples indicate that a *guanxi* base is prerequisite to the establishment of steady business relations.*

When we turn the question around and ask if *guanxi* based on economic relations can be politically useful, the evidence from Mazu is inconclusive. Politically-active businessmen suggest that if "people do business together", they will support each other. In the December 1972 election, former Township Assemblyman Lin Gujian of Village A supported Mr Xu, the party's nominee for Provincial Assemblyman from North Market Town, because Mr Xu wholesaled goods for Mr Lin's store. A township assemblyman stated he received votes in other villages because he did business there. But in Mazu Township most business is small-scale. Those few merchants who ran for office generally believed their customers *qua* customers offered no base of support. (Of course, customers might support a businessman *qua* kinsman or fellow-villager). One merchant believed he gained support by acting as a guarantor for Farmers' Association loans, but another believed giving people credit did not necessarily assure him of votes.

Further research must ask two questions about economically-based *guanxi*. First, are economically-based *guanxi* more important in areas with greater commercialization and industrialization than rural Mazu? Second, are such economically-based *guanxi* really other particularistically-based *guanxi* which have been utilized for economic purposes and thus have become close because of the economic utilization? (The discussion of *guanxi* dynamics below shows "utilization" helps make a *guanxi* closer).

Public *Guanxi*   In Mazu Township the native Taiwanese political leaders share no *guanxi* bases with the few Mainlanders who have been sent into the township by various political and governmental organs. To overcome this gap, the native and non-native leaders establish "public" *guanxi* (*gonggong guanxi*; Hokkien: *kong-kiong kuan-he*). In contrast to other *guanxi* which tie people in the community political system, public *guanxi* exist only within bureaucratic arenas. Yet public *guanxi* differ from co-worker *guanxi* in that public *guanxi* tie people working in different organs. The most important public *guanxi* in Mazu Township tie leaders of the Public Office, the Farmers' Association, and the Township Assembly on one hand to leaders of the Party Office, the police, and the schools on the other. Of course, where

---

*On this point see the excellent analysis of DeGlopper and the sources he cites on p. 301.[17]

other *guanxi* exist, such as between leaders of the Public Office and the Farmers' Association, public *guanxi* are unnecessary.

Public *guanxi* enable coordination between bureaucratically separate, but mutually dependent, organs. The *guanxi* themselves, like other *guanxi*, are mutually beneficial. In a township, the Township Executive might arrange for the Public Office to budget a motorcycle for the Party Secretary's use and even help with the Party Office's upkeep. In return, the Party Secretary may help get the Township Executive a nomination or use his influence to have the township selected for some special governmental programme. Thus, the phenomenon of public *guanxi* resembles the "family circles" or "family groups" reported in the Soviet polity.

Public *guanxi* in Mazu seem to lack strong affective content (*ganqing*) and thus are less useful for general political organization than the more particularistic *guanxi* discussed above. Yet the need to cultivate public *guanxi* suggests the tremendous importance *guanxi* play in Mazu politics. The determination of whether or not public *guanxi* are a new, emerging type of *guanxi* base must await further research.*

A Comparison of *Guanxi* Typologies   My confidence in the general applicability of this typology increased substantially after comparing it with two other independently formulated typologies concerned with different periods and levels and based on different sources. The Mazu typology derived from a field study in a local-level, rural Taiwanese township during 1971-1973. The typologies of Nathan and Ch'i relied primarily on documentary research to describe *guanxi* bases at the provincial and central levels during the late Qing and early Republican periods.[18] Yet, despite these substantial differences in time, level, and research method, the three typologies, as Table 8.2 indicates, are almost identical. If we exclude the items which Nathan and I suggest are not true *guanxi* bases, then only two differences in the three typologies appear. First, Nathan and Ch'i omit the same surname *guanxi* which, as noted above, plays no role in Mazu anyway. Second, Nathan includes family friendship of former generations which Ch'i and I both omit.
and I both omit.

Comparison between the relative importance of the various *guanxi* bases in Mazu and the warlord factions also reveals only two important differences. (Nathan does not rank his *guanxi* by importance). The locality *guanxi* base, important in Mazu, seems relatively unimportant in the warlord factions, while the teacher-student *guanxi* base important to the warlords has little importance in contemporary Mazu politics. Sworn brotherhood also seems to have been somewhat more important in warlord poli-

---

*The term "public *guanxi*" had a different meaning in Taiwan during the Japanese period (1895-1945). According to informants, it meant a willingness to be active in public affairs, such as a willingness to serve as Village Head, help the poor, donate land for a school or cemetery, etc.

TABLE 8.2
A Comparison of Three *Guanxi* Typologies

Mazu, 1970s[a]	*Beijing, 1910s–1920s[b]*	*Warlord Factions, 1910s–1920s[c]*
Locality	Locality	Same country or district of origin (9)
		Same province of origin (11)
Kinship: Agnatic	Lineage	Father-son (1)
		Brothers (2)
		Clansmen and kinsmen (5)
: Affinal	In-law	In-laws (6)
Co-worker	Bureaucratic superior-subordinate	Direct institutional superior-subordinate relationship (8)
	Bureaucratic colleagues	Colleagues (10)
Classmate	Schoolmate	Schoolmate (12), classmate would rank slightly higher
Sworn brotherhood	Sworn brotherhood	Sworn brotherhood (7)
Surname	—	—
Teacher-student	Teacher-student	Teacher-student (3)
—	Family friendship of former generations	—
	(More Questionable *Guanxi* Bases)	—
Economic	—	—
Public (similar to co-worker)	—	—
—	Master-disciple (similar to teacher-student)	—
—	Patronage	Patron-protege (4)

[a]In approximate order of importance in Mazu politics.
[b]*Source:* Nathan, *Peking Politics*, pp. 50–55.
[c]*Source:* Ch'i *Warlord Politics*, p. 68. The numbers in parentheses indicate Ch'i's approximate ranking of the relative importance of *guanxi* bases in the warlord factions (lower numbers being more important).

tics than in Mazu politics. Unfortunately, the various hypotheses concerning variation in importance of *guanxi* bases according to level, persons tied, and arena, whihc have been suggested above, seem neither confirmed nor disproved by the Ch'i typology (which become available only after the hypotheses were formulated). Only further research can show whether or not Ch'i's ranking of the relative importance of *guanxi* bases would change if applied to relatively stable, civilian-controlled provincial and central-level politics.

Friendship   The inclusion of family friendship of former generations as a *guanxi* base in Nathan's typology raises the important question of friendship. Scholars have disagreed about the subject of friendship in Chinese society. Some almost deny its existence. Stover, for example, calls friendship "formalized informality," while Solomon says his informants agreed "it was most difficult to establish really close friendships".[19] Possibly the absence of friendship discovered by Stover and Solomon results from their having worked with refugee informants. Those who conduct field research in Chinese society cannot but discover friendship. Fried, for example, found friendship "clearly exists on all levels of Ch'uhsien society" and he makes frequent reference to the subject in his classic study of a Mainland community.[20] Pasternak and Diamond found friendship common in the Taiwanese villages they studied, while Wolf emphasizes the importance of friendship between women in rural Taiwan.[21] And, according to Vogel, friendship, albeit more guarded, still exists in the People's Republic, despite the intense pressure of rectification campaigns.[22]

In Mazu Township, where numerous friendships exist, friendship occurs as a result of fairly sustained social interaction. This interaction is of a particular kind, however, because (1) the term friend cannot be applied to agnates or affines, (2) friends almost invariably are of similar social status, (3) friends are usually of the same age and sex, and (4) friends tend to have similar inclinations and values. Most Mazu friendships tend to develop in school, the military, during work, or during the evening when villagers relax and chat in a shop or someone's home. Mazu residents distinguish two general categories of friendship. Most friendships are ordinary and would not, for example, be sustained if one of the friends moved away. Good friendships are more durable and bound by affect (*ganqing*). Very close friends may become sworn brothers or sisters.

Though one can occasionally hear the term "friendship *guanxi*" (*pengyou guanxi*; Hokkien: *pieng-iu kuan-he*) in Mazu, friendship is not a true *guanxi* base. Rather a *guanxi* base such as classmate, co-worker, or fellow-villager seems prerequisite to the establishment of friendship. Friends are people of similar age, social status, and interests tied by a non-kin *guanxi* base who spend their leisure time together. Political allies can be friends—Mazu has many examples—but alliances are based on close *guanxi*, not on close friendships. However, we should note (anticipating the analyses of *ganqing* and *guanxi* dynamics below) that friendship can make a *guanxi* closer by (1) improving the *ganqing* which a close *guanxi* requires and (2) providing the social interaction necessary for the development and maintenance of a close *guanxi*.

IMPLICATIONS OF THE *GUANXI* BASE TYPOLOGY

The field research and typology of *guanxi* bases suggest two important points about *guanxi* which must be noted. First, *guanxi* can be the basis of group as well as dyadic activity. Second, although ideology and/or issues rarely play a role in the formation of political alliances based on *guanxi*, such political alliances can become involved in issue-based political conflict.

Groups and Dyads The utilization of the patron-client model in political science has provided the discipline with some important insights. Several persons including Nathan, Lerman, and Thaxton have greatly improved our understanding of Chinese politics by applying the model.[23] Obviously *guanxi* closely resemble patron-client ties, but in one important aspect the two models differ substantially.

In the patron-client model all relationships are analyzed as *dyads*. In Mazu Township, however, political alliances based on *guanxi*, often consist of *groups*. Five men, for example, all from the same village, may organize to achieve some political objective. They have organized on the basis of the same-locality *guanxi* and, of course, each has a same-locality *guanxi* with all of the others. However, the suggestion that these men have attempted to reach their political goal by organizing themselves into ten dyads, each based on the same-locality *guanxi*, incorrectly describes Mazu politics. They have organized themselves into one group of five based on a same-locality *guanxi*, not into ten dyads.

The inappropriateness of much of the patron-client literature to Mazu Township (and, I believe, to most Chinese settings) becomes clear when we examine George Foster's original formulation of the "dyadic contract". ("Patron-client" contracts, according to Foster, are hierarchical dyadic contracts, while "colleague" contracts are horizontal dyadic contracts). Foster stresses repeatedly that dyadic contracts "bind pairs . . . rather than groups" and give "rise to no feeling of group association". The reason, Foster notes, is that in the Mexican village of Tzintzuntzan, where he formulated the concept of dyadic contract, "there are no vigorous voluntary associations or institutions in which an individual recognizes identical or comparable obligations to two or more people".[24]

In contrast, each of the *guanxi* bases in our typology (with the possible exception of the teacher-student base) can give rise to a group identification. Chinese readily form associations based on *guanxi*, e.g., native-place associations, classmate associations, alumni associations, guilds and trade associations, lineages, etc. These associations based on *guanxi*, I believe, constitute an important organizational form used by Chinese to reach political goals. The establishment of a formal association is not prerequisite, however, to this sense of group identity; a Mazu citizen is villager, kinsman, classmate, alumnus, or co-worker even if a formal association is not chartered. Thus, unlike the villagers of Tzintzuntzan, Chinese do form voluntary associations.

Furthermore, the conditions in Southeast Asian and Mediterranean societies, which have led scholars to emphasize the role of dyads in those cultures, generally do not exist in Chinese society. Landé, for example, points to four conditions common to Southeast Asian societies which "show a marked tendency to employ dyadic structures . . ."[25] Landé first suggests bilateral or cognatic kinship systems, in contrast to unilineal kinship systems, are basically dyadic and thus cultures with bilateral kinship systems are more likely to use dyadic models in non-kin relationships than cultures with unilineal kinship systems. (In another article, Landé discusses this stimulating hypothesis at greater length).[26] Of course, the Chinese kinship system is unilineal and we therefore would not expect the Chinese kinship system to induce Chinese to favour dyadic models.

Landé's second condition, a "shortage of manpower in relationship to available land", also does not apply to China. Most regions of China have had a surplus of labour and a shortage of land. The third condition, the "endemic nature of private violence," likewise does not apply to China. Chinese generally attempt to resolve disputes peacefully; they do not have "a conception of honor which requires that personal affronts and injuries be avenged by force . . ." Only the fourth condition, a " 'zero sum' view of the resources available in a community," has some relevance to China. Thus, three of the four conditions by which Landé explains "the proliferation of dyadic structures" in some Southeast Asian societies do not exist in Chinese culture.*

My emphasis on group activity in Mazu Township (and Chinese society) does not mean, of course, that all *guanxi* tie more than two persons. Dyads constitute an important element in Chinese politics. But *guanxi* do provide the bases for group activity in Chinese politics. In Mazu Township, for example, both the North and South factions had group leaderships consisting of five to six men. No single man could be labelled the primary leader.

---

*For two useful, recent collections of articles discussing patron-client ties, see Schmidt *et.al.*, and Gellner and Waterbury. The Schmidt volume has an excellent bibliographical essay by James Scott.[27]

Guanxi **Alliances and Issue-Based Politics**   Political alliances formed on the basis of *guanxi*, rather than in pursuit of ideological commitments or policy preferences, tend to be concerned with a politics of elite selection rather than a politics of issues. Yet *guanxi*-based political alliances can become issue-oriented in two types of situations. In the first situation, the issue affects the *guanxi* base itself. For example, a lineage may unite against other villagers over the location of a new lineage temple; villagers may work together in support of a paved road; alumni may oppose the closing of their alma mater; or the supervisory personnel in the Public Office may work together to become the site of an experimental programme. In such a situation, where do *guanxi* bases end and issues begin as the basis for political organization? In Mazu the *guanxi* base makes possible the political alliances, but clearly these examples may involve issues as well.

In the second situation the shared experience with which people identify and thus base a *guanxi* may have programmatic consequences. Many of the "progressives" in Taiwan's central level went to school together. Their shared identification with this educational experience seems to facilitate the organization of their joint political activity. But the shared experience itself, their university education, may have played an important role in the development of their "progressive" views.

The discovery of a common *guanxi* base only establishes that two or more persons have a *guanxi*. To be politically useful, a "distant "*guanxi* must first be made "close "and then maintained. We now turn to a description and analysis of these dynamic *guanxi* processes.

THE DYNAMICS OF *GUANXI*

The *guanxi* model consists of three *variables*. The independent variable, the existence or absence of a *guanxi* base, determines whether or not a *guanxi* exists and is simply a nominal variable. If a *guanxi* exists, its value, i.e., its "closeness" or "distance" also depends on an intervening variable, the element of affect or *ganqing*. Both the intervening variable *ganqing*, and the dependent variable, the value of a *guanxi*, are ordinal variables. In other words, the quality of *ganqing* and the values of *guanxi* in various relationships can be compared, ranked, and thus measured.* According to Mazu residents, any outsider able to observe social interaction between those having *ganqing* or a *guanxi* can evaluate the relative "goodness" of the *ganqing* or the relative "closeness" of the *guanxi*. The social scientist may make these observations himself and/or ask the opinions of others. If a social scientist

---

*"[A]bsolute, isolated measurement is meaningless. In all useful measurement, an implicit comparison exists when an explicit one is not visible. 'Absolute' measurement is a convenient fiction and usually is nothing more than a shorthand summary. . ."[31]

can determine the relative "goodness" of the *ganqing* or the relative "close-ness" of *guanxi*, he can predict who is more likely to form political alliances with whom. The ability to predict, of course, suggests the development of theory. We must remember, however, the values of the variables of *ganqing* and *guanxi* do not remain static; their values change over time because they tie human beings. The "occurrence" of *ganqing* and the development of "close" *guanxi* depend upon two dynamic processes: (1) social interaction and (2) utilization and helping. We describe and analyze these processes after first defining and describing the variable of *ganqing*.

The concept of *ganqing* (Hokkien: *kam-cieng*), as a Chinese concept without an English equivalent, cannot be adequately translated. Rather than use such inadequate translations as "sentiment", "feelings", and "emotion", we shall simply state that *ganqing* is the "affective component" of a *guanxi* and define the concept through description.[28]

The classic analysis of *ganqing* appears in Fried's study of a pre-1949 mainland Chinese county seat, Chuxian.[29] *Ganqing*, according to Fried, is the "quality of a relationship".[30] It tends to tie people of different social classes who have no kinship ties, though the term can occasionally be used between friends of equal social status and between distantly related kin.[32] "*Kan-ch'ing* [*ganqing*] differs from friendship in that it presumes a much more specific common interest, much less warmth and more formality of contact, and includes a recognized degree of exploitation". *Ganqing* varies in warmth and intensity and frequently improves over time. It can be described as "good", "not bad", "not good", or "absent".[33]

In Mazu Township the term *ganqing* has a broader application than in Chuxian. Like *ganqing* in Chuxian, *ganqing* in Mazu can tie non-kin of different social classes, but *ganqing* in Mazu can also be used to describe the affective component between agnates, between affines, between non-kin of similar social status, and between non-kin of similar age. Thus Mazu usage appears comparable to that of Lugang.*

Ganqing can occur in two kinds of hierarchical relationships, between those of different social status and between those of different ages.** *Ganqing* between landlords and tenants was common in Mazu before the land reform of the early 1950s just as in pre-Communist Chuxian. Because the government now sets rent rates, *ganqing* in landlord-tenant relationships is less important than in the past, but former landlords and tenants describe landlord-tenant *ganqing* in a similar way. The tenant works hard to take care of the land and produce a good crop. In exchange the landlord "does not

---

*"*Kan-ch'ing* [ganqing] as the term is used in Lukang [Lugang], refers to the affective component of *all* human relations" (emphasis added). In Xin Xing, *ganqing* occurs in agnatic and affinal kinship relationships, but the relationships must be hierarchical.[36]

**Many Mazu informants note the word *ganqing* can also be used to describe love between man and woman, but they say this type of *ganqing* is not the same as the *ganqing* we are presently analyzing.

calculate to the last dollar", but charges less than the agreed rent. When negotiating a new rent contract, the landlord may even set the rent below the normal rate. If *ganqing* exists between landlord and tenant, or in other socially hierarchical relationships such as between factory owner and worker, there are no fights or disputes between the parties.

In hierarchical relationships between those of different ages having *ganqing*, Mazu residents characterize the younger as "respecting" (*zunjing*; Hokkien: *cun-kieng*) the elder. The elder in turn "loves" the younger in a protective way.* In bureaucratic settings the elder "trusts" (*xinren*; Hokkien: *sin-zim*) the younger.

Because Chinese kinship terminology invariably ranks people differentially, either by generation or by age within a generation, truly egalitarian relations between kin are practically impossible. Between non-kin, however, such horizontal relationships are common, as we noted in our earlier discussion of friendship. Not all friendships have *ganqing*, but in Mazu all close friendships are seen as having *ganqing*.

Although Fried specifically analyzes *ganqing* in terms of dyads, some Mazu informants refer to the *ganqing* of a group.[34] If "everyone" (*dajia*; Hokkien: *tak-ke*) works well together, then they all have *ganqing*. During my 1976 visit to Mazu, *ganqing* among villagers in Village A improved as they worked together to build a new village temple. DeGlopper refers to the *ganqing* of another group, the family.[37] The "connective" (*lianjie*; Hokkien: *lian-kiat*) nature of *ganqing* also ties more than two parties. If A and B have good *ganqing* and A and Z also have good *ganqing*, B and Z will probably have *ganqing*. For example, if A and his maternal uncle, Z, have good *ganqing* and if A and B are close friends, B will probably have good *ganqing* with Z and may even address Z with the same kinship terminology that A uses. The applicability of the concept of *ganqing* to groups as well as dyads reinforces the earlier analysis that political alliances based on *guanxi* often consists of groups.

Just as in Chuxian, *ganqing* in Mazu varies along a dimension of "goodness" being "good" (*hao*; Hokkien: *hou*), "not good" (*buhao*; Hokkien: *m hou*) or absent.** The values of *guanxi* are described as being "close" (*miqie*; Hokkien: *chin-bit* for which the Mandarin is *qinmi*) or "distant" (*shuyuan*; Hokkien: *so-uan*). The paucity of adjectives to describe these variables does not preclude fine measurement. The number of values equals the number of relationships being compared. The reasons for this great variability become apparent when we examine the two dynamic processes of "social interaction" and "utilization and helping".

---

*A variety of terms are used: e.g., *teng* (Hokkien: *thia:*), *aihu* (Hokkien: *ai-ho*), *renci* (Hokkien: *zin-chu*).

**A few Mazu informants say *ganqing* can also be "bad" (*huai*: Hokkien: *phai:*). However, most Mazu people feel unsure or simply reject this usage. In Mazu people do say that *ganqing* has "become bad" (*huaile*; Hokkien: *phai:-le*).

Social Interaction *Ganqing* can only "occur" (*fasheng*: Hokkien: *huat-sieng*) following social interaction (*laiwang*; Hokkien: *lai-ong*). It is most likely to occur when people work together, cooperate, and are good to each other. Thus, any effort to make a *guanxi* close must involve social interaction. The strategies employed by various Mazu leaders show remarkable similarity. If, for example, a township leader wishes to make his *guanxi* with a village leader closer, the township leader will attempt to increase the social interaction between them by inviting the village leader to banquets on such occasions as weddings in the township leader's family and festivals in his home village. Should a wedding occur in the village leader's family, the township leader will be sure to send a wedding gift, usually a "red envelope" (*hongbao*; Hokkien: *ang-pao*) containing money and he may also send a signed scroll which the village leader can hang in his ancestral hall for his guests to see. If the township leader receives an invitation to attend a banquet at the village leader's home, the township leader will attend and thus give prestige or "face" to the village leader. Provided the social interaction continues, *ganqing* between the township leader and village leader will occur and become better. Then the township leader can expect the village leader's support in an election (unless the village leader has a closer *guanxi* with the other township faction) and the village leader can expect the township leader's support at the township level (unless a competing, closer *guanxi* has precedence). This example should not imply that only a status superior can purposely attempt to make *guanxi* closer. Merchants, for example, will try to get contracts with the Farmers' Association by attempting to develop close *guanxi* with leading Farmers' Association personnel through the sending of presents and invitations to go drinking together. As a general rule, the higher the status of the person, the more attempts others will make to develop close *guanxi* with him.

Social interaction is important not only to the development of close *guanxi*, but to the maintenance of close *guanxi* as well. Without social interaction the *guanxi* withers and becomes more distant. This means practical limits imposed by time and financial abilities restrict the number of close *guanxi* any individual can develop and maintain. Time is most critical. A person can only attend so many weddings or banquets or visit with so many people. The costs of "red envelopes" and hosting large banquets also tend to limit the social interaction of even the very rich in Mazu, but money is not so important as time in the development and maintenance of close *guanxi*. Close *guanxi* can be developed without expenditure of money, but no close *guanxi* can develop without the expenditure of time in social interaction. Thus a person must choose with whom to develop close *guanxi*. He considers who will be able to help him in reaching his goals, but, of course, he must also consider if the other person will regard their commonality a sufficiently important *guanxi* base on which to build a close *guanxi*.

One technique to insure continued social interaction is to add another base to the *guanxi*. As Barbara Ward has noted, Chinese prefer "multiplex rather than single-stranded relationships".[38] In Mazu Township the close *guanxi* between Township Executive Huang and Construction Section Chief Lai was based on their co-worker *guanxi* developed while Huang worked under Lai. They desired to solidify their close *guanxi* and Township Executive Huang's sister married Construction Section Chief Lai's son. But, despite the addition of an affinal kinship *guanxi* base, both men maintained the primary basc of thcir *guanxi* was that of co worker. Another very close multi-based *guanxi* existed between Township Executive Huang and another leader of his faction, Guo Shangjing, Director of the Raw Materials District. They were both from Village JK and were classmates. One of them described how their close friendship developed as they walked the six-kilometre roundtrip from Village JK to the Village A primary school every day for six years. Multi-stranded *guanxi* bases increase the opportunities for social interaction. They also increase the feelings of commonality between the parties and make it easier for *ganqing* to occur. Multi-based *guanxi* are closer and more consolidated, and thus more resistant to deterioration than single-stranded *guanxi*.

Utilization and Helping *Ganqing* has truly emotional aspects. If one of two persons having *ganqing* dies, the other will feel very sad. These emotional aspects of *ganqing* seem to conflict with Fried's harsher emphasis on "a recognized degree of exploitation" in *ganqing*.[39] In an effort to study these more instrumental aspects of *ganqing*, I asked informants if *ganqing* could be "utilized".* Without exception, each informant confirmed Fried's analysis by saying *ganqing* is "utilized". The explanation becomes simple if we remember *ganqing* occurs when people work together and cooperate. With the existence of *ganqing*, there are no disputes or fights. But, *ganqing*, according to Mazu informants, is necessary for more than just peace; it is essential for successfully carrying out any activities (*zuoshi*; Hokkien: *cou tai-ci*). Without *ganqing* one cannot do things. Without *ganqing* lots of problems and possibly arguments occur. In other words, the concept of "utilization" (*liyong*) implies the prior existence of *ganqing*. As one younger leader explained, "Of course one can use *ganqing*. If *ganqing* can't be used it isn't *ganqing*!" I do not wish to suggest that Mazu Township residents develop emotional attachments solely for the purpose of reaching selfish objectives. Another important element of *ganqing* in Mazu is "helping" (*bangmang*; Hokkien: *pang-bang*) each other. But Mazu residents convey a Hobbesian view of the world because they say people will not help unless *ganqing* is present. In their somewhat hostile society, Mazu's people believe they can only rely on those with whom they have an emotional attachment, *ganqing*, to protect them in times of difficulties and to help them reach their goals in

---

*I used the word *liyong* (Hokkien: *li-iong*) which means "utilize," or "use," and connotes self-interest, because the usual Chinese word for "exploitation" (*boxiao*; Hokkien: *pak-siaq*) has very strong implications as well as political overtones.

better times. Of course, political leaders, too, rely on those with whom they have *ganqing* to reach their political goals.

We have already explained how social interaction can be used to develop and maintain close *guanxi*. As the discussion of the instrumental aspects of *ganqing* suggests, a second, related method of developing and maintaining close *guanxi* is to "utilize" the *guanxi* in a mutually beneficial way. People attempt to develop close *guanxi* for the same reasons they develop *ganqing*; with close *guanxi* they can attain their objectives more easily. A politician develops close *guanxi* in order to get electoral support and help in carrying out projects. Close *guanxi* help a merchant develop his business and improve his reputation. He can even charge a bit more and people will say his goods are better (even though they are identical to those of his competitors). Close *guanxi* will help a man arrange good marriages for his children or get workers for a factory owner or work-gang boss.

The converse of "utilizing" *guanxi* is "helping". In attempting to develop a close *guanxi*, a political leader will go beyond simply increasing social interaction and seek to find out what the person needs and then go to help him. Thus the leader shows both capacity and willingness to help. Ultimately, if a close *guanxi* is to be maintained, the help must be mutually beneficial though it need not be equally beneficial to both parties. The "helping" or "utilization" of *guanxi* may even be uni-directional and the *guanxi* maintained as long as the "helping" person does not suffer loss from the *guanxi* and knows he can rely on the other person in time of need. A person never knows when he will need help and therefore, except perhaps in *guanxi* between merchants, people tend not to keep balance sheets of benefits.

Being intensive forms of social interaction at important moments in the lives of the parties, the "help" and "utilization" of *guanxi* go far towards the development and maintenance of close *guanxi*. In this development and maintenance of close *guanxi*, a person must take two precautions. First, he must be careful not to so overuse a *guanxi* that it becomes a burden for the other person. Second, he must be dependable when the other person needs help.

Dependability or reliability (*xinyong*; Hokkien: *sin-iong*) is essential to the maintenance of close *guanxi*.* Nothing transforms a close *guanxi* into a distant one faster than unreliability. Only if a person will himself suffer great loss or if he has competing demands from an equally close *guanxi* can he be excused from being reliable. Reliability varies directly with the closeness of the *guanxi*. The closer the *guanxi*, the more reliable it is; the more distant the *guanxi*, the less reliable.

Deterioration and Repair of *Guanxi*   Just as *guanxi* can become closer and must be maintained, they can also deteriorate and become more distant. The

---

*See DeGlopper's superb analysis of *xinyong (hsin-yung)* in business relations.[40]

process can be gradual as when a politician retires and reduces his social interaction. Or the deterioration can be sudden following a dispute or a severe conflict of interest.

Such a conflict of interest is called a "profit and loss *guanxi*" (*lihai guanxi*; Hokkien: *li-hai kuan-he*) and technically has nothing to do with *guanxi* at all, since the people involved need not be tied by a *guanxi* base. "Profit and loss guanxi" means A and B are in a zero-sum situation; if A gains, B loses and vice-versa. For example, A and B work in a Public Office Section and both want to fill the vacant post of Section Chief. But only one can be successful. The person who loses, according to informants in Mazu and around Taiwan, harbours resentment against the winner. The disputants rarely will come to blows, but they also lack a "let's make up spirit," and the loser will await an opportunity for revenge. This, according to Taiwan analysts, accounts for political factions in Taiwan. The electoral loser refuses to make peace and the dispute continues for years both in elections and in government and assemblies.*

This difficulty in dispute resolution originally led me to conclude the repair of "destroyed" guanxi would be very difficult. This finding must now be modified. First, because a *guanxi* base cannot be destroyed, a *guanxi* itself cannot be "destroyed", only made distant. Second, the reason for the dispute must be considered. If the dispute arose because one party did the other wrong, then repair of the *guanxi* remains difficult. However, if the dispute arose because of a misunderstanding, then the *guanxi* can be repaired, though the process of resolution is not easy and requires a third party with fairly close *guanxi* to both parties. Should the misunderstanding be resolved and the *guanxi* repaired, the *guanxi* can even become closer than before the misunderstanding.

"Pulling" *Guanxi*   To say "everyone knows everyone else" in Mazu Township overstates the truth, but within villages everyone does know everyone else while township leaders know leaders in each of the villages. A political leader desiring to develop a *guanxi* within the township can usually find a *guanxi* base, since within the North and South sections of the township political leaders can always rely on the locality base while affinal kinship, co-worker, and classmate bases increase the density of *guanxi* available for developing. At higher levels and, more importantly for Mazu, between lower and higher levels, the bases of *guanxi* are more sparse. Mazu citizens and Chinese in general overcome this problem by "pulling" (*la*; Hokkien: *thua* for which the Mandarin is *tuo*) or "seeking" (*zhao*; Hokkien: *chue*) *guanxi*.

---

*One-candidate elections are an attempt to overcome electoral loss and the consequent loss of face which causes resentment and protracted conflict. If a pre-election agreement can be made, the "winner" gains office and usually saves considerable campaign funds. The "loser" also wins because he obtains a new post, the promise of a future uncontested election, and/or money.

"Pulling" *guanxi* works because *guanxi* must be reliable. A needs something from Z, but no *guanxi* ties them. Therefore A considers his various *guanxi* and finds M who has a *guanxi* with Z. M helps A and goes to Z who helps A in order to help M. If none of A's *guanxi* has *guanxi* with Z, A may ask help from H who also has a *guanxi* with J who has a *guanxi* with K . . . who has a *guanxi* with Z.

Suppose Mr. Lin needs help from the County Executive with whom he has no *guanxi*. He goes to Mr. Wang, with whom he has a close *guanxi* and who also has a close *guanxi* with the County Executive. Mr. Wang, the intermediary, can use several strategies to press Mr. Lin's request. He can go directly to the County Executive. If the County Executive agrees, Mr. Wang may then bring Mr. Lin to visit the County Executive. Mr. Wang can also write a letter to the County Executive. Or he can go to relatives and friends of the County Executive and seek their help.

This last method worked well in Mazu Township. Residents in Village A wanted to move the village temple from its site of the past century and a half to the old eighteenth-century site. Unfortunately, the Township Party Office now occupied the land. The villagers "pulled" *guanxi* at the County Party level and obtained some support there, but Township Party Secretary Miu demurred not wanting to give encouragement to "superstition" or put up with the inconvenience of moving the building in which he both lived with his family and worked. Party Secretary Miu's wife had become fairly well integrated in Village A's life and the villagers asked her to talk with her husband. Ultimately, Party Secretary Miu not only agreed to the new temple site, he even made a NT$2000 contribution to the new temple fund.

In Taiwan the Provincial Governor is one of the island's most powerful men. No one in Mazu, even those who have met him personally, feels they have a *guanxi* with him. "How," I asked several township leaders, "would you try to get help from the Provincial Governor?" The answers were remarkably similar. First, the township leaders would seek help from an elected representative, most probably a Provincial Assemblyman. Of course, as important township leaders, they had each helped get one or more Provincial Assemblymen elected. Secondly, they would try to reach relatives of the Governor. Thirdly, those holding jobs with bureaucratic channels to the Governor would utilize these *guanxi*. Finally, a man with the Governor's surname would use a same-surname association. But, it should be emphasized, even should the Mazu Township leader reach his objective and obtain help from the Governor, he would still not have a *guanxi* with the Governor and in the future would again need to rely on intermediaries.

THE RESOLUTION OF COMPETING *GUANXI*: CASE STUDIES

Cross-pressures by competing *guanxi* in political situations can be resolved either by taking a neutral stance or by making a decision in favour of one *guanxi.* As a general rule, the more politically involved the person is, the less likely he will opt for neutrality.

One family of former tenant farmers tended to opt for neutrality during elections. They did not belong to a lineage, and being of modest means had no particular status within the village. Their "strategy" could be described as avoiding factional disputes and remaining friendly with all of the village's groupings. The family had four adults, and during one Village Head election with three candidates the family demonstrated its neutrality by allocating one vote to each candidate, and keeping the fourth voter at home.

Township faction leaders show sensitivity to cross-pressures on their supporters in villages. A village leader, for example, wants to support his township faction's candidate, but the opposing faction's candidate is an affine, being from the same village and lineage as his wife. Unless the election promises to be very close, the township faction leaders will make no demands upon their village supporter and allow him to remain neutral realizing that, if the opposing candidate does not obtain a few votes in the village, the village leader's father-in-law will lose face, a development which will severely damage the *guanxi* between the village leader and his father-in-law. The township leaders calculate their *guanxi* with the village leader will be closer in the future because they have helped him now. Conversely, if they force him to damage his affinal kinship *guanxi* with his father-in-law, they will also damage their *guanxi* with him. Of course, if the village leader does not remain neutral and helps his affine, then he will damage his *guanxi* with the township faction leaders.

One important Village A lineage leader did not opt for neutrality in the face of competing *guanxi.* The Deng, who account for about one third of the Village A population, had become supporters of the South Faction because of various affinal kinship *guanxi*, despite their residence in North Mazu. The sharp village dispute over temple property however, brought the new, young Deng lineage leader, Deng Helai, together with another young village leader, the newly-elected Village Head, Cai Ligao.[41] Village Head Cai was very closely associated with the North Faction as his affine, Construction Section Chief Lai, was a key North Faction leader. In their efforts to solve the temple question, the two young village leaders, Deng Helai and Village Head Cai, relied heavily on Construction Section Chief Lai's advice and during the process Deng's locality *guanxi* with Village Head Cai, Construction Section Chief Lai, and other North Faction leaders including Township Executive Huang gradually became very close.

In late 1972 during the preliminary maneuvering for the March 17, 1973 township executive election, former Township Executive Su Dijian of the South Faction threatened to run against the North Faction's incumbent, Township Executive Huang. Deng now had developed very close locality-based *guanxi* with Township Executive Huang and with the entire North Faction leadership. Yet former Executive Su of the South Faction was his affine.

If former Township Executive Su challenged Huang, whom would Deng support?

Deng said he had decided to support incumbent Township Executive Huang. In the event of a contest, he would go to Su and explain that he had to support Huang due to the need for local solidarity. Deng said he would urge Su to allow Huang a second term. If Su insisted on running, Deng would note that Su had obtained his original job in the Public Office through Deng's late father, former Township Secretary Deng Suobang (meaning Su owed the Deng lineage a debt). At this time Deng Helai was most concerned with solving the Village A temple question and local solidarity was essential to this task. Su's candidacy could wait. Deng thus based his decision on two calculations. First, his locality *guanxi* with Village Head Cai and Township Executive Huang were closer than his affinal kinship *guanxi* with Su. Secondly, the consequences of damaging these locality *guanxi* would have been much more destructive to his political objectives (solving the temple question) than would damaging his affinal kinship *guanxi*. Thus, Deng made his decision to support the incumbent Township Executive.

CONCLUSION

This study has presented an analysis of Chinese particularistic ties called *guanxi*. Mazu citizens, when seeking political allies, prefer to ally with persons sharing a *guanxi* base. In the analysis of *guanxi* bases we have shown which *guanxi* bases political participants in Mazu Township utilize and suggested hypotheses which might account for variation in level, persons tied, political arena, and historical period. Yet, as noted, to be politically useful a *guanxi* must be made "close" through the accretion of affect (*ganqing*). Mazu residents deliberately nurture *ganqing* and make *guanxi* closer through two dynamic processes: social interaction and utilization. Temporal and, to a lesser extent, financial restraints limit the number of close *guanxi* any individual can develop and maintain. Outsiders, including social scientists, can observe and compare the relative closeness of *guanxi* and thus predict who will ally with whom.

An understanding of the concept of *guanxi* thus enables us to analyze politics in Mazu Township and contributes, I believe to an understanding of Chinese politics in other places, times, and levels.[42]

NOTES

1. Harold Lasswell, *Politics: Who Gets What, When, How* (New York: The World Publishing Company, 1958).

2. Andrew J. Nathan, *Peking Politics, 1918-1923: Factionalism and the Failure of Constitutionalism* (Berkeley: University of California Press, 1976), pp. 51–52; Kenneth E. Folsom, *Friends, Guests and Colleagues: the Mu-fu System in the Late Ch'ing Period* (Berkeley: University of California Press, 1968), p. 19; Morton H. Fried, "China: An Anthropological Overview," in *An Introduction to Chinese Civilization*, ed. John Meskill (Lexington, Mass.:

D.C. Heath and Company, 1973), pp. 373–74; Ho Ping-ti, *Zhongguo huiguan shilun* (Taibei: Xuesheng shuju, 1966); G. William Skinner, *The City in Late Imperial China* (Stanford: Stanford University Press, 1977), pp. 270–72; 538–46; J. Bruce Jacobs, "Recent Leadership and Political Trends in Taiwan," *The China Quarterly*, 45 (1971): 136–43.

   3. See Chapters VI, VII, and VIII in J. Bruce Jacobs, *Local Politics in a Rural Chinese Cultural Setting: A Field Study of Mazu Township, Taiwan* (Canberra: Contemporary China Centre, Research School of Pacific Studies, Australian National University, 1980).

   4. Ibid., Chapter VII.

   5. Skinner, *The City in Late Imperial China*, pp. 541–42.

   6. Margery Wolf, "Child Training and the Chinese Family," in *Family and Kinship in Chinese Society*, ed. Maurice Freedman (Stanford: Stanford University Press, 1970), pp. 53–54; 61.

   7. Bernard Gallin, *Hsin Hsing, Taiwan: A Chinese Village in Change* (Berkeley: University of California Press, 1966), p. 151.

   8. See Chapter V in Jacobs, *Local Politics*, pp. 85–113; See also J. Bruce Jacobs, "The Cultural Bases of Factional Alignment and Division in a Rural Taiwanese Township," *The Journal of Asian Studies*, 36 (1976): 86–88; 96–97.

   9. Matthew Ricci, *China in the Sixteenth Century: The Journals of Matthew Ricci: 1583–1610* (New York: Random House, 1953), p. 70.

   10. Chen, Shao-hsing and Morton H. Fried, *The Distribution of Family Names in Taiwan* (Taibei and New York: Jointly published by the Department of Sociology, College of Law, National Taiwan University and the Department of Anthropology and East Asian Institute, Columbia University, 1970), II, The Maps, p. 44.

   11. Morton H. Fried, "Clans and Lineages: How to Tell Them Apart and Why with Special Reference to Chinese Society," *Bulletin of the Institute of Ethnology, Academia Sinica*, 29 (1970): 27.

   12. Morton H. Fried, "Some Political Aspects of Clanship in a Modern Chinese City," in *Political Anthropology*, eds. Marc J. Swartz, Victor W. Turner, and Arthur Tuden (Chicago: Aldine Publishers, 1966), pp. 292–93; Hugh D. R. Baker, "Extended Kinship in the Traditional City," in Skinner, *The City in Late Imperial China*, pp. 504–5.

   13. Fried, "Some Political Aspects of Clanship."

   14. Donald R. DeGlopper, "City on the Sands: Social Structure in a Nineteenth Century Chinese City," Diss. Cornell University 1973, pp. 190–211; "Social Structure in a Nineteenth Century Taiwanese Port City," in Skinner, *The City in Late Imperial China*, pp. 638–42.

   15. Donald R. DeGlopper, "Doing Business in Lukang," in *Economic Organization in Chinese Society*, ed. W. E. Willmott (Stanford: Stanford University Press, 1972), p. 302.

   16. Li Teng-yue, *Taiwan sheng tongzhi gao* (Taibei: Taiwan sheng wenxian weiyuanhui, 1960) II, *renmin zhi shizu pian*, pp. 280–86.

   17. DeGlopper, "Doing Business in Lukang," pp. 301–5.

   18. Nathan, *Peking Politics*, pp. 50–55; Chi'i, Hsi-sheng, *Warlord Politics in China, 1916–1928* (Stanford: Stanford University Press, 1976), p. 68.

   19. Leon Eugene Stover, " 'Face' and Verbal Analogues of Interaction in Chinese Culture: A Theory of Formalized Social Behavior Based Upon Participant-Observation of an Upper-class Chinese Household, Together with a Biographical Study of the Primary Informant," Diss. Columbia University 1962, pp. 245–60; *The Cultural Ecology of Chinese Civilization: Peasants and Elites in the Last of the Agrarian States* (New York: New American Library, 1974), p. 261; Richard H. Solomon, *Mao's Revolution and the Chinese Political Culture* (Berkeley: University of California Press, 1971), pp. 124–25.

   20. Morton H. Fried, *The Fabric of Chinese Society: A Study of the Social Life of a Chinese County Seat* (New York: Praeger, 1953), p. 226.

   21. Burton Pasternak, *Kinship and Community in Two Chinese Villages* (Stanford: Stanford University Press, 1972), pp. 65–66, 72; 105–10; Norma Diamond, *K'un Shen: A Taiwan Village* (New York: Holt, Rinehart and Winston, 1969), pp. 75–76; Margery Wolf, *Women*

and the Family in Rural Taiwan (Stanford: Stanford University Press, 1972), pp. 42–52; 75; 146–47.

22. Ezra F. Vogel, "From Friendship to Comradeship: The Change in Personal Relations in Communist China," *The China Quarterly*, 21 (1965): 46–60.

23. Nathan, *Peking Politics*, pp. 29–32; Arthur J. Lerman, "National Elite and Local Politician in Taiwan," *American Political Science Review*, 71 (1977): 1406–22; Ralph Thaxton, "Tenants in Revolution: The Tenacity of Traditional Morality," *Modern China*, I (1975): 323–58.

24. George M. Foster, "The Dyadic Contract: A Model for the Social Structure of the Mexican Peasant Village," in *Peasant Society: A Reader*, eds. Jack M. Potter, May N. Diaz, and George M. Foster (Boston: Little, Brown and Company, 1967), pp. 215–16.

25. Carl H. Lande, "Networks and Groups in Southeast Asia: Some Observations on the Group Theory of Politics," *The American Political Science Review*, 67 (1973): 119.

26. Carl H. Lande, "Kinship and Politics in Pre-Modern and Non-Western Societies," in *Southeast Asia: The Politics of Integration*, ed. John T. McAlister, Jr. (New York: Random House, 1973), pp. 219–33.

27. Steffen W. Schmid, *et. al.*, *Friends, Followers, and Factions: A Reader in Political Clientalism* (Berkeley: University of California Press, 1977); Ernest Gellner and John Waterbury, eds., *Patrons and Clients in Mediterranean Societies* (London: Duckworth, 1977).

28. DeGlopper, "Doing Business in Lukang," p. 318.

29. Fried, *The Fabric of Chinese Society*.

30. Ibid., p. 103.

31. Eugene J. Webb, *et. al.*, *Unobtrusive Measures: Nonreactive Research in the Social Sciences* (Chicago: Rand McNally and Company, 1966), p. 5.

32. Fried, *The Fabric of Chinese Society*, pp. 103; 227.

33. Ibid., pp. 103–04.

34. Ibid., p. 103.

35. DeGlopper, "Doing Business in Lakang," p. 318.

36. Gallin, *Hsin Hsing, Taiwan*, p. 171.

37. DeGlopper, "Doing Business in Lukang," p. 318.

38. Barbara E. Ward, "A Small Factory in Hong Kong: Some Aspects of Its Internal Organization," in *Economic Organization in Chinese Society*, pp. 371; 382; 385.

39. Fried, *The Fabric of Chinese Society*, p. 226.

40. DeGlopper, "Doing Business in Lukang," pp. 304–11.

41. See Chapter VI in Jacobs, *Local Politics*, pp. 114–46.

42. J. Bruce Jacobs, "A Preliminary Model of Particularistic Ties in Chinese Political Alliances: *Kan-ch'ing* and *Kuan-hsi* in a Rural Taiwanese Township," *The China Quarterly*, 78 (1979): 237–40; 269–73.

9 POPULAR VALUES AND POLITICAL REFORM: THE "CRISIS OF FAITH" IN CONTEMPORARY CHINA

Victor C. Falkenheim

INTRODUCTION

Virtually from the first days following the Gang of Four era, the Chinese leadership has stressed the importance of moral and spiritual renewal in China. The nation, it was said, had entered a "new era" in which, confronted by "new tasks," it would have to blaze a "new road." Charting a distinctive "Chinese" road to modernization would demand not simply new structures of administration and governance but a renewed dedication to Party-defined guiding values. In calling for all Chinese to "unite to look forward," the emphasis has been on the simultaneous development of a "material" and a "spiritual civilization" (*jingshen wenming*) as complementary dimensions of the process of economic and political reform.

Yet less than two decades from target date of the year 2000, much of the early enthusiasm and optimism generated by the vision of a new order has been dissipated. The thrust towards economic reform has faltered in the face of inflation and bureaucratic opposition. The political reforms have also slowed down, partly because of a lack of agreement over the new institutional structures, partly because of administrative footdragging at lower levels. But nowhere has the problem of regeneration been more manifest than on the plane of public attitudes and values. Instead of the hoped-for, renewed popular mandate, journalists, students, and other foreign observers report a corrosive cynicism and alienation, both within the ruling elite and at the level of the mass public. The Chinese press itself has openly referred to the existence of twin crises of "faith" and "confidence." Complaints about the deteriorating "social atmosphere" and "the tarnished Party image" reinforce the impression of eroding popular morale and regime credibility.

For those assessing the prospects for modernization and reform in China, the question of popular attitudes, both towards the Party leadership and the program of "Four Modernization," has become a central concern, inasmuch as the unwillingness of many to accept Party-defined standards, values, and priorities would appear to be a major impediment to the goal of "mobilizing all positive factors" in a broad-based modernization drive. Yet interestingly, discussions in the Chinese press over the ostensible "crisis of faith" reveal widely-divergent views regarding its scope, severity, and significance as well as over the appropriate remedies for it. To some, the new skepticism represents a healthy and essential process of ferment, while to others it constitutes a menacing "ideological confusion" to be vigorously suppressed.

The aim of this essay is to look at the character of the current "authority crisis" on the basis of current press discussion in China. In particular, it will seek to explore the implications of the flux in popular values for the goals of modernization and reform, placing it in the context of conflicting leadership perspectives on the appropriate attitudinal correlates deemed necessary to the process of institutional and policy reform. Given the documentary basis of the study few firm judgments will be possible with regard to the scope, intensity, and forms of the purported alienation. Yet to the extent that the leadership has become concerned about public opinion and has sought to probe its shifts, a study of the press can supply data against which independent observers and researchers can judge their own findings. The essay will concentrate primarily on reported attitudes and values, though clearly behavioral indicators of alienation are also both relevant and important to any full analysis.

ANATOMY OF CRISIS

Whatever the disagreement among Chinese leaders over the nature of the current "crisis of faith" there is widespread agreement that the fabric of public life and values (encompassed in the term "social atmosphere") has sharply altered for the worse in the thirty-odd years since liberation. The "fine social atmosphere of the 1950s"[1] is now an object of intense nostalgia, representing a lost era in which the Party stood for widely affirmed values, people could be moved by heroic example, and norms of civic responsibility guided social interaction. In contrast, the current "social atmosphere" is frequently described as "polluted," marked by the decline of "socialist norms of behavior and moral standards."[2] The main features of this decline are, in the official view, "indifference to state interests," "unwillingness to undertake social labor," and on the part of "many people" the lack of even "rudimentary concepts of law, discipline, and morality."[3] This "lack of heed to social morals" is seen as an outgrowth of a new "individualism," and an unwillingness to "consciously subordinate individual interests to those of the collective."[4] Among the more pernicious manifestations of this egoism is an unprecedented resistance to unpalatable job assignments by graduates, but equally symptomatic is the tendency, particularly among the youth, to "argue with the leadership, attack government offices and interfere with social production," when individual grievances or demands are not met by the government.[5] The fact that 1979 quarterly statistics revealed juvenile crime running at ten times the pre-Cultural Revolution level indicates the magnitude, as well as another dimension of this decline.[6]

Perhaps more alarming to China's leaders is the erosion of doctrinal allegiance and the growing skepticism regarding the relevance and utility of guiding Marxist values. An investigation group sent by the propaganda department of the Party Central Committee to survey the problems of teaching Marxist principles in institutions of higher learning reported on the basis of a three-province survey that "quite a large number of students take no interest in fundamental Marxist principles" nor do they "take them seriously." An investigation at South China Normal College revealed that one third of the students failed to listen to theory lectures and instead used lecture time to "till their own private plots," "studying foreign languages, doing homework, studying technical books, reading novels, writing letters and so forth." In part, the report noted, this inattention was a function of poor teaching and inappropriate curricular materials, as well as the heavy burden of school work which forced students to make choices among priorities. For many students, neglecting political study was a deliberate decision to sacrifice "the pawn to save the chariot."[7] But this lack of interest in ideology also arose from the students' perception that political theory was "too abstract" to offer solutions to concrete current problems, and had "no consequence" in an era when science and technology were supreme.[8] While this latter view was derided as "stupid," it drew less-scathing fire than the reported outright revulsion against politics and political study which was exhibited by some students. The leadership acknowledged the "dread and detestation" of political work and conceded that the "distaste with which youth react to any teachings about proletarian politics"[9] was a natural reaction to the Gang of Four. It nonetheless denied the view that "theory had no basis" (i.e., "he who is in power is always right").

While one element in the putative "crisis of faith" has been an outright skepticism with regard to claims of doctrine, a no less noted feature has been the tendency to dispute the economic and political merits of the socialist system itself, as Deng Xiaoping remarked in early 1980.[10] This skepticism moreover was not confined to the relatively apolitical generation of aspiring students, but showed up among Communist Youth League members in factories as well.[11] A Shanghai Party journal noted that even among party members, some "have doubts about the ultimate triumph of socialism and communism," believing that "marxism is something too abstract, socialism not guided by any example, and communism too empty."[12] Still others, "misled" by the comparatively fast growth of capitalism, "think that the theory of scientific socialism doesn't work."[13] A Nanking secondary school teacher of political theory lamented, "When I talk about the superiority of socialism, they laugh!"[14] Reinforcing this cynicism about socialism according to the press has been the continuing gap between ideals and reality. One group of secondary-school students characterized politics as "cheating," precisely on the grounds that "theory is theory; reality is different."[15] This gap, in particular, has contributed to the much-deplored decline in the Party "image" which appears as a major feature of the new credibility gap. The loss of Party prestige which is held to represent the cumulative impact of the Party's defects, mistakes, and "unhealthy tendencies" is now treated as a matter of "survival" by Party leaders, and a critical impediment to efforts to rally support for its beleaguered programs.[16]

The last major element in the "crisis of faith" has been the loss of public confidence in Party-led modernization. "Despair about the future" and pessimism appear to be major morale factors, undermining the effort to mobilize support for a program of sacrifice and struggle. Among the youth this "lack of ideals and ambition" appears as a particularly striking phenomenon.

Taken cumulatively, these growing doubts which focus on the deficiencies of the leadership, the political system, and its moral and doctrinal basis would appear so encompassing as to cut at the very core of the regime's legitimacy. Certainly, the rise of a dissenting movement, the infatuation with foreign ideologies and life styles, the new materialism and individualism, and more direct and forcible patterns of interest articulation all have very great implications, both for the stability of the system as well as for the efforts at building a new "spiritual civilization."

SCOPE OF THE CRISIS

But how widespread is the alienation and disenchantment described above? In the official view, it is clearly a minority phenomenon. While the press discussion seldom touches precisely on the magnitudes involved, the conventional formula ascribes such dissenting or deviant views and behavior to a "very small number" of "black sheep" or class enemies, with the "vast majority" "cherishing the state and its interests." To a certain degree the press also had tended to treat alienation as a generational phenomenon, disproportionately affecting the young, particularly those youth whose formative period of moral and political development coincided with the most chaotic years of the "decade of disaster." Often the analysis extends the generational umbrella to encompass potentially all the current youth, by suggesting that those with little "social experience" or "knowledge of old China" are more easily deceived, and hence likely, to impute without thinking "all of the problems arising in socialist modernization and economic life to the socialist system, the dictatorship of the proletariat, party leadership and Mao Zedong thought." "Older workers, cadres and poor and lower middle peasants" on the other hand, it is asserted, can "easily see through and reject" such simplistic notions.[17] Thus, the press contends that the "masses of the people did not lose faith "in the Party even during the Gang-of-Four years, and that the majority remains confident of success in modernization.[18]

In stark contrast to this official optimism, foreign observers offer a far more dispiriting picture of virtually universal pessimism and despair, one American observer noting that among his acquaintances, "I found no youths, workers or students who were optimistic about the future or the successful implementation of the four modernizations." Instead, even the most favored and fortunate "had substituted personal striving after material possessions for higher ideals of service."[19] Given these conflicting assertions, there is little evidence to resolve debate over the size of the "silent" supportive majority, or the extent of non-conformity in values and behavior among the others. Some data, however, has been assembled by units professionally concerned with youth behavior and attitudes, which is worth briefly summarizing. One such study sponsored by the Central Discipline Inspection Committee sought to probe the extent of deviant behavior among the children of high ranking cadres (*gaogan zidi*), examining two groups of children, the first involving 740 respondents and the second, 1,221 youngters, in terms of their "political behavior." The results were held to confirm the positive view of youth behavior, since only 1.3% of the youth studied had a rating of "not good," while the remainder, over 98%, were rated "good" or "average," of which 11% were rated "progressive."[20] A comparable poll focusing on values, conducted by a CYL research department among a group of 1,001 young people between the ages of 14 and 28 in four cities and two counties, drawn from factories, production, brigades, colleges, middle schools and a commercial unit, generated similar results. Only 1.6% of those polled indicated "no ambition in life" or disillusionment, while 78.4% indicated that their foremost goals were to "build up the nation, work for the people, work for the country's modernization, or for communism." On "social questions," 54.8% of the same group expressed a primary concern with "the development of science and technology in China," and the next largest group, with preventing bureaucratic ills and developing democracy.[21] In a smaller plant-wide poll in Beijing, among 482 workers between the ages of 17–25, 65.14% were concerned about the "future of the country" and "the four modernizations," 10% expressed a concern with the "peoples' standard of living," and a few expressed more personal concerns, e.g., "with whether the next promotion includes me."[22]

In one poll, 810 young people were asked to choose a favorite proverb from a list provided. Of them, 53% chose service-oriented proverbs, for example, "the rise or decline of a country is the responsibility of its citizens," or "a life without lofty ideals is wasted," while 37.9% chose a neutral proverb related to science and technology and its importance. Ten percent of the respondents, however, endorsed such hedonistic sentiments as "life is nothing more than eating and drinking," or "when men stop looking after themselves, that will be the end of the world."[23] A canvass of letters to the editor reveals a similar pattern. In response to the city-wide discussion in Peking in 1978 involving 400,000 young people on the subject "What shall I do for my country?", a number of trade unionists who had been arrested at Tiananmen in 1976 wrote: "To us, politics means loyalty and service to the people."[24] Similar views were expressed in wallposters and letters to the press after the demonstrations of early 1979, by calling for unity and stability and deploring such "unhealthy phenomena" as abuse of public order.[25]

While one might be tempted to dismiss such statements as orchestrated, my own 1977 interview-study among thirty-seven emigres, revealed a stong desire among respondents for a return to order, routine, and predictability. These reflected not only disenchantment with the chaos of the late 1960s, but more positively the central importance of nationalism and public-oriented values.[26] One former Red Guard interviewed in 1977 expressed a characteristic view when he noted that it had been the state's disregard of private needs in the late 1960s and early 1970s that had compelled his generation, against their will, bent, and preference, to become self-regarding.

Wall posters by "democratic movement" activists deploring the "trusting attitude" of the people[27] lend further support to the supposition that a significant popular tendency exists, which is supportive of state authority. In a telling assessment of the "democratic movement" by a participant, its major weakness is seen as arising from the fact that the movement arose out of "anger at the backwardness of the motherland" and that the existing system was "the only one [the] people could grasp" and the only "credible" cause.[28]

On the other hand, along with this statist orientation, the surveys cited below suggested a significant degree of institutional skepticism as well, more widespread than indicated by the conventional references to "a handful of dissenters." A survey of 987 young people on their judgments regarding the merits of the socialist system was striking. Although 65.4% judged it a superior system, 35.4% judged it either not very superior or possessing no superiority. Similarly, when queried on the feasibility of China's attaining its modernization targets by the end of this century, although 53.4% indicated they had confidence in its achievement, 39.5% took a more agnostic stance, indicating that they thought it possible, while 6.7% judged it unlikely.[29] It may well be that this greater degree of skepticism in 1979–80 reflects short-run fluctuations in perception sensitive to the economic and employment situation. If one compares, for example, the letters to the editor of *Zhongguo Qingnian* between May and December 1980 (111 were published of 57,000 received), the tone of disillusionment is notably stronger than in the comparable discussion of 1978 cited above.

While the general results of these surveys, however questionable their value as instruments of measurement, must afford some comfort to the leadership in suggesting a high degree of public concern by the youth polled, the agnostic position of significant numbers on the virtues of the socialist system and its prospects must give the leadership serious pause. This is particularly so since the general discussion of public attitudes elsewhere in the press suggests that this skepticism cuts across social and political strata, affecting both workers and students, Communist Youth League (CYL) and Party members as well as non-members, and urban and rural sectors. Although the polling instruments did include at least some suburban respondents, the published results provided no breakdown by unit or occupation. But there are ample materials suggesting that the social atmosphere in the countryside is no better than in the city. One article, which noted in 1979 that "feudal and superstitious activities" were "gaining ground in the countryside" and in some localities had "become quite prevalent,"[30] offers at least partial substantiation on this point.

Given the uncertainties in connection with quantitative estimates of the magnitude of the crisis of faith, there seems to be little point in reviewing further the evidence at hand, particularly since the precise magnitudes are less important than their perceived significance. While all of the writers dealing with this issue treat the crisis of faith with seriousness and while all employ the conventional description of this trend as numerically negligible, they diverge in their judgments as to its import. To some, the fact that a reactionary trend of thought is a product of "a very few people" is less significant than the "momentum" it generates. As one account put it, "though only a very few people are black sheep, the fact is that a single black sheep can disturb a whole flock."[31] The contrary point of view holds that while black sheep are a matter of concern, "we should make no great fuss over a few."[32] In general this more liberal position calls for examining closely the composition and motives of the alienated. One such effort discerned several categories of people who were not in fact black sheep at all but who were dissatisfied because "their problems were unsolved." Some even could be characterized as having "relatively good" attitudes of "caring for the future and fate of the state" but "lack knowledge and perspective."[33]

The most positive views of the young, generally held by political education authorities, tend to deny the equation between skepticism and a "crisis of faith". "Students," one writer asserted, "do not reject theories"; rather they reject irrelevant and poorly taught theories. Teachers at Hunan Normal College characterized the students of the 1980s as "more advanced" than the university students during the Cultural Revolution, (they want to "answer questions raised by real life . . .").[34] "Some teachers and leading comrades have indiscriminately treated the emergence of these questions as signs of 'confusion of ideology' and 'crisis of faith.' They are prejudiced."[35] As a senior provincial leader of similar persuasion put it, "youth should be credited with its ability to discern things." "Comrades who are getting up in age should refrain from setting demands for youth that simply mirror their own views."[36]

THE CRISIS OF FAITH AND THE DEBATE ON REFORM

As one article summarized the main lines of disagreement, in what it characterized as a "controversial debate," views on the character of the current generation "vary from person to person," some called it "a perplexing generation with shaky faith and a dismal view of the future," and others a "thoughtful generation probing for ways to make their country prosperous and strong after surviving a disaster." "Some shake their heads with regard to this generation—others are pinning their hopes on it."[37] As this summary suggests, judgments about the decline in social atmosphere and youthful morals are likely to be quite individual. But the lines of divergence in *official* perspectives on the "crisis of faith" appear to be more sharply defined, linked to the broader position, with regard to the problems of reform in the political system. To a large degree, a leadership perspective on the wider issues of institutional reform appears to shape their position on how to evaluate and deal with the evident flux in values.

Since 1978, two distinct views regarding the problem of political reform have emerged, each with distinct implications for issues of doctrine and values posed by the "crisis of faith." Both positions can be characterized as reformist; one, however, is markedly more conservative in its orientation than the other. This conservative orientation tends to perceive the central problems of the political system as party and leadership centered, manifest in terms of a decline in cadre standards of behavior, slack organizational discipline, and lack of ideological commitment resulting from the post-1957 neglect of traditional Party work methods, compounded by the assault on Party authority during the "ten-year catastrophe." The results, pervasive defects in cadre "working style," and defective and unpopular public policies, are seen as crucial factors in the serious decline in the credibility and legitimacy of the Party. As Huang Kecheng noted at the November 1980 meeting of the Central Discipline Inspection Committee:

In the 1950s we would send cars to take our children home from the primary boarding schools on weekends without hearing any complaints from the masses. Now things are different. Even sending an orderly to take the children home from school is criticised by the masses.[38]

But to conservatives, these problems are remediable without drastic reform. Huang, in the same speech, was critical both of those who viewed the Party's "unhealthy tendencies" as a "minor issue" and those who claimed that the Party had "caught an incurable disease." The solution was painstaking ideological and organizational work to rectify the Party's work style along lines set forth by Mao in 1942. The essential point was to firmly uphold Party leadership and restore Party primacy, which in the view of these conservatives is the political premise on which modernization has to proceed. The restoration of effective Party leadership requires, in turn, a reassertion of Leninist norms, the elimination of factionalism, the reimposition of tight discipline under Central Committee leadership. Thus conservatives stress a return to traditional methods of criticism and self-criticism and to norms of open debate within the Party and collective leadership as a way of maintaining internal organizational balance and cohesion. In addition, this prescription for reform calls for the restoration and more effective utilization of united-front organizations and mass organizations, both to temper and to extend Party-society ties. As the "Guiding Principles" set forth in February 1980 put it, a key to reform is the willing acceptance by the Party of public criticism and supervision.[39]

In institutional terms, the conservatives endorse the dismantling of Cultural Revolution innovations as well as constructive efforts at extending legal reforms. But the focus of reform in their view must be on Party "work style." In an era in which "bourgeois ideas and a decadent way of life" are "sweeping like a wind everywhere," and in which the Party is moving to implement a variety of unorthodox economic reforms, "strict organization and discipline" is "an even greater imperative," and political experimentation particularly dangerous. As one article put it, the Party has to work cautiously, "fording the river by feeling the rocks," since "many problems are interrelated in an intricate manner and very often a slight move in one direction may affect the situation as a whole."[40]

The position of Party institutionalizers thus articulates to a significant degree the corporate interest of the Party apparatus, stressing a return to the organizational emphases of the 1950s and the 8th CCP Congress, emphasizing the need for painstaking political construction (*jian zheng*) along the lines sketched out by Zhou Enlai in 1957. Their conservatism is manifest in their distrust of wider changes, in their particular sensitivity to the interdependence of political and economic reforms, in their aversion to experimentation, and in their preoccupation with issues of control. To this group the "crisis of faith" is a major impediment to reinstitutionalization, and hence they are committed to a reassertion of Party orthodoxy.

REFORMERS

The reformers on the other hand, a disparate Deng-led group, centered *inter alia* in the Party Policy Research Office and the Social Science Academy, perceive the problems of reform quite differently. To be sure, they endorse much of the conservative position, including the principle of Party rectification, but their focus is far broader. Their main slogan emphasizes that to "uphold Party leadership" one must "improve party leadership." Moreover, as Deng Xiaoping suggested in January 1980, improvement meant not simply organizational tightening but also attention to the "leadership system."[41] Thus, a primary difference between the two groups is the latter's focus on the political system as a whole as the target of reform. As one editorial put it, for a long time "we admitted shortcomings in certain links of the state system," but held that "they have nothing to do with the leadership organs of the Party," or we "conceded that specific rules and systems had defects but that the political system as a whole is faultless." This view, the reformers urge, must be dispelled. "Systematic reform" is not only necessary but "important and urgent."[42]

This more encompassing notion of reform reflects the reformers' different sense of the problem, which in their view is not simply enfeebled institutions and public cynicism, but the problem of adaptation to a new era and new problems for which older solutions are inadequate. They are thus scathingly critical of "nostalgic" people who "can't bear to part with old methods" and who believe that if the methods of the "first seventeen years" are restored "everything will be all right."[43] In the reformers' view, the new era requires new departures to be developed, partly through experimentation and partly through selective adaptation of foreign models. Rather than looking back to 1956 and domestic solutions, reform proponents have been canvassing both bourgeois and socialist political practice and thought for innovative ideas. Like the institutionalizers, they concede the interconnectedness of Party and state economic and administrative structures as a barrier to reform, but unlike institutionalizers, they see it as a spur to approach reform in an appropriately holistic manner.

The watchword of the reformers is systematization. Their proposals envisage strengthening the autonomy and coherence of government institutions generally, creating "a strong hierarchical working system from the State Council to peoples' governments."[44] As one writer noted, "all organizations in socialist countries are tools to realize the people's interests. They must be given powers and duties. They are by no means just ornaments."[45] This stress on formalization of powers and the rejection of "nihilism with respect to forms" is based on a commitment to an appropriate "social division of labor" whose aim is partly the rationalization of authority, but more importantly its institutional limitation. Reform advocates show a fascinating preoccupation with the division of powers and with the notion of countervailing and mutually restraining institutions. This Madisonian perspective which underlies the proposals for the separation of Party and state, and for the clearer differentiation of legislative and executive functions, reflects the reformers' belief that historically the central problem of the polity has been the "over-concentration of power."[46] The conviction that countervailing powers represents a solution is reflected in some of the more far-reaching proposals, for example, the proposal to replace the unwieldy single-chamber N.P.C. with a streamlined bicameral legislature, whose two houses, a House of Regional Representatives and a House of Social Representatives, would exercise mutual veto powers. One proposal for the reform of Central Party organization similarly calls for the creation of three "mutually restraining" central Party governing bodies to replace the unitary central committee format.[47] This stress on countervailing powers is also reflected in the greater degree of autonomy and self-management accorded to economic and social subsystems. Like the institutionalizers, the reformers stress the importance of mass organizations, but their emphasis is on their representational and interest-articulating functions. Thus the proposal to create a House of Social Representatives adds the suggestion that a prerequisite for an effective peasant voice within that assembly is likely to be the formation of independent peasant associations, which it strongly endorses.

Virtually all the concrete proposals for deconcentrating power, whether for strengthening and reforming the legislature, increasing the effectiveness of legislative oversight, or enhancing judicial independence, are premised on a more circumscribed direct role for the Party, hence the critical importance accorded to the separation of Party and state. Thus proposals for subordinating the managers to Worker Congresses at the enterprise level, or for decreasing the number of concurrent Party-state appointments, are all seen as steps towards abolishing the *de facto* fusion of powers which is perceived as a major impediment to reform.[48]

To reformers, relatively unfettered public debate and genuine mass activism is a *sine qua non* in pushing towards a full revitalization of doctrines and institutions.

IMPLICATIONS

These wider views on reform clearly shape very different perspectives on the character of the "crisis of faith." The conservatives who are committed to restoration of a 1950s-style system are alarmed by the erosion of faith, both in values and institutions. They concede that the damage caused by the "era of disaster" is responsible, but their preference is to attack the problem vigorously by prohibiting disruptive forms of behavior, limiting the dissemination of heretical views, and by defining political orthodoxy relatively narrowly. They are committed to applying the full force of the educational and propaganda apparatus to assert these values and to using legal sanctions when necessary. They pin their long-run hopes on later generations of Chinese and in the short term seek to defuse what they perceive as a volatile situation by satisfying the material aspirations of youth for jobs and employment. But the key to their position is control. As one editorial put it, "a society's mood is not based on isolated phenomena. It is a comprehensive reflection of a society's political, economic and cultural conditions." Thus while "grasping economic construction is important," the "socialist legal system is an important lever" to be applied in all areas.

> A song, a painting, a book, a class, art, school, a film, a play—all these exert an influence on popular thinking. Now popular songs are heard in some places. Some of them are rubbish from capitalist society, while others are lewd music and songs reminiscent of the singing and dancing halls in old Shanghai. If we let them go rampant, they will certainly adversely affect society's present mood.[49]

The characteristic conservative view is that whatever the origins of the "crisis of faith," the problems it poses are magnified by cultural and economic liberalization and by foreign contacts. No solutions are possible which do not recognize and constrain these sources of infection.

The reformers' view on the other hand is predicated on exploration and openness. The "crisis of faith" is a positive thing. When "students want to answer questions raised by real life they act as a great motive force in pushing forward theoretical circles."[50] The 1980 Annual Meeting of the Guangdong Society of Education noted that "young students do not do things the same way as the students of the '50s and '60s; in some ways they fall short, in some ways they are superior. . . In general they can think for themselves . . . do not readily believe or blindly follow; they stress reality and put no faith in empty words, they are dissatisfied with the way things are and want to change them."[51] In this sense they are natural allies of the reformers.

This positive point of view was put most directly by Lin Honglin in *Renmin Ribao* in November 1980, in an essay entitled "What does the 'confidence crisis' show?"[52] The essay begins boldly with a brief dialogue which serves as a point of departure for a general discussion of orthodoxy and truth. The argument starts with a syllogism whose premise is that Marxism is science. As a science it owes its vitality to its conformity with objective law. Since ideas which conform to objective law must ultimately triumph over doubt, any idea that withers in face of doubt cannot be Marxism, "no matter what it is called." The author concludes that the "change in ideological circles" signifies in fact the triumph of genuine Marxism over sham Marxism and thus must be seen not as a 'Marxist crisis' but a 'Marxist victory'." The main significance of current doubts about Marxism is that under the surface of an apparent "confidence crisis," a "new development" in Marxism "is brewing." Just as the triumph of Marxism in China in 1949 resulted from the break with old orthodoxy, the current era requires China to "break a new path similar to what we did in the Jinggan Shan mountains." In short, the current ferment involves "the new replacing the old."

> The doubt, the exploration, the indifference and enthusiasm mean a change is taking place in social thought. The masses are turning towards marxism seeking the truth that can lead China to prosperity and strength. Yearning of the masses for truth has never been so intense as today.

Thus concludes Lin, what has been regarded as a "confidence crisis" is in fact "a process of emancipation."

To a certain extent then, the debate over the "crisis of faith" has been a veiled debate over liberalization in relation to reform. Yet despite the seesaw-ing nature of the public discussion, in practice a more or less mainstream approach has been adopted to deal with the real alienation which does exist. Both sides see employment difficulties as a critical factor underlying the ex-isting alienation and unrest.

> Practice since the founding of the country has proved that our social atmosphere is relatively good when production forces develop rapidly and the national economy is prosperous. Conversely, evil winds tend to spread easily when production is stagnant, the problem of employment cannot be solved, and large numbers of the unemployed wander about everywhere. In all cities today there are many young people who are awaiting assignments and also those who are idle and hanging around in society. They see no way out, find life difficult, have too much unspent energy and are spiritually exhausted. This is an important factor leading to some young people's committing crimes and causing social unrest.[53]

Both see a return to moral and political education as an essential comple-ment to economic recovery measures, although they divide over pedagogical approaches. The reformers encourage students' questioning in order to meet them head on in dialogue, rather than employing doctrinal forcefeeding, which is closer to the conservative position. Both strongly invoke patriotism as a basis for reform. The youth journal, in its Youth Day editorial, called on youth to show confidence in the country, noting that before liberation, when China was genuinely in a hopeless state, the youth took responsibility for building an ideal China, "believing in a bright future." "The same need exists today." "National confidence," the editorial stressed is "most important, without it how can a nation continue its existence?"[54] While the two groups divide over how to define the limits of public debate, they are in fact united in the view that the gap between reality and ideals is the critical factor producing alienation. Thus, reform of Party working style and the correction of "unhealthy tendencies" is central to both approaches to political renewal. But the liberal reform position, which sees far more sweeping change as essential in the long run to push China towards modernization, stresses enlisting citizens in a more meaningful joint search for more effective programs and institutions. Less committed to the orthodoxy of the 1950s, they are more willing to accept a less quiescent citizenry and a more open political process. And, as in the past in China, it will be precisely the interaction between leadership factions and such mass constituencies which will determine the pace of change. The evidence from the current debate over issues of public confidence suggests however that in the coming years this interaction may involve a far more assertive mass constituency than before. The very significance of the generational shift that appears to be at hand is that the break with the past that is so deplored by many conservatives is both permanent and likely to acquire a momentum of its own, independent of the perception and desires of leadership groups with their own agendas for change.

NOTES

1. *Renmin Ribao*, 8 June 1979 [*FBIS*, 11 June 1979], L 12.

2. *Renmin Ribao*, 23 July 1980 [*FBIS*, 29 July 1980], L 4.

3. *Renmin Ribao*, 6 May 1979 [*FBIS*, 9 May 1979], L 17.

4. *Beijing Ribao*, 3 April 1979 [*FBIS*, 17 April, 1979], R 1.

5. Radio Harbin, 14 May 1979 [*FBIS*, 18 May 1979], S 1.

6. *Xinhua*, 5 April 1979 [*FBIS*, 5 April 1979], L 9.

7. *Guangming Ribao*, 3 November 1980 [*FBIS*, 14 November 1980], P 3.

8. Ibid., also *Renmin Ribao*, 24 April 1979 [*FBIS*, 24 April 1979], L 2.

9. *Renmin Ribao*, 24 February 1981 [translated in *China Report* No. 179, *JPRS* 77764], P 38.

10. Deng Xiaoping, "The Current Situation and Tasks," *Cheng ming*, No. 29, 1 March 1980 [*FBIS*, 11 March 1980, Supplement].

11. Ivan London, Ta-ling Lee, and Miriam London, "China's post-thaw Blues," *American Spectator.*

12. *Renmin Ribao*, 5 January 1981 [*FBIS*, 7 January 1981].

13. Radio Changsha, 13 May 1979 [*FBIS*, 19 May 1979], P 3.

14. *China News Analysis*, No. 1189 [September 12, 1980], p. 2.

15. *China News Analysis*, No. 1189 [September 12, 1980], p. 2.

16. *Renmin Ribao*, 28 February 1981 [*FBIS*, 10 March 1981, 10 March 1981].

17. Radio Tianjin, 25 May 1979 [*FBIS*, 17 June 1979], R 2.

18. *Beijing Ribao*, 24 December 1980 [*FBIS*, 5 January 1981], L 1.

19. Tom Gold, "Back to the City: The Return of Shanghai's Education Youth," unpublished paper, 1980.

20. *Ta Kung Pao* [Hong Kong], 23 March 1981 [*FBIS*, 25 March 1981], U 2.

21. *Xinhua*, 15 October 1980 [*FBIS*, 15 October 1980], L 8.

22. *Xinhua*, 28 March 1980 [*FBIS*, 1 April 1980].

23. *Renmin Ribao*, 24 February 1981 [*JPRS*, No. 77764], p. 38.

24. *Xinhua*, 23 October 1978 [*FBIS*, 24 October 1978].

25. Radio Shanghai, 2 March 1979 [*FBIS*, 2 March 1979]; Radio Shanghai, 24 March 1979 [*FBIS*, 26 March 1979].

26. Victor C. Falkenheim, "Political Participation in the People's Republic of China," *Problems of Communism*, XXVII, 3 (May-June 1978), 18–32.

27. *AFP*, 28 March 1979 [*FBIS*, 29 March 1979].

28. *AFP*, 28 May 1979 [*FBIS*, 29 May 1979].

29. *Ren Ribao*, 24 February 1981 [*JPRS*, No. 77764], p. 38.

30. Radio Beijing, 31 January 1980 [*FBIS*, 6 February 1980].

31. Radio Jinan, 15 April 1979 [*FBIS*, 24 April 1979], O 1.

32. *Renmin Ribao*, 9 May 1979 [*FBIS*, 31 May 1979], L 4.

33. Radio Tianjin, 25 May 1979 [*FBIS*, 7 June 1979], R 6.

34. *Guangming Ribao*, 3 November 1980 [*FBIS*, 14 November 1980], L 7.

35. Ibid.; see also, *Nanfang Ribao*, 21 December 1980 [*JPRS*, No. 77474], p. 46.

36. Radio Shenyang, 5 June 1980 [*FBIS*, 9 June 1980], S 2.

37. *Renmin Ribao*, 24 February 1981 [*JPRS*, No. 77764], p. 32.

38. *Renmin Ribao*, 28 February 1981 [*FBIS*, 10 March 1981], 28.

39. *Xinhua*, 14 March 1980 [*FBIS*, 17 March 1980].

40. *Renmin Ribao*, 28 February 1981 [*FBIS*, 10 March 1981], L 9.

41. *Renmin Ribao*, 23 February 1981 [*FBIS*, 4 March 1981], L 10.

42. Deng Xiaoping, "The Current Situation and its Tasks."

43. *Hongqi*, No. 21 [November 1980], [*FBIS*, 17 November 1980], L 21.

44. Ibid., L 22.

45. "It is Impermissible to Replace the Government with the Party," *Honqi*, No. 21 (1 November 1980), [*FBIS*, 2 December 1980].

46. "On the Division of Work Between Party and Government," *Renmin Ribao*, 18 December 1980 [*FBIS*, 19 December 1980], L 38.

47. Ibid., L 42.

48. "Overconcentration of Power is Not to be Permitted," *Renmin Ribao*, 14 November 1980 [*FBIS*, 3 December 1980], L 2.

49. *Wenhui Bao*, (Shenghai), 11 February 1980 [*FBIS*, 13 February 1980].

50. *Guangming Ribao*, 3 November 1980 [*FBIS*, 14 November 1980], L 7.

51. *Nanfang Ribao*, 21 December 1980 [*China Report*, No. 166 in *JPRS*, No. 77474], p. 46.

52. *Renmin Ribao*, 11 November 1980 [*FBIS*, 13 November 1980], L 8-11.

53. *Renmin Ribao*, 8 June 1979 [*FBIS*, 11 June 1979], L 13.

54. *Zhongguo Qingnian*, 1 June 1980 [*FBIS*, 6 June 1980], L 26.

INDEX

ABOUT THE EDITORS AND CONTRIBUTORS

SIDNEY L. GREENBLATT, associate professor of sociology at Drew University, Madison, New Jersey, is editor of *Chinese Sociology and Anthropology*. He is also editor of *The People of Taihang: An Anthology of Family Histories* (1976); co-editor of *Deviance and Social Control in Chinese Society* (1977), *Value Change in Chinese Society* (1979), *Social Interaction: An Introductory Reader in Sociology* (1979), as well as *Organizational Behavior in Chinese Society* (1981).

AMY AUERBACHER WILSON has been Professional Associate at the Committee for Scholarly Communication with the People's Republic of China since 1979 and is Editor of *China Exchange News*, issued quarterly by the Committee. She has published a number of articles concerning contemporary China and has been co-editor of the Praeger volumes *Deviance and Social Control in Chinese Society* (1977), *Value Change in Chinese Society* (1979), *Organizational Behavior in Chinese Society* (1981), *Moral Behavior in Chinese Society* (1981), and *Methodological Issues in Chinese Studies* (forthcoming). Dr. Wilson holds a Ph.D. from Princeton University.

RICHARD W. WILSON is professor of political science at Rutgers University. He has published widely in the area of political behavior and moral development. In addition to writing numerous articles, Wilson is author of *Learning to be Chinese* (1970) and *The Moral State* (1974) and is co-editor of *Deviance and Social Control in Chinese Society* (1977), *Value Change in Chinese Society* (1979), *Moral Development and Politics* (1980), *Organizational Behavior in Chinese Society* (1981), and *Moral Behavior in Chinese Society* (1981).

VICTOR C. FALKENHEIM is associate professor of political science at Scarborough College, University of Toronto, and chairman of the East Asian Studies Committee, University of Toronto.

BERNARD GALLIN is professor and chairman of anthropology at Michigan State University, East Lansing, Michigan.

Dr. Gallin has published widely in the area of anthropology, particularly dealing with Chinese culture and society. He is the author of *Hsin Hsing, Taiwan: A Chinese Village in Change* and numerous articles in journals such as the *American Anthropologist, Human Organization, Journal of Asian and African Studies* and in a number of edited volumes on China and anthropology.

Dr. Gallin holds a B.S.S. from City College of New York and a Ph.D. from Cornell University, Ithaca, New York.

RITA S. GALLIN, a sociologist, is assistant professor in the graduate program of the College of Nursing at Michigan State University, East Lansing, Michigan.

Dr. Gallin has published in the areas of Chinese culture and society and in the American health care delivery system. Her articles have appeared in *Culture, Medicine and Psychiatry, Inquiry, American Journal of Health Planning*, and in several edited volumes in the social sciences on China.

Dr. Gallin holds a B.S. degree from Columbia University and a M.A. and Ph.D. from Michigan State University, East Lansing, Michigan.

J. BRUCE JACOBS is a senior lecturer in politics at La Trobe University, Melbourne, Australia. He received his Ph.D. from Columbia University. He first went to Taiwan in 1965–1966 as a post-graduate in history at National Taiwan University and returned for field research in the period 1971–73, and again each year from 1976 to 1980. Dr. Jacobs is the author of *Local Politics in a Rural Chinese Cultural Setting: A Field Study of Mazu Township, Taiwan* (1980), from which this essay was drawn. He has published numerous scholarly articles on Chinese and Taiwanese politics and society.

RICHARD C. KAGAN has a diploma from the University of Judaism, Los Angeles, where he studied religion, and a Ph.D. from the University of Pennsylvania, where he studied Asian history. He has lived in Israel, Taiwan, Hong Kong, and Japan. Currently he teaches East Asian history at Hamline University, St. Paul, Minnesota. His research on shamanism began in 1978 during a summer visit to Taiwan. He was accompanied by Jerry Schultz, who conducted the interviews and kindly contributed his observations. Mr. Schultz is now a graduate student in anthropology at the University of Kansas, Lawrence.

NISHAN J. NAJARIAN is director of the Division of Continuing Education and Off-campus Academic Programs, Fairleigh Dickinson University, Madison, New Jersey. He is an ordained minister of the United Methodist Church, having served as a missionary in Taiwan (1965–68), where he was associate professor at Soochow University, Taipei. From 1969–74 he was director of the East Asian Summer Institute, Fairleigh Dickinson University.

ANNE WANG PUSEY was born in China in 1946. As an undergraduate she attended Tunghai University, Nanyang University, and Oberlin College. In 1969 she received her bachelor's degree in social relations from Radcliffe College and in 1977 her master's degree in social psychology from Bucknell University.

JON L. SAARI is associate professor of history at Northern Michigan University in Marquette, Michigan. He is the author of several articles; this essay is drawn from his dissertation research on the early years and inner lives of the transitional generation in Republican China. Dr. Saari holds a B.A. from Yale College and an M.A. and Ph.D. from Harvard University.

JANET W. SALAFF is associate professor of sociology at the University of Toronto. Dr. Salaff researches family formation among Chinese populations, and her most recent book is *Working Daughters of Hong Kong: Filial Piety or Power in the Family?* (1981).

Dr. Salaff holds a B.A., M.A., and Ph.D. from the University of California, Berkeley.

ANNA WASESCHA is an assistant dean of student affairs at Hamline University, St. Paul. Her undergraduate and graduate work have been in the areas of literature, psychology, and myth. She holds a bachelor's degree from the University of Minnesota, Minneapolis.